irreverent

Ch

G000122728

irreverent

Chi

guides

cago

BY

DAN SANTOW
AND
TODD SAVAGE

A BALLIETT & FITZGERALD BOOK

MACMILLAN • USA

Where to crash with a lake view...

The Surf Hotel, see Accommodations

Make waves...

Windward Sports, see Shopping

Cool your heels with Al Capone...

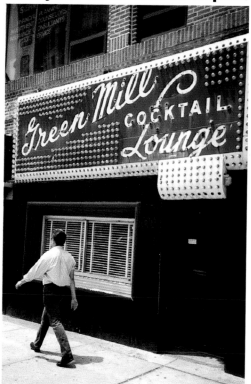

Green Mill, see Nightlife

Land a room with a view...

The Fairmont Hotel, see Accommodations

Go where da beau monde goes...

Marché, see Dining

Stay where dey stay...

Four Seasons, see Accommodations

Eat like Mike...

Michael Jordan's Restaurant, see Dining

Melt your plastic on Michigan Avenue...

Crate & Barrel, see Shopping

Rethink the Prairie style...

Mario Villa, see Shopping

See stars.

The Adler Planetarium, see Diversions

what's so irreverent?

It's up to you.

You can buy a traditional guidebook with its fluff, its promotional hype, its let's-find-something-nice-to-say-about-everything point of view. Or you can buy an Irreverent guide.

What the Irreverents give you is the lowdown, the inside story. They have nothing to sell but the truth, which includes a balance of good and bad. They praise, they trash, they weigh, and leave the final decisions up to you. No tourist board, no chamber of commerce will ever recommend them.

Our writers are insiders, who feel passionate about the cities they live in, and have strong opinions they want to share with you. They take a special pleasure leading you where other guides fear to tread.

How irreverent are they? One of our authors insisted on writing under a pseudonym. "I couldn't show my face in town again if I used my own name," she told me. "My friends would never speak to me." Such is the price of honesty. She, like you, should know she'll always have a friend at Frommer's.

Warm regards,

Michael Spring

Michael Spring
Publisher

a disclaimer

Prices fluctuate in the course of time, and travel information changes under the impact of the varied and volatile factors that influence the travel industry. Neither the author nor the publisher can be held responsible for the experiences of readers while traveling. Readers are invited to write to the publisher with ideas, comments, and suggestions for future editions.

about the authors

Dan Santow was a senior editor at *Chicago* magazine and an on-air correspondent for the city's Fox network news. After *Chicago,* Santow was a producer for "The Oprah Winfrey Show" and a staffwriter for *People*. He is currently the managing editor of a health care magazine published in Chicago.

Todd Savage is a freelance writer and researcher based in Chicago who has contributed to *Chicago* magazine, *Chicago Tribune, Chicago Reader, Town and Country,* and *Outside*.

photo credits

Page 1: Peter J. Schulz/City of Chicago; Page 2: Peter J. Schulz/City of Chicago; Page 4, top and bottom: © f-stop Fitzgerald Inc.; Page 5, top: © f-stop Fitzgerald Inc., bottom: courtesy of the Farimont Hotel; Page 6, top: © f-stop Fitzgerald Inc., bottom: courtesy of The Four Seasons Hotel; Page 7, top and bottom: © f-stop Fitzgerald Inc.; Page 8, top: courtesy of Mario Villa, bottom: Willy Schmidt/City of Chicago.

Balliett & Fitzgerald, Inc.
Series editor: Holly Hughes / Executive editor: Tom Dyja / Managing editor: Duncan Bock / Production editor: Howard Slatkin / Photo editors: Rachel Florman, Sue Canavan / Assistant editor: Maria Fernandez / Editorial assistants: Sam Weinman, Jennifer Leben
Macmillan Travel Art director: Michele Laseau

Design by Tsang Seymour Design Studio
The map on p. 73 was adapted from maps belonging to GEOSYSTEMS Global Corporation © 1995. Unauthorized use, including copying by technical means, is expressly prohibited.
All other maps © Simon & Schuster, Inc.

Air travel assistance courtesy of Continental Airlines

MACMILLAN TRAVEL
A Simon & Schuster Macmillan Company
1633 Broadway
New York, NY 10019

ISBN 0-02-860687-6
ISSN 1085-4797

special sales

Bulk purchase (10+ copies) of Frommer's Travel Guides are available to corporations at special discounts. The Special Sales Department can produce custom editions to be used as premiums and/or for sales promotions to suit individual needs. Existing editions can be produced with custom cover imprints such as corporate logos. For more information write to: Special Sales, Simon & Schuster, 1633 Broadway, New York, NY 10019.

Manufactured in the United States of America

contents

introduction

In Yiddish to "schmy" means to walk around, window shop, stop for a cup of coffee and maybe a tuna club, window shop some more, stop and have another cup of coffee, maybe a nice piece of carrot cake… you buy a little here, a little there. You check out everyone else schmying around and try to decide if they're wearing Anne Klein or Calvin Klein, whether their fur is real or fake. You go into fancy stores and five-and-dimes. You schmy.

Half the fun of visiting Chicago is schmying around, checking out the neighborhoods, itineraries and agendas be damned. To get to know the people, the architecture, the parks, you have to be willing to explore (on foot if possible, though this is a driving town).

The first thing that will strike you is Lake Michigan, so immense you can't see across to Indiana or Michigan (much to the surprise of many who've never been here). The lake is always east and the city faces that way. Early this century, the great architect Louis Sullivan wrote, "Chicago can pull itself down and rebuild itself in a generation, if it will:… a dream born of the incomparable lake…" Nearly 80 years later, as new towers cast shadows over his creations, his words are still true. The water—and the open sky over it—give Chicagoans room to breathe, room to think, room to hope. Stand on Oak Street Beach, a backdrop of high-rises and hotels behind you, and stare out at the vastness. Sit along the rocks at Belmont Harbor and watch the sailboats gracefully lope across the horizon on an early summer morning. It will clear your head for sure, maybe even calm your soul.

Turn away from the vastness, and you'll learn that Chicago is a city of neighborhoods: The Loop, Lincoln Park, Hyde Park, Lake View, Andersonville, Ravenswood Manor—the list could fill a page (now more than ever, as old-time neighborhoods get carved up and renamed to give developers and other real estate sharks a new sales handle). But just a list of names would be meaningless. Canaryville sounds quaint, doesn't it? Well, it's not; it's a tough Irish enclave. Streeterville is a pretty lumpy neighborhood moniker, right? Well, it's the ritzy neighborhood where Oprah Winfrey lives.

It was in these neighborhoods that the city's successive waves of immigrants hunkered down and tried to recreate their homeland in the face of the next influx. The neighborhood known as Pilsen, for instance, began as an immigrant Czech area, but starting in the 1950s, Mexicans moved in, and today its main drag, 18th Street, is lined with Mexican diners, taquerias, and music shops blaring salsa. Rogers Park still has kosher delis, bakeries, and butchers with window signs in Hebrew, but in the past decade it's been infiltrated by East Indian restaurants, sari shops (which, mysteriously, often sell small appliances, too), and video stores trafficking in Indian films. Wicker Park, touted by many as the successor to Seattle and its grunge scene, was once a well-to-do German neighborhood.

The South and West Sides were prime destinations for the great black migration earlier in this century, partly explaining why Chicago has contributed so much to African-American culture. This is the home of the Nation of Islam, Johnson Publications *(Ebony* and *Jet)*, Oprah's Harpo Productions, the late novelist Richard Wright, author of *Native Son,* and the blues of Muddy Waters and Howlin' Wolf. This is also the home of grinding poverty and some of the most notoriously crime-ridden housing projects in the country, as anyone who's read Alex Kotlowitz's sobering bestseller *There Are No Children Here,* or at least anyone who's seen the 1994 documentary *Hoop Dreams,* knows. Though long reputed to be America's most segregated big city, the races here seems to have reached a detente, as Mayor Richard Daley the younger's popularity has, in Harold Washington's wake, spread across racial lines and Michael Jordan and Oprah Winfrey are role models for kids of all colors. The increasing Hispanic population forms the other third of the racial balance here, its visibility and power growing accordingly.

Chicago has the variety you'd expect in America's third largest city—rich ditzy socialites, yuppie advertising copywriters, drug dealers, 21–year–old Porsche–driving millionaire commodity traders, dowdy gay men and lipstick lesbians, jet-skiers, Tibetan refugees, Pakistani taxi drivers, grocery store clerks, sports giants and more. But though its people are diverse in race and interests, the city's ethos is remarkably unified. It is—and don't laugh—a reasonably happy place. Not a mindlessly smiley–face kind of place, but a place where people try to be pleasant and get on with it. Sure, it's had its serious, even tragic, moments—the riots during the '68 Democratic convention; the day in the mid-'70s when the *Daily News,* one of the most intelligent newspapers Americans have ever read, closed down; the week in July 1995 when hundreds of people died because of a brutal heat wave—but overall, Chicago is a seat-of-the-pants kind of town. If you have troubles, they're your troubles, not Chicago's.

Being pleasant doesn't mean that Chicagoans don't have an attitude, though. A few years ago, a boutique called Fiorucci—full of metallic leather bustiers and feathered mules—closed here after a short run, despite successes in New York and Los Angeles. As a local wag said, "Chicago's too real a place for a store like that." One of Chicago's great literary offspring (and there are many), Nelson Algren, wrote about his home, "Like loving a woman with a broken nose, you may well find lovelier lovelies. But never a lovely so real."

Chicago's residents genuinely take advantage of the city, broken nose or not, from the crazy ferris wheel on Navy Pier to the sailboat harbors along the lake to the bleachers of Wrigley Field, watching the Cubbies lose another one. The art museums are jammed with locals; so is Orchestra Hall and the Lyric Opera. Everybody schmys on Michigan Avenue, not just the swells who can afford to actually buy things at Nieman-Marcus. Civic festivals, from the over-hyped "Taste of Chicago" to the huge jazz, gospel, and blues fests, draw millions of Chicagoans from every possible race and status, all sitting affably together on their blankets, under the stars.

Still, residents don't often take lazy boat tours of the Chicago River, or gawk at the top of the Sears Tower, currently the world's tallest building. We tell ourselves that those obvious pleasures are just for tourists—that is, until Uncle Jerry and Aunt Elaine come in from out of town and we have to show them "American Gothic" at the Art Institute and stand in line forever around Christmastime for a table in the Walnut Room at Marshall Field's on State Street, just so we can sit under the huge tree. We grumble and groan about looking like tourists, and we love it. We love the excuse to schmy in our own city.

Schmying here means, of course, dealing with Chicago's climate. One of the great myths about Chicago is that the weather stinks. Yes, winter lasts a long time—it's freezing or below that about a third of the year—and the skies can be gray for weeks. But the annual low temperatures usually aren't as bad as those in Denver, Minneapolis, Spokane, and Omaha—they're more on the level of Kansas City and Albuquerque. Don't get scared by the fact that it was 27 degrees below zero (without the wind chill factored in) on New Year's Day 1985, or that Chicagoans are 177 percent more likely to own a snow-blower than the rest of the country. Be like a Chicagoan and dress for the season. It's winter—it's supposed to be cold. People here take a perverse pride in their ability to handle the elements, though they don't exactly revel in the cold like Montrealers or Minnesotans, throwing carnivals, for god's sake, amid heaps of snow. No, the pleasure here comes in facing down the annual invasion of ice and cold and slush and still doing business as usual. It takes a lot to shut this city down, so pile on the fur, duck down, wool, and electric socks and bun-warmers, no matter how stupid you end up looking. Summers can be, and generally are, hot and humid—the average high in July is over 85 degrees—but those lucky enough to live near the lake (or play near it) don't suffer so much. The phrase "cooler by the lake" really means what it says—in fact, it can be up to 10 degrees cooler along the shore. (And the opposite is true as well—in winter it can be up to 10 degrees warmer.)

Summer allows you to hang at Oak Street Beach, schmying with tanned and toned natives who can look surprisingly like the real-life cast of *Baywatch*. In winter you can cross-country ski through Lincoln Park and then sip a hot chocolate overlooking a lagoon so picturesque that it would make even Fragonard's teeth hurt. In spring you can

inhale the scent of the formal gardens in Grant Park beginning to bloom. And in autumn... well, September, October,
and November all are consistently gorgeous. Acres of trees
lining the shores of Lake Michigan become a living, breathing Impressionist painting, their muted colors blending in
with one another in a way that would have awed Monet.
The air is crisp as an apple and a cool, pristine breeze settles
over the city.

So enjoy being a tourist here. Prepare to be tired, because
you will be—if you schmy like you're supposed to.

Central Chicago Neighborhoods

you probably didn't know

Why do they call Chicago the Second City?... If you're speaking in terms of population, these days Los Angeles beats Chicago. (New York still wins, though). Legend has it, though, that the term "Second City" refers to more than just population. After the Great Fire in 1871, much of the city was rebuilt, and locals starting referring to the new, glistening sections of town as the "second city." The phrase eventually caught on to describe the city as a whole, maybe because it fits a certain state of mind— Chicagoans' decades-long low self-esteem binge—implying that the city lacks the beauty, excitement, grandeur, and power of New York. The truth of that, of course, you'll have to decide for yourself.

Why do they call it the Windy City?... No doubt, Chicago is windy—it sits on a big body of water, and winds whip across it throughout the year. But other cities are just as windy, if not windier (Oklahoma City and Atlanta, for example, annually average faster winds than Chicago). Although a record 69mph wind blew through the city on April 14, 1984, the average is a measly 10.2 miles an hour. There are various legends as to why Chicago became known as the "Windy City," but the most popular ascribes it to the fact that over the decades it has hosted so many presidential nominating conventions, with all those politicians generating so much hot air that they were referred to as "windy-mouthed." That certainly hasn't changed.

What is "The Loop"?... The name may have originally come from the loop made by the el tracks as they circle a compact and dense area of downtown, but the encircled area long ago burst at its seams. Nowadays when Chicagoans speak of the Loop, they're not just referring to the real estate encircled by the tracks, but to anywhere east and south of the Y-shaped Chicago River, north of Roosevelt Street, and west of Lake Michigan. It includes many of Chicago's landmarks and nerve centers—its civic arenas, its finest cultural venues, its smartest hotels, and its most important financial centers.

Why does the Loop seem so empty?... Chicagoans may claim that they like the great outdoors, but every day thousands of Loop office workers and shoppers never see a shred of sunlight. That's because they're underground squirreling through the **Pedway**, a subterranean maze of covered walkways that connect numerous train stops, much of the Loop, and its environs on weekdays, from 6am to 6:30pm. The tunnels are marked with "You are Here" signs throughout, though getting lost is half the fun, or at least half the adventure, of being there.

What's so great about State Street?... Lots, actually. When the glitz and glam of North Michigan Avenue becomes too much to take, State Street's old-time urban aura can be a pleasant antidote. Its current strength lies not so much in the reflection of its past, but in its current reincarnation as a middle-class, bargain-hunters' paradise, upscale **Marshall Field's** notwithstanding. In the last few years a gargantuan three-story **Toys 'R' Us** opened (10 S. State St.), which caused a brouhaha among purists who saw this as the final step in the suburbanization of the street. It's been a huge success, though, and has made it possible for other popular discount stores to move in. A few architectural gems have avoided the wrecker's ball lo these many years, and are worth a look up: **Carson Pirie Scott & Co.** (1 S. State St.), designed by Louis Sullivan and completed in 1904, and Daniel Burnham's 1890, 15-story **Reliance Building** (32 N. State St.), both of which presaged much of today's modern architecture. Architectural insignificance, however, is the key to one of the street's other highlights—called **Block 37**, just across the street from Field's. Starting out as an urban nightmare when it was cleared to make room for a huge shopping-and-office development that never got off the ground—literally—the square block has evolved into one of the most pleasant oases in the area, with an outdoor art gallery during the summer months and an ice skating rink in winter.

What's so magnificent about the Magnificent Mile?... The Magnificent Mile isn't, in fact, a mile at all—it's the stretch of Michigan Avenue starting at Oak Street and running south to the Chicago River, which measures slightly less than a mile in length. What's real, however, is its magnificence. Once lined with some of the city's most renowned architecture, the street has evolved over the years from a sleepy yet chic thoroughfare of five-story limestone buildings, to a bustling, traffic-choked canyon of cash-cow retailers and gleaming office buildings. Yet, it's still elegant, wide, and surprisingly light-filled, with water on both ends (the lake at the north end, the river at the south). The Mag Mile is the true retail center of the city, as well as a business center and an upscale residential neighborhood. And at Christmas time, when the trees are strung with tiny white lights that make the street glitter like a diamond necklace, it's an especially gorgeous sight.

Is there anyone in town who doesn't idolize Michael Jordan?... No.

Well, I brought my car—now where am I going to park it?... Parking on the street in most neighborhoods is a huge pain in the kiester—meters are enforced by an army of persnickety meter readers, and a parking space on

Chicago in the movies, part 1—downtown
The 1938 period piece In Old Chicago starred Tyrone Power and Don Ameche as two sons of Mrs. O'Leary, the lady who accidentally started the Chicago Fire. Brian DePalma's mob pic The Untouchables (1987), starring Kevin Costner, Sean Connery, and Robert De Niro, had one great shootout scene with a baby carriage bouncing down the steps at Union Station. Chicago almost saw its destruction during 1980's The Blues Brothers, when John Belushi and Dan Aykroyd drove their Blues-mobile through Daley Plaza. And who could forget The Beginning of the End, a horrible 1957 sci-fi flick with Peter Graves in which giant grass-hoppers invade Chicago?

CHICAGO | YOU PROBABLY DIDN'T KNOW

side streets, where it's free, is a rare commodity. In addition, the city of Chicago loves, loves, loves to have cars towed, and the companies that do the actual towing are not known for service with a smile. (It'll cost you at least $100 to ransom your car.) Most decent restaurants have valet parking for $4 or $5, which is generally a good deal considering the cost to your psyche of driving around the block for a half-hour looking for a space. There are privately owned parking garages all over the city, which are generally well-lit, safe, and convenient, if pricey. Municipal lots, where the prices are generally lower than the private garages' (how does $5 for 24 hours sound to you?), are mostly downtown; see Hotlines for a list.

Does Chicago really have more Polish people than anywhere save Warsaw?... Well, there are about two million people in Warsaw—presumably almost all Poles, right?—and, according to the librarian at the Polish Museum of America (tel 312/384–3352, 984 N. Milwaukee Ave.), about 1,000,000 Poles and Polish-Americans living in Chicago. Nowhere else comes close.

How can I sound like a real Chicagoan?... Pronounce the city's name Chicawgo, not Chicahgo.

What's "coffee and"?... A Chicago idiom, the phrase means coffee and a piece of cake, coffee and a pastrami sandwich, coffee and a slice of pie—whatever you might have after a movie or play. "Come on," you might say, "let's get some coffee and." I know, it sounds like a word is missing, but trust me, it's not.

And how about "come with"?... Another idiom. It means come with me, or us, so when a Chicagoan asks, "Do you want to come with?" it's actually an invitation of some sort.

Where can I hear music for free?... While there are clubs all over town that feature live music (see Entertainment), the city itself sponsors some of the best sounds every summer—and it's free. Chicago's line-up of three-day music festivals, which takes place at the **Petrillo Music Shell in Grant Park**, rivals the music you'll hear anywhere else in town. The best events are the **Chicago Blues Festival** and the **Chicago Gospel Festival**, both in June; the **Chicago Country Music Festival** in July; the **Chicago Jazz Festival** in August; and **Viva! Chicago**, the Latin music festival, in September. In addition, the **Grant Park Music Festival**

(also at the Petrillo Music Shell) includes nighttime outdoor concerts ranging from classical to show tunes, performed by the **Grant Park Symphony and Chorus**;
they're on Wednesday, Friday, Saturday, and Sunday
evenings throughout the summer.

**Can I go to the opera and the symphony when
I'm in town?...** It depends on when you come. Just like
the weather, Chicago's cultural resources have seasons,
too. The **Lyric Opera of Chicago** (tel 312/332–2244),
for instance, performs September through February, the
Chicago Opera Theater's (tel 312/292–7521) season is
June through July, so neither of them will be around if
you're here in the spring. The **Chicago Symphony Orchestra** (tel 312/435–6666 or 800/223–7114) plays September through June; in the summer they retire to
Ravinia, while downtown the **Grant Park Symphony
and Chorus** (tel 312/742–7638) concerts begin in June
and run through August.

What if I gotta go?... Chicago's a pretty user-friendly
place when it comes to finding decent, clean public bathrooms. Hotels, of course, are the best bets. **The Drake**,
the **Park Hyatt**, the **Ritz-Carlton**, and **Four Seasons** are
all reliable way stations. There are little-known and very
private bathrooms at **Crate & Barrel** on Michigan
Avenue, and at the **Starbucks** coffee shop on Rush Street.
And, of course, there are bathrooms within all the department stores and malls, such as **Water Tower Place**.

accomm

1

odations

Chicago hosts
more conven-
tions—especially
the really big
ones—than
almost any
other city. That

situation has both its ups and its downs. On the upside it means that there are many, many hotels catering to people and corporations with various budgets, from deluxe to demure to depressing (though none of the latter are listed here). The sheer number of hotels also has meant that there is a wide breadth of styles available, from small and intimate European-style inns to you-know-what-you're-gonna-get chain hotels to showy chintz-furnished palaces. The downside, of course, is that some hotels—especially the you-know-what-you're-gonna-getniks—can be about as personal as a K-Mart. They're used to dealing in volume, so don't expect a French-accented concierge who'll remember your name, or rooms with much dash. Because of the number of conventions the city hosts, there are times of year that it is almost impossible to book a room if you haven't done so way in advance. Blocks of hundreds of rooms in many of the bigger hotels are reserved annually for conventioneers. If you are lucky (or unlucky, depending on your attitude) enough to visit the city when one of the big conventions is in town, you may be sharing your temporary home with hordes of mid-level vice-presidents traipsing the halls in starchy white shirts, rep ties, and plastic name-tags.

Overall, the selection of hotels in Chicago outshines that of most other cities. In the past decade or so, there has been a hotel building boom, and thousands of newly available (mostly upscale) rooms in such hotels as the **Four Seasons**, **Hotel Nikko**, **The Fairmont**, and **Swissotel** have forced the old stalwarts—like **The Palmer House Hilton**, which had fallen on musty times—to invest millions of dollars in renovations just to remain viable. And, perhaps because of the competition, even in the biggest of the big convention sleep warehouses, service is more often with a smile than a sneer. After all, the city's hotel employees are aware that the conventioneers only return to Chicago year after year because the service is so consistently good.

Winning the Reservations Game

There's only one real rule when making a hotel reservation in Chicago: don't be a chump. In other words, don't agree to pay what are referred to in the hotel business as "rack prices," meaning the highest nightly fee at which rooms are rented—which is the one you'll be quoted. It's not that you can exactly haggle with the reservations clerk—though you've got nothing to lose by trying—but there are many ways to get a better price. Most hotels have special corporate rates, which may be 10 percent lower than the rack rate. In most cases, you'll have to prove you're really there on business, but some hotels will simply take you at your word. There are often deals for frequent fliers, the elderly, auto-club members, people in the military, or teachers and others who work in education. It pays, literally, to ask about any of these.

Because most conventions occur during the week, Chicago hotels are relatively uninhabited on weekends, even during peak season. Most offer weekend hotel packages year-round, so if you're in town for an entire week you could stay the weekdays at a bland-but-not-too-expensive chain hotel and then move to a fancier place for about the same price or less for the weekend. Some hotels in Chicago also offer special tie-ins with various events and exhibitions. The **Stouffer Renaissance**, for example, works closely with the Art Institute to create weekends geared toward art lovers who may be visiting Chicago just to see the museum's latest blockbuster show. Theater tie-ins are another popular way hotels lure guests.

Hotels well known for the views offered from one side of their building may discount the rooms on the other side, so it's always smart to ask if you can get a cheaper room if you face the city instead of the lake. (After all, there are other ways to see the lake.) Making reservations early is imperative, especially if you are traveling during peak season—January, April, May, and June, when the weather is the most pleasant and/or when the biggest conventions take over the town. During non-peak months, however, rooms may be discounted up to 50 percent off the rack price. You can also get a 50-percent-or-more discount if you go through **Hot Rooms** (tel 800/468–3500), a Chicago-based service that works with about 15 downtown and Gold Coast hotels such as the Drake, the Blackstone, and the Knickerbocker. You can call Hot Rooms 24 hours a day, seven days a week, and there's no fee (though if you make a confirmed reservation and then cancel there is a $25 fee). Hot Rooms operators are familiar with other local hotels as well, and can direct you to similar sites should your first choice be unavailable, though of course they'll try to get you into another Hot Rooms hotel if possible.

Is There a Right Address?

Most of the city's best (and most expensive) hotels are along or at least nearby the **Magnificent Mile**, from **The Drake** at the street's northern tip to the **Chicago Hilton and Towers** farther south. Recent additions to the city's hotel scene, including the **Four Seasons**, are in the **North Michigan Avenue** area, the retailing center of the city, which has many of the best restaurants within walking distance as well. In addition, it's one of the city's safest neighborhoods. But busting out of the Mag Mile area and staying in other neighborhoods can make for a different perspective, especially if you've visited the city before. If you want to be near the action, but not in the center of the storm, you might try staying in the **Gold Coast** neighborhood just north of Michigan Avenue. Its quiet, tree-lined streets are some of the city's poshest. It's peaceful and understated, yet near enough to the beach and shopping that you won't need a cab every time you walk out the door of your hotel. If you're a glutton for punishment, and your plans include a three-day stint attending Cubs games, you're better off staying in **Lake View**, which has a few small, inexpensive places within walking distance of Wrigley Field. Ditto Lake View if your shopping tastes lean more towards the funky than the fancy. Nightclubs, bars, and jazz and blues clubs all proliferate here. For business trips or museum-hopping, **the Loop** is a good bet, given its proximity to the financial district, convention center, and the Art Institute et al, but keep in mind that there aren't too many restaurants in the area, and nightlife will most likely require a cab ride. The Loop is so dead after-hours and on weekends, it can seem eerie. Some of the city's newest high-rise hotels—including the **Sheraton**, **The Fairmont**, and **Swissotel**—are way east of Michigan Avenue in quasi-neighborhoods such as **Illinois Center** and **Cityfront Center**. They

Chicago in the movies, part 2—the neighborhoods

About Last Night *(1986)*, one of the more stupid-but-famous movies made here, takes place in and around Lincoln Park, with brat packers Demi Moore, Rob Lowe, real Chicagoan James Belushi, and Elizabeth Perkins. The movie's set designer went loco and decorated an el stop—usually grungy and in need of paint—with Christmas lights and bunting during a holiday scene (a good use of our tax dollars, right?). While You Were Sleeping propelled Sandra Bullock to stardom, but the 1995 movie, filmed in Lake View, is totally implausible—believe me, real el token clerks are never as cute as the one she played. The first ten minutes of 1989's When Harry Met Sally take place in Hyde Park at the University of Chicago (though Billy Crystal and Meg Ryan behave so stupidly, it's hard to believe they even got into the U of C to begin with). And for a taste of the South Side, try the 1975 comedy Cooley High (set in 1964), or the riveting 1994 documentary Hoop Dreams, which chronicled the lives of two ghetto b-ball stars.

have great views all around, but it's a trek (usually involving a cab) to get anywhere; there's nothing to do in the immediate area, so it can assume a surreal, where-is-everybody feel. The hotels near **O'Hare Airport** are, well, near the airport. They cater to a business crowd (though they attempt to be attractive to others as well by offering weekend packages), and basically are convenient, safe, clean, and about as dull as a dishrag.

The Lowdown

Big bucks de luxe... Guests schlep Marshall Field's and Lord & Taylor bags right upstairs from Water Tower Place to the twelfth floor, where they enter the enormous greenhouse lobby of **The Ritz-Carlton**. The tone is set by plush furnishings, an oddly loud but fanciful fountain, English tea carts piled high with pastries and dainty sandwiches, and other guests surrounded by mountains of Louis Vuitton luggage and hovering uniformed bellhops. The hotel spends a quarter-million dollars a year just on flowers, and it shows. You'll probably feel every cent was well spent, though it does seem pretty chintzy that guests paying upwards of a couple hundred dollars a night have to fork over another $8 for each visit to the hotel's health club—especially considering that the **Four Seasons** across the street, which is owned by the same company, doesn't charge guests to use its facility. The Four Seasons—which sits atop Bloomingdale's, if that's your shopping preference—in many ways seems like a huge English country manor in the sky. The beds here are so comfortable that a few years ago guests began to ask where they could buy one; now they can, believe it or not, through the hotel's gift shop. The intimate (some might say the low-ceilinged guest rooms are cramped) **Park Hyatt**, located directly across the street from the Water Tower on Michigan Avenue, throws in a free car wash, of all things, with its high rates. But some guests, such as Elizabeth Taylor (when she hits town she always stays in the hotel's Penthouse Suite, complete with 14 phones and a Steinway piano) think it's worth it. The regular rooms are pretty, though nothing special, but the service could spoil you permanently—your luggage is unpacked for you; bottled water and fresh fruit and a newspaper are delivered every day; rooms are stocked with fresh flowers, jelly beans, fax machines, free coffee, and shoe shines; and

CHICAGO | ACCOMMODATIONS

there's *three*-times-a-day maid service. Unlike the rest of the city's expensive hotels, **The Drake** has an old-timey, aristocratic feel that some might find dowdy. But if you like the kind of environment where old ladies in white gloves and Republicans wearing wingtips feel comfortable, then this is the place. The barber shop, or as they call it, gentleman's grooming service, shouldn't be missed.

The grande dames... The huge pink neon sign on the roof of **The Drake** has become as much a part of the city skyline as the nearby Hancock Center, which is about five times as tall. Built in 1920 by Ben Marshall, the famous architect to Chicago's rich and famous, and modelled after Renaissance palaces, the Drake hasn't lost its elegance. Its guest rooms, decorated in reproduction English furniture, aren't as plush as some other luxe sleeperies, but few can match it in inherent grace. Similarly, **The Palmer House Hilton**, the city's oldest hotel and the longest continually running hotel on the continent, still offers a pretty fabulous welcome to the jillions of businesspeople passing through its portal, especially after a $120 million top-to-toe renovation. Located smack in the middle of the Loop, this Chicago institution has a spectacular gilded lobby with a soaring, mural-covered ceiling, sweeping staircases, and furniture covered in thick velvet brocades and moire taffetas. The sprawling **Chicago Hilton and Towers** is the sort of place where waiters have been known to work for 50 years, where one doorman started the day the hotel opened in 1927 and retired decades later when he was 95 years old. Though the ornate lobby is rife with square conventioneers and tour groups dressed for a big day on the bus, the hotel has plenty of big-city glamour. Unlike the other Chicago classics, the **Omni Ambassador East** is small enough that the concierge will remember your name. When you mention to a local that you're staying here, they nod a knowing nod and just say, "Ahhhh." At The **Knickerbocker**, another venerable smaller hotel, gangsters and socialites once partied, and later, Hugh Hefner ruled his Playboy empire; nowadays it's trying to make a comeback with a multi-million-dollar renovation, this time molding its image as a business hotel. If you have a good imagination, you might be able to conjure the grandeur that once was the **Congress Hotel** and not focus on its current shabby state.

Dowdy but lovable... Originally built in 1924 as a private men's club, the enormous **Allerton** is, while clean, on the shabby—but not shabby-chic—side. It's been rehabbed in chunks, at different times over the decades, giving it a dotty, old-fashioned charm. (Its room rates are the best bargains on Michigan Avenue, which doesn't hurt.) The **Blackstone,** by no means a first-class hotel, is campy in its nod to the past, with loads of red velvet and polished wood and giant brass wall sconces; it's so old and over-the-top it's hip. All sorts of movies have been shot here, including scenes from *The Untouchables* and *The Hudsucker Proxy.* **The Raphael** also has a dowdy charm, with a slighty goofy staff—well-meaning but just a bit odd—and the lobby's gloomy tapestries and Gothic-style decorative features. **The Talbott Hotel**'s fox hunt decorating theme is a tad on the twee side, but the hotel—converted in 1989 from a 1920s-vintage apartment building—has the casual comfort of a well-worn blazer. For post-modern dowdiness, there's the **Sutton Place Hotel,** which opened in 1988 and quickly became the city's trendiest hotel; it has managed to hold onto that cachet despite a less than stellar atmosphere. Where once it had slim muscle guys with really good haircuts garbed in Armani-inspired uniforms scurrying about, now there are garishly red-coated people with big boufs and tacky little name-tags. Some of the furniture is nicked up and really could use an upgrade—which, supposedly, it's getting. Even so, with the great location (a block from Oak Street beach and around the corner from the city's best shopping) and a restaurant that's ground-zero for fabulous people-watching, the Sutton Place continues to attract a fast-talking, deal-cutting clientele.

Best views... There are only three things you really want to see out your windows in Chicago: the lake, the skyline, or the Chicago River. At the **Stouffer Renaissance** you can get all of the above, and sometimes from the same room (ask to face north), at least if you stay on one of the top floors. It helps that all the rooms have bay windows, which add a 3-D drama to the panorama. Ditto at the modern but luxurious **Fairmont,** at least from its suites, which are lined up on the east side of the hotel to monopolize the best vistas of the lake (and of the city's downtown nine-hole golf course, the Illinois Center Golf Course). Also in Illinois Center, there are unobstructed views from every angle of the triangularly shaped **Swissotel,** even from the forty-second-floor health club and pool, though otherwise the Swissotel is bland as vanilla. There are great lake views from the **Chicago Hilton and Towers**, too, but its perspective of Grant Park and its gorgeous formal and wildflower gardens is the real knock-out. Though more expensive, the north-facing rooms at **The Drake** are the only ones in the city to overlook the lake, the Gold Coast, and Lincoln Park. At the **Sheraton Chicago**, the views are pretty terrific from both sides—it's how far up or down you are that makes all the difference. If you're facing north try to get a room on a high floor for best views of North Michigan Avenue and the lake, but if you're on the south side, book a lower floor for spectacular views of the Chicago River. Expensive hotels don't have a monopoly on spectacular views, either; you can go as cheap as the **Congress Hotel** and get a clear, wide-open view of Grant Park and Lake Michigan, while the reasonably priced **Days Inn** gives you an eyeful of the lake and of Navy Pier from east-facing rooms; face west and your city panorama is one of the finest.

Gold Coasters... Spiffy, uniformed doormen greet you beneath a dramatic, old-fashioned gold-and-creamy-white canopy at the Georgian-style **Omni Ambassador East**, located on a quiet residential street only a block from the lake in the affluent Gold Coast. The neighborhood location gives this Chicago classic an air of seclusion that helps endear it to celebrities. Nearby, **The Claridge** offers the same neighborhood feel, convenience, and personal attention, all at lower prices, though its plainer furnishings move it a couple of notches down on the glamour scale. Both hotels are far enough away from the hustle and hassle of Michigan Avenue, yet close enough to walk there.

If everyone else stays on Michigan Avenue, I don't want to... The **Hyatt on Printers Row** is too hip for Michigan Avenue and extremely un-Hyatt-y—a small hotel in a national historic landmark, built in a South Loop neighborhood constructed right after the Great Fire, and recently gentrified with condos, a few trendy boutiques, and bookstores. Don't worry about being far from restaurants—downstairs is one of the city's best, Prairie. Also south of the river, though on the north bank of the Loop, the contemporary-style **Clarion Executive Plaza** offers great city- and riverscapes; the boxlike gray **Stouffer Renaissance** is on the same street, but two blocks farther in from the lake; and the sleek **Hotel Nikko** sits across the river from them, well inland from Michigan Avenue. In trendy River North, there's the **Best Western River North** and the **Ohio House Motel**—good for those who'll spend most of their time out enjoying the neighborhood, rather than basking in the standard motel-issue rooms. A trio of quaint, quiet, quirky hotels run by the same management, the **Park Brompton**, **The Surf Hotel**, and the **City Suites Hotel Chicago** are smart choices for budget-minded travelers willing to stay far from the downtown crowd. Each is within walking distance of many of the city's gay bars and dance clubs, Wrigley Field, the Lincoln Park Zoo, and only a few blocks from the lake, tennis courts, and the Waveland Golf Course (and only a 15-minute bus ride from the Mag Mile). It's even folksier at **Arlington House**, which isn't so much a hotel as a hostel in Lincoln Park. Way off in Hyde Park, near the University of Chicago and the Museum of Science and Industry, there's not much lodging choice except for the **Ramada Inn Lakeshore**. Though it's isolated from the rest of the city (you shouldn't walk to other neighborhoods from here, though trains and buses are an option), you get a great view of the whole downtown skyline in the distance.

Lobbies to die for... You may feel breathless when you enter the gigantic lobby of the the **Chicago Hilton and Towers**, all gilded and full of green and pink marble. The octagonal sunken lobby of **The Fairmont** is conspicuously filled with cushy velvet divans, glass-top tables, and flowers that fill the high-ceilinged space with a faintly sweet aroma. Step off the seventh-floor elevator at the **Four Seasons**, and room after room, salon after salon, unfolds before you as if you're in some Merchant-Ivory film—tufted sofas and chairs, inlaid marble floors, highly polished English-y furniture, Chinese porcelain bowls, and a legion of uniformed men and women dashing about, presumably carrying out every whim of every guest. In a radically different vein, one of the city's most beautiful gathering places is the **Hotel Nikko**'s sleek black-granite lobby, outfitted with chic black leather sofas and Asian art and artifacts, and overlooking an extensive Japanese rock garden and the Chicago River.

Family values... Suite hotels are generally a great solution when you've got kids in tow, giving you what amounts to two rooms for the price of one, usually with cooking facilities to boot. For families on a budget, the **Lenox Suites**, located just a block off Michigan Avenue, has one- and two-room suites with kitchenettes (stocked with free coffee and juice) and separate sitting- and dining areas. Somewhat pricier but still handy are the **Doubletree Guest Suites** and the **Embassy Suites**, which have indoor pools as a bonus. If cooking for yourself is about the furthest thing from your mind, and you've got the money, the family suite at the **Four Seasons** is definitely the way to go. There's a king-size bedroom for Mom and Dad and a smaller kids' bedroom with twin beds. Each suite has Nintendo, two bathrooms, kid-sized bathrobes, and a minibar filled with jelly beans, chocolate chip cookies, and M&Ms; milk and cookies for the kids (and the adults, if requested) is served at bedtime. In addition, the hotel provides guests in all rooms with a crib, diapers, strollers, formula, and baby food on request, and arranges for babysitting. At the **Hotel Nikko**, kids under 18 stay free with their parents and get a gift bag at check-in, which includes an inflatable frisbee. The **Holiday Inn Chicago City Centre**'s spacious and bright—if standard—rooms are kid-friendly (and free for children under 18), and the location near the beach will save you on transportation. The hotel is big enough that if the kids run around and get out of hand for a while, no one will notice.

For lovers and those who want to be... When you and your companion need to get away from it all (the office, the wife, the husband, the kids, the other lover), discretion is the key ingredient. At the **Sutton Place Hotel** you'll find everything you need in your room—including a VCR (rent a steamy movie) and, in the chic black-and-white tiled bathrooms, a deep-soaking tub big enough for two. Take a left out the front door and you'll be in the center of a lot of neon-lit nightlife, but if you opt to take a right and walk down the otherwise quiet street, there's little chance of running into whomever it is you're trying to avoid. The ceilings in the guest rooms of the **Park Hyatt** seem low, which makes those blandly pretty rooms feel cozy. It's cozy and intimate at **The Tremont**, whose traditionally furnished rooms are done up with abandon in Laura Ashley–like chintz, all matching frilly bedskirts and flowered draperies and valences. Etched-glass double doors divide the bedroom from the living room in the suites at the **Four Seasons**, adding just the right tone of romance to the sumptuously furnished rooms; the room-service food here is so good you never really have to leave your room at all, and the beds are reportedly the most comfortable in town. But the ultimate key to romance may be at the **Chicago Hilton** and the **Knickerbocker**, where many guest rooms have two bathrooms—a set-up that not-so-scientifically has been proven to reduce the number of lovers' quarrels.

Suite deals... If you're travelling with the kids or insist on fixing your own eggs in the morning, try an all-suite hotel. Chicago has a number of them, where every guest room has at least a separate sitting area and some kind of kitchenette. Tops in this category are the sleek **Embassy Suites** with its echoing atrium, the crisply modern **Omni Chicago** on Michigan Avenue, and the traditionally furnished **Doubletree Guest Suites** hotel, a high-rise right off Michigan Avenue that has some of the best views in town. All three also have pools and some kind of gym or health club, as does the somewhat smaller and more personal **Summerfield Suites**. The roomy and reasonably priced quarters at the **Lenox Suites** are downright homey, with sofabeds, kitchenettes, and microwaves (but no gym, nor pool). If you're talking suites—as in "I'm taking a suite of rooms for my entourage,"—that's a different and more luxurious story. The opulent **Conrad Hilton Suite**, named after the former owner of the **Chicago Hilton and Towers**, sits like a birthday cake on the top of the hotel. With its Jacuzzi overlooking Lake Michigan, grand salon, enormous crystal chandeliers, two bedrooms, library, and 17th-century Flemish tapestries on the walls, it's an exaggerated version of all the regular rooms and suites, which are top-of-the-line themselves, with Chippendale-style furniture and great soothing views of the parks and harbors. Best feature of the **Anniversary Suites** at **The Ritz-Carlton**: awe-inspiring, all-marble oversized bathtubs facing floor-to-ceiling windows overlooking the city. At the **Hotel Nikko**, special tatami suites include a futon for sleeping, a private rock garden, an oversize soaking tub, and even an elaborate traditional tea/sake/sushi ceremony.

Pet accompli... It's not easy to find a hotel that will allow you to stay over with Fido, but the French-accented **Hotel Sofitel** out near O'Hare is one of them, at least if said dog

CHICAGO | ACCOMMODATIONS

is small (like a French poodle, oui?). Unfortunately, no cats are allowed.

Mega-hotels for conventioneers... If you're here at a convention, you're probably staying at whatever place your company put you. At least you've been saved from having to decide among the massive, charm-free convention hotels. If you've been given that unfortunate duty, though, here are the ones to keep in mind. For sheer size, the standouts are the **Chicago Marriott**, with more than 1,000 rooms and 55,000 square feet of exhibition space, and the **Hyatt Regency**, a mega-hotel with more than 2,000 cookie-cutter guest rooms (each of which includes an ironing board and iron so you can get spiffed up for that 7:30am seminar) and 188,000 square feet of meeting space. Both have about as much charm as a freeway, and you may feel stupid not wearing a "Hello, my name is..." tag pinned to your gray pinstripe. The Hyatt's attached to the Illinois Center business complex by an underground maze of hallways, which also links it to the **Swissotel**, with more than 600 rooms, creating one big convention megalopolis. An enormous line of yellow cabs snaking around the **Chicago Hilton and Towers** is a sure sign a convention has just hit town, since that hotel is the closest of the bunch to McCormick Place, the city's main exhibition and convention hall. Unlike the others, the Hilton's rooms are outfitted in residential-like furniture that won't make you feel you're so far from home. Ditto **The Palmer House Hilton**, well located in the Loop, whose more than 1,600 guest rooms fill up during peak convention season. The shiny gold **Hyatt Regency O'Hare** has only two things going for it: size (1,100 rooms and 81,000 square feet of exhibition space) and direct access to the O'Hare Expocenter.

Taking care of business... It seems as though every Chicago hotel is trying to be a "business hotel." Whereas the convention hotels succeed by having hanger-like amounts of space to handle the crowds, business hotels make an effort to see business travelers as individuals. The **Radisson Hotel and Suites**, for example, has computer modem hook-ups in the rooms, voice mail, and halogen lamps so you can actually see your work. Most rooms in the **Omni Chicago Hotel** have fax machines. The **Knicker-**

bocker is going beyond modems by actually installing computers in some rooms; it's also outfitting those business rooms with fax machines. For an extra $15 a night, the **Hyatt on Printers Row** provides a room with a computer modem jack, a coffeemaker, newspaper delivery, and an express Continental breakfast. You'll find in-room fax machines/copiers, modem hookups, and shoe buffers at **The Fairmont**, as well as a slew of homier touches, such as real art on the walls, lots of plants in the rooms, and windows that actually open to catch the breeze. As tony and almost as well-equipped is the **Stouffer Renaissance**, where about a fifth of the rooms have multiple phone lines, data ports for modems, and fax machines; to help harried business travelers stay on schedule, they guarantee room-service delivery within 25 minutes or it's on the house (now if they could get that down to 10 minutes…). The Stouffer offers another rare freebie, too: it waives telephone surcharges on 800-, credit card-, and collect calls, which can save a bundle. The dining table in the two-room suites at the **Doubletree Guest Suites** easily doubles as a large work space, and the hotel offers what it calls "female traveler suites," complete with hairdryers, irons, ironing boards, and upgraded bathroom amenities. (So what are men with fly-away hair and wrinkled shirts supposed to do?)

Gym dandies... Well-equipped gym facilities (with Lifecycles, rowers, a Gravitron, treadmills, Nautilus weight stations, Stairmasters, and free weights) and swimming pools—or at least lap pools—are almost de riguer nowadays, so it's no surprise that many of the city's best hotels, including the **Stouffer Renaissance**, **Chicago Hilton and Towers**, **Embassy Suites**, **Omni Chicago**, **Palmer House**, **Summerfield Suites**, and **Hotel Nikko**, have such high-end perks (though the Nikko has no pool). Most will even lend you workout clothes. A few other hotels, though, have even more going for them. The **Swissotel**'s forty-second-floor health club has dynamite views, and the **Doubletree Guest Suites** has a great rooftop gym and pool. The **Four Seasons** has a quarter-mile outdoor running track and and sundeck, as well as a glass-domed eighth-floor 50-foot swimming pool, surrounded by columns and windows overlooking the city. But even it can't compete with the utter fabulousness of the thirteenth-floor swimming pool at the **Hotel Inter-Continental Chicago**. Surrounded by stained-glass windows, mosaics, wicker chaise longues, huge potted palms, and wrought-metal sconces, the Italianate junior Olympic-size pool (75 feet) was the training ground for the original Tarzan, Johnny Weissmuller. Even if you're not staying here, you should make a special trip to see it. It's that cool.

Cheap sleeps... You don't get much in the way of luxurious perks by staying at the **Park Brompton**, **The Surf Hotel**, and the **City Suites Hotel Chicago**, three small, eccentric Lake View hotels, but you do get to go to bed each evening knowing that you're not spending much. Convenient to the galleries and eateries of River North are two more decent bargains: the **Best Western River North**, which has a rooftop pool, and **Ohio House Motel**, which has a coffeeshop were you can get a $2.95 breakfast of two eggs, two strips of bacon, two sausages, and two pancakes (attention, hearty eaters). If a central location is important to you, by far the cheapest place to stay along Michigan Avenue is the **Allerton**—what the hotel obviously saves in decorating costs it apparently passes on to guests. Within spitting distance of Michigan Avenue, the **Motel 6** is a bargain, if you're willing to go for generic furnishings and minimal service. Or if you'd like to be south of the river, near the Loop and the museums, there's the **Essex Inn**, the **Best Western Grant Park**, and the econo-model motel **The Avenue** (the latter two do have outdoor pools). But the hands-down cheapest place to stay in town is **Arlington House**, a hostel with both private rooms and dormitory sleeping arrangements, where the clientele is mainly backpacking students and foreigners. Bring your own linen, or rent theirs—it's that kind of place (though the coffee is free).

May I get that for you, sir?... At the **Four Seasons** they really service you, so to speak. Forget your entire wardrobe? No problem. The hotel has a deal with Bloomingdale's, which is in the same building, through which you can get a new wardrobe delivered to your room (though you'll pay through the proverbial nose). Got a hankering to work out at a great gym with a personal trainer? No problem. They've got those, too. Each room even has a private safe for those traveling with jewels à la the Duchess of Windsor. **The Tremont** will lend its guests a cellular phone for the day. At the **Sutton Place**

Hotel, a BMW is available on a first-come, first-served basis for guests to use during their stay. Ditto at the **Park Hyatt**, except the car choice there is a dark Mercedes, and if you've brought your own car, they'll wash it for you for free. Anything else I can do for you, sir?

Oh so near O'Hare... Staying near the airport is usually a matter of convenience—you need to make an early morning flight, or you're forced to stay an extra day because your flight's been delayed or the wing fell off the plane. A courtesy van shuttles people and luggage between the airport and the nearby hotels, which are many but undistinguished. You can while away the hours in your room at the **Sheraton Gateway Suites** by playing Nintendo, which is included in each room; the two-room suites at the **Radisson Plaza O'Hare** include a microwave, for those too travel-weary to face another restaurant. The **Hyatt Regency O'Hare** offers an automated check-in and check-out machine (like an ATM) that takes about 90 seconds; you just stick in your credit card, punch a few buttons, and you're on your way. Give the relatively small and civilized (for an airport hotel, anyhow) **Hotel Sofitel** a round of applause for trying to create a little excitement for its guests: you get a rose on your bed each night at turndown, and a loaf of French bread when you check out. If nothing else, that could help you skip the airline's mystery-meal-on-a-tray on your flight home.

ACCOMMODATIONS | CHICAGO

The Index

$$$$$	over $250
$$$$	$200–$250
$$$	$140–$200
$$	$100–$140
$	under $100

Price applies to a standard double room for one night.

Allerton. Though the decor's pretty tired-looking, this big hotel does have a spectacular location right on Michigan Avenue and room rates about as cheap as they come.... *Tel 312/ 440–1500 and 800/621–8311. 701 N. Michigan Ave., Chicago, IL 60611. 450 rms. $$*

Arlington House. This friendly and cheap little hostel is on a leafy Lincoln Park Street, about a 15-minute bus ride from downtown and within walking distance of many of the city's best blues, jazz, and dance clubs. There are both private rooms and dormitory sleeping arrangements. What this place lacks in amenities (which is just about everything), it makes up for in low rates, which are even lower if you're a member of the American Youth Hostel Federation.... *Tel 312/929–5380 and 800/538–0074. 616 W. Arlington Place, Chicago, IL 60614. 200 beds, 40 private rms. $*

The Avenue. A motel in every sense of the word—rather sterile decor, and not all that new, though clean enough— the Avenue's most attractive feature is its price. The neighborhood's not one you should stroll around much at night, and there are Illinois Central train tracks right across the street, but it's also a short distance from the three museums anchoring Grant Park, not to mention Soldier Field, and it has an outdoor pool.... *Tel 312/427–8200. 1154 S. Michigan Ave., Chicago, IL 60605. 78 rms. $*

Best Western Grant Park. Once a dive called the Ascot, the Best Western Grant Park got a facelift and is now respectable, albeit with standard-issue motel furnishings, but the rates are still pretty cheap. The location is a little too deep-south for many travelers' taste, but it's convenient to some key museums—the Field, the Shedd Aquarium, and the Adler Planetarium. The hotel also has an outdoor pool and workout facilities.... *Tel 312/922–2900 and 800/528–1234. 1100 S. Michigan Ave., Chicago, IL 60605. 172 rms. $$*

Best Western River North Hotel. The two main things the Best Western has going for it are its location amid trendy galleries and restaurants and its price—weekend rates begin at $69. There's also an all-season rooftop pool.... *Tel 312/467–0800 and 800/528–1234, fax 312/467–1665.*

125 W. Ohio St. (at the corner of LaSalle), Chicago, IL 60610. 152 rms. $

Blackstone Hotel. Perhaps the only hotel remaining in Chicago where you could actually make believe you were living in the gangster days of Prohibition. Rooms are large and comfortable and generally have good views.... *Tel 312/427–4300 and 800/622–6330. 636 S. Michigan Ave., Chicago, IL 60605. 305 rms. $$*

Chicago Hilton and Towers. This imposing hotel is full of the sort of big-city pomp that others have to hire art directors and public relations flacks to create. Grand in every way, from the ornate lobby with its 60-foot ceiling to the gilded ballrooms, it has very well-appointed rooms—cherrywood cabinets and quilted bedspreads—and a terrific health club (unfortunately named the "Fun & Fitness Center").... *Tel 312/922–4400 and 800-HILTONS, fax 312/922–5240. 730 S. Michigan Ave., Chicago, IL 60605. 1,543 rms. $$$*

Chicago Marriott. Quite possibly the ugliest hotel in the city, this mega-sleepery has one thing going for it: location, location, location. It's also one of the more reasonably priced hotels on the Magnificent Mile. Otherwise, this white marble box is totally bland. There is, however, outdoor paddle tennis.... *Tel 312/836–0100 and 800/831–4004, fax 312/ 836–6139. 540 N. Michigan Ave., Chicago, IL 60611. 1,172 rms. $$$$*

City Suites Hotel Chicago. There aren't too many hotels that would boast about their former incarnation as the home to gangsters and their molls, but this small, funky place does. And why not, considering its location right on busy Belmont Avenue amidst restaurants, coffeehouses, night clubs, and stores selling everything from Doc Martens to sun-dried tomato bagels. With the floors heavily carpeted and the windows equally draped, the fact that the el rumbles by 24 hours a day only a few hundred yards away doesn't seem to bug anyone. Simply decorated rooms, suave black-and-white tile bathrooms.... *Tel 312/404–3400. 933 W. Belmont Ave., Chicago, IL 60657. 45 rms. $*

The Claridge. A small hotel on a beautiful Gold Coast street, its rooms are all plainly decorated in beiges and maroons,

CHICAGO | ACCOMMODATIONS

though a few suites do have fireplaces. Basically, this is a very pleasant, no-thrill, no-frill place. Continental breakfast and newspaper are delivered to your room daily.... *Tel 312/787–4980 and 800/245–1258, fax 312/266–0978. 244 N. Dearborn Pkwy., Chicago, IL 60610. 170 rms. $$$*

Clarion Executive Plaza. This contemporary hotel gets away with higher tariffs largely because it's situated on the Loop's southern bank of the Chicago River. Rooms are tasteful if not spiffy, but if you stay here, you won't be looking at the furniture—you'll be looking out the window at those city and river views.... *Tel 346–7100, fax 346–1721. 71 E. Wacker Dr., Chicago, IL 60601. 417 rms. $$$*

Congress Hotel. Open since the days of the World Columbian Exposition in 1893, the Congress looks like it hasn't been renovated since. But the location is still prime—across from Grant Park, on the edge of the Loop, an easy walk from numerous museums.... *Tel 312/427–3800 and 800/635–1666. 520 S. Michigan Ave., Chicago, IL 60605. 850 rms. $$*

Days Inn. Another one of those hotels with nothing really going for it but incredible views (at least if you're facing east) and very reasonable room rates. Rooms are clean and functional. You won't think you're at the Ritz, but then again, many of the rooms here have far, far better views of the lake than the Ritz does. Noise from Lake Shore Drive may keep you up at night. There's an outdoor swimming pool, and you're only two blocks north of the small beach at Olive Park.... *Tel 312/943–9200 and 800/325–2525. 644 N. Lake Shore Dr., Chicago, IL 60611. 578 rms. $$*

Doubletree Guest Suites. What this all-suite hotel lacks in drama, compared to many of its neighbors such as The Drake, Four Seasons, and Ritz-Carlton, it makes up for with two-room suites, lotsa service, panoramic views, and an excellent rooftop gym facility and pool. Plus, the hotel houses the Park Avenue Café, one of the city's best and trendiest restaurants. White-gloved bellhops hanging around the lobby are a nice touch, though the Muzak ruins the effect.... *Tel 312/664–1100 and 800/424–2900, fax 312/664–9881. 198 E. Delaware Place, Chicago, IL 60611. 345 suites. $$$$*

The Drake. Quite possibly the city's most famous hotel, this limestone edifice is so gracious you feel like you have to whisper. The oak-paneled, crimson-carpeted lobby is as ornate as a palace (perhaps that's why Queen Elizabeth once stayed here); the rooms, none of which are decorated exactly the same, are quietly elegant, with fancy draperies and furniture that's expensive but not showy. The hotel's bar, Le Coq D'Or, is one of—if not the—best hotel bars in the city. Dig those martinis.... *Tel 312/787–2200 and 800/445–8667. 140 E. Walton Place, Chicago, IL 60611. 535 rms. $$$$*

Embassy Suites. You'll see a lot of suits and maybe even a few convention badges running around the huge central atrium, but the Embassy Suites has plenty to offer non-corporate travelers. All suites have a living room with a sleeper sofa and a bedroom with either a king-size or two double beds, as well as mini-kitchens, and a complimentary breakfast buffet serves good stuff like thick waffles and smooth scrambled eggs. There's also a nice indoor pool and workout room and a very good restaurant, Papagus Greek Taverna.... *Tel 312/943–3800, fax 312/943–7629. 600 N. State St., Chicago, IL 60610. 358 suites. $$$*

Essex Inn. Far from fancy, but not exactly seedy, the Essex is a good medium-priced choice. Rooms are clean if spare (the closet has no door, just a space in the wall).... *Tel 312/791–1901 and 800/621–6909. 800 S. Michigan Ave. (at 8th St.), Chicago, IL 60605. 225 rms. $$*

The Fairmont Hotel. Overlooking Grant Park, this pink granite high-rise hotel has bigger-than-usual rooms flooded with sunlight. God is in the details here—feather and foam pillows, bedsheets of premium 200-count cotton, standing butlers, tie racks, and the best thick terry robes in town, one edged in light blue, the other in pink (an odd sexist touch, that). Superbly outfitted bathrooms come complete with Neutrogena beauty products, a heat lamp, and (rare for most Chicago hotels) a television. There's a wide choice of restaurants, including one that's very fancy and one where the waitstaff occasionally bursts into song.... *Tel 312/565–8000 and 800/527–4727, fax 312/856–9020. 200 N. Columbus Dr., Chicago, IL 60601. 692 rms. $$$$*

Four Seasons Hotel. Located in the same postmodern go-go eighties building that houses Bloomingdale's, Henri Bendel, and Gucci, this hotel is one of the few that Chicagoans themselves frequent—the restaurants are top-notch and the bar and lounge are nightlife destinations for folks dressed in anything from jeans to tuxes. Guest rooms are done up in muted peaches, foam greens, and pinks, with shiny English furniture, heavily draped windows, and botanical prints; the minibar supplies not only the requisite booze and nuts but a disposable camera.... *Tel 312/280–8800 and 800/332–3442, fax 312/280—1748. 120 E. Delaware Place, Chicago, IL 60611–0142. 343 rms. $$$$$*

Holiday Inn Chicago City Centre. A huge high-rise a few blocks from Michigan Avenue, this glass-clad, 26-story monolith hosts lots of tour groups and business travelers. The attached McClung Court apartment complex has a top-drawer sports complex, tennis and raquetball courts, and an outdoor pool, free for guests to use. Room decor is innocuous, so ask for one with the wonderful, airy city and lake views.... *Tel 312/787–6100 and 800/HOLIDAY. 300 E. Ohio St., Chicago, IL 60611. 500 rms. $$*

Hotel Inter-Continental Chicago. This dual personality palace is actually two side-by-side hotels—one modern, one built in 1929—joined together in 1994. Though the lobby is blandly contemporary, rooms in the older section (recently refurbished) are laden with Biedermeier furniture, heavy draperies, and brass lamps. The second-floor restaurant looks like an old-fashioned gentleman's club but serves up-to-date Mediterranean food.... *Tel 312/944–4100 and 800/327–0200, fax 312/944–3050. 505 N. Michigan Ave., Chicago, IL 60611. 844 rms. $$$*

Hotel Nikko Chicago. This glamorously simple Japanese-owned hotel operates at a considerably lower decibel level than its competitors. After its stunning Zen-like black granite lobby, it's a surprise that the guest rooms have so little character, though they do have bay windows and panoramas. (Ask to face south for the best views.) There's an excellent Japanese restaurant on the ground level and a great gym for working off all that teriyaki.... *Tel 312/744–1900 and 800/645–5687, fax 312/527–2650. 320 N. Dearborn St., Chicago, IL 60610. 421 rms. $$$$*

Hotel Sofitel. A little bit of French-fried hospitality near O'Hare Airport—they answer their phones, "Bonjour." The marble-floored lobby with its babbling fountain creates a calm, surprisingly un-airport-like atmosphere. Despite the blond wood armoires and floral-print padded headboards, the rooms are pretty ugly; each has a bay window—too bad the view is of the featureless town of Rosemont. Still, the bathrooms have telephones and Nina Ricci toiletries.... *Tel 708/678–4488 and 800/233–5959, fax 708/678–4244. 5550 N. River Rd., Rosemont, IL 60018. 304 rms. $$$*

Hyatt on Printers Row. Located in a National Historic Landmark—two industrial red-brick buildings, built right after the Chicago Fire, now joined together—this small Hyatt is nevertheless very much in the here-and-now. Rooms are good-sized, with modern monochromatic decor, and equipped with two TVs and a VCR. The Hyatt also happens to be home to one of the best restaurants in the city, Prairie.... *Tel 312/986–1234 and 800/233–1234, fax 312/939–2468. 500 S. Dearborn St., Chicago, IL 60605. 161 rms. $$$*

Hyatt Regency Chicago. The lobby lounge covers half an acre; its greenhouse look, fountains, pools, and restaurants seem cool for about five minutes, after which you start feeling as if you're still at O'Hare. This entire hotel complex is so big, and signage is so bad, that you can't help but get lost at least once during your stay. Room service includes glatt kosher meals.... *Tel 312/565–1234 and 800/228–9000, fax 312/565–2966. 151 E. Wacker Dr., Chicago, IL 60601. 2,019 rms. $$$$*

Hyatt Regency O'Hare. When this hotel opened in 1971 its major draw was the huge 11-story skylit atrium lobby with four glass elevators and catwalks dripping with vines and ivy. It's still a sight—though not necessarily a pretty one—to behold. Otherwise, this gargantuan convention hotel (there are 89 meeting rooms) is pretty standard stuff: contemporary pinkish and brownish rooms, sprawling restaurants serving adequate food, and lots of people wearing name tags.... *Tel 708/696–1234 and 800/233–1234, fax 708/380–4890. 300 W. Bryn Mawr Ave., Rosemont, IL, 60018. 1,100 rms. $$$*

Knickerbocker Hotel. Once a grand hotel, the Knickerbocker has lost much of its luster, but it's spending big bucks to shed its image as a has-been social hotel in favor of one as a serious business hotel. A $10.5 million renovation in 1995 and 1996 will redecorate all sleeping rooms and add fax machines and computers to a number of them. One unusual feature: about one-third of the rooms have two bathrooms, a result of a previous renovation.... *Tel 312/751–8100 and 800/621–8140, fax 312/751–0370. 163 E. Walton St., Chicago, IL 60611. 254 rms. $$$*

Lenox Suites. Well-located (just off Michigan Avenue), this all-suite venue has clean but profoundly dull-looking rooms done up in dreary shades of blue and purple. One nice touch: the couches in the living rooms are all sofabeds. There's no gym, no pool, no parking (and parking in this neighborhood is pricey). Skip Houston's, the trying-to-be-swinging singlesy restaurant.... *Tel 312/337–1000 and 800/445–6669. 616 N. Rush St., Chicago, IL 60611. 325 suites. $$*

Motel 6. You're not going to get any cheaper than this unless you're willing to stay in a place that rents by the hour—and even then, you won't find one so near Michigan Avenue. Rooms are clean, with no frills, and the safe neighborhood gives this a definite edge over The Avenue (see above). It's hard to get a haircut these days for what Motel 6 charges for a bed.... *Tel 312/787–3580, fax 312/787–1299. 162 E. Ontario St., Chicago, IL 60611. 191 rms. $*

Ohio House Motel. Attention budget travelers: this little courtyard motel is hard to beat. Rooms start at $62; the most expensive (a four-person occupancy) is $80. Like a roadside motor inn, right down to the room doors opening onto the parking lot, it's an incongruous property for River North, only a few blocks from the Loop and the Magnificent Mile.... *Tel 312/943–6000. 600 N. LaSalle St., Chicago, IL 60610. 76 rms. $*

Omni Ambassador East. Home to the world-famous Pump Room, where everyone from Judy Garland to Rob Lowe has eaten, this quiet hotel ranks high on glitz as well as refinement. Guest rooms, though all outfitted with classic furnishings, are not cookie-cutter similar. It doesn't take itself too seriously: the management has the temerity to claim that every guest who really pays attention will see a celebrity, and the minibars are stocked with frozen Snickers Bars. The Muzak in the lobby is the only false note.... *Tel 312/*

*787–7200 and 800/843–6664, fax 312/787–4760. 1301
N. State Pkwy., Chicago, IL 60610. 274 rms. $$$*

Omni Chicago Hotel. Within sneezing distance of Saks Fifth
Avenue, Neiman Marcus, and Tiffany & Co., the Omni hov-
ers three floors above Michigan Avenue shops. Considering
that every room is a suite and that guests are free to use
the full health club (including lap pool), it's something of a
bargain. The Italian restaurant, Cielo, has one of the best
views of the Magnificent Mile around.... *Tel 312/944–
6664, fax 312/266–3015. 676 N. Michigan Ave., Chicago,
IL 60611. 357 suites. $$$*

The Palmer House Hilton. Once one of the city's grandest
hotels, the huge Palmer House has recaptured some of its
elegance with a $120 million renovation. Most of the
rooms, while spacious, are pretty standard-issue, with traditional upscale walnut furniture. A bar and a couple of good-
looking but so-so restaurants help feed the hordes.... *Tel
312/726–7500 and 800/445–8667, fax 312/263–2556.
17 E. Monroe St., Chicago, IL 60603. 1,639 rms. $$$*

Park Brompton Hotel. Done up to resemble a countryside
English inn, this small out-of-the-way hotel in Lake View is
more inspiring for its low prices than its decor, despite the
four-poster beds and tapestry-upholstered chairs. The man-
ager says it evokes "Dickensian spirit," whatever that
implies. Hold the gruel—there's no restaurant or room ser-
vice here.... *Tel 312/404–3499. 528 W. Brompton St.,
Chicago, IL 60657. 30 rms. $*

Park Hyatt. The smallness of this hotel is in inverse proportion
to its high-end glamour. Its two-story lobby has one of the
hugest, ugliest Lalique chandeliers you've ever seen, but it's
a great place to hang around and people-watch, drink, or
play backgammon (boards are all set up for you). Guest
rooms, most of which have terrific views, are pretty small but
well-appointed. The restaurant is home to the city's "power
breakfast," with rafts of wheeler-dealers eating egg-white
omelets and scribbling important memos on note pads the
hotel provides. No gym, but they'll deliver a stationary bicy-
cle, Stairmaster, or rowing machine to your room.... *Tel 312/
280–2222 and 800/228–9000, fax 312/649–2290. 800
N. Michigan Ave., Chicago, IL 60611. 255 rms. $$$$*

Radisson Hotel and Suites. Renovated in 1995, the hotel boasts upscale, spacious, well-lit rooms. Sleeping rooms begin on the fourteenth floor (offices and stores occupy the lower floors), so you get some truly beautiful views of the lake and the city. An extra $25 will get you an upgrade to a suite. The Radisson has both a fitness center and an outdoor rooftop pool, where guests can arrange for barbecue or cocktail parties.... *Tel 312/787–2900, fax 312/787–5758. 160 E. Huron St., Chicago, IL 60611. 334 rms. $$$*

Radisson Plaza O'Hare. Give this place a bit of credit: it's the only hotel in the Chicago area trying to evoke Frank Lloyd Wright's Prairie-style decor, using mahogany trim, barrel chairs, and stained-glass windows. Even the terrazzo marble floor in the lobby is designed after a rug Wright once created. Spiffy forest-green, beige, and burgundy two-room suites are clean-lined and bright, and have sofabeds, a microwave and refrigerator, and two TVs. You get a free full breakfast every morning delivered to your suite.... *Tel 708/678–4000 and 800/333–3333, fax 708/928–7678. 5500 N. River Rd., Rosemont, IL 60018. 296 suites. $$$*

Ramada Inn Lakeshore. If you want to stay in Hyde Park— near the University of Chicago, the DuSable Museum, and the Museum of Science and Industry—the Ramada is your best bet. This high-rise hotel has unexceptional cookie-cutter rooms, but there is an outdoor pool, and many rooms have views of the city skyline and the lake.... *Tel 312/288– 5800 and 800/228–2828, fax 312/288–5745. 4900 S. Lake Shore Dr., Chicago, IL 60615. 330 rms. $*

The Raphael. Tucked away in the residential neighborhood east of Michigan Avenue, the Raphael has friendly service and an oddball charm. The lobby features an enormous wood chandelier and tapestries; guest room interiors range from contemporary to ornate. Business people predominate during the week, but there are plenty of leisure travelers on weekends.... *Tel 312/943–5000 and 800/821–5343, fax 312/943–9483. 201 E. Delaware Place, Chicago, IL 60611. 172 rms. $$$*

The Ritz-Carlton. Located above the windowless, marble-clad behemoth known as Water Tower Place shopping mall, this ultra-deluxe hotel offers handsomely outfitted rooms—

wingback chairs, brass lamps, and traditional mahogany and cherrywood furniture set against a backdrop of drop-dead city and lake views. There's a grade-A restaurant and a cafe, and daily high tea is served in the splendid twelfth-floor lobby. There's also a well-equipped gym facility and small pool, though they charge a daily fee to use them.... *Tel 312/ 266–1000 and 800/621–6906, fax 312/266–1194. 160 E. Pearson St., Chicago, IL 60611–0124. 431 rms. $$$$$*

Sheraton Chicago. Along the flower- and shrub-lined Chicago River promenade, this postmodern hotel is a blight, but it succeeds where it really counts, with its interiors and service. The main lobby is all pretty wood trim and huge expanses of glass taking in the gorgeous riverscapes outside; there are separate check-in areas for conventioneers and regular guests. The rooms are pretty standard, in muted peaches, browns, and creams, but they're more comfortable than many rooms in competing hotels.... *Tel 312/464– 1000 and 800/325–3535, fax 312/464–9140. 301 E. North Water St., Chicago, IL 60611. 1,200 rms. $$$*

Sheraton Gateway Suites. About as generic as possible, this all-suite hotel has one thing going for it: proximity to O'Hare. Otherwise, you get a grim concrete atrium surrounded by drab beige-and-greenish rooms with tacky little wallpaper borders at the ceiling. Sofabeds, refrigerator, coffeemaker, and two TVs complete the picture. Free shuttle to and from O'Hare.... *Tel 708/699–6300 and 800/548–4193, fax 708/699–0391. 6501 N. Mannheim Rd., Rosemont, IL 60018. 300 suites. $$$*

Stouffer Renaissance Hotel. Gray and dreary-looking, this relatively new hotel sits prominently on the Chicago River; inside it's high glitz, with faux French-provincial furniture, oversize dripping crystal chandeliers, a wishing fountain, uniformed bellhops scurrying about, and ashtray sand branded with a curlicue "R." Guest rooms have marvelous views of the river and/or city from almost every window (though they're nothing special in the decor department). The bathrooms offer environmentally correct amenities.... *Tel 312/ 372–7200, fax 312/372–0834. One W. Wacker Dr., Chicago, IL 60601. 550 rms. $$$$*

Summerfield Suites Hotel. A nice combination of a small, European-style hotel with room-to-stretch-out suites, the

Summerfield (formerly the Barclay) is cozy and charming. A book-lined lounge downstairs sets the homey tone, but it's also modern, with VCRs in every room, kitchens in most, and a health club and rooftop pool. Complimentary Continental breakfasts and hors d'oeuvres; room service is from Gino's East pizzeria and Benihana of Japan.... *Tel 312/787–6000 and 800/621–8004, fax 312/787–4331. 166 E. Superior St., Chicago, IL 60611. 120 suites. $$$*

The Surf Hotel. Instead of a doorman, this out-of-the-way hotel greets guests with an imposing bust of Louis XIV, or XV, or some other wig-wearing poufed-up French guy. He adds just the right loony touch to this small, quirky (and inexpensive) hotel on a sleepy residential Lake View side street. The rooms and suites, though simple, have all the requisite amenities; there's nearby parking for less than $10 a day (and staying out here, you'll probably want a car).... *Tel 312/528–8400. 555 W. Surf St., Chicago, IL 60657. 36 rms. $*

Sutton Place Hotel. The foster child of Chicago hotels, this place has gone through three name changes since its 1988 opening, so it's no surprise that it seems to have an identity crisis. It still looks postmodern, but that's a trend that's come and gone—the framed Robert Mappelthorpe photographs seem a bit passé, and the fake plants in the lobby are definitely tacky. The rooms have some chic amenities, though, like Sony CD players and VCRs, and black-and-white checkerboard tile bathrooms with deep-soaking tubs and separate glass-enclosed showers.... *Tel 312/266–2100 and 800/543–4300. 21 E. Bellevue Place, Chicago, IL 60611. 246 rms. $$$$*

Swissotel. This wedge-shaped, glass-clad tower takes advantage of the views at the far eastern tip of Wacker Drive, a few blocks off Michigan Avenue, but though it's attached underground to Illinois Center and the Hyatt Regency, it's otherwise rather isolated. Exactly what you'd expect from the Swiss: well-ordered, clean, and with all the usual luxury amenities (king-size beds, remote-controlled TVs, marble baths). One nice twist: each room has its own doorbell. Don't miss the authentic *konditorei* in the lobby, which serves fabulous home-baked goods. The rest of the restaurants here are forgettable.... *Tel 312/565–0565 and 800/*

654–7263, fax 312/565–0540. 323 E. Wacker Dr., Chicago, IL 60601. 630 rms. $$$

The Talbott Hotel. Built as an apartment building in the 1920s and converted to a hotel in 1989, the Talbott offers large rooms with a variety of layouts that include either kitchenettes or full kitchens. If the decor's a tad shabby, that just adds to the comfy, unpretentious air of the place, a nice antithesis to its Gold Coast neighbors. Complimentary Continental breakfast and evening brownies and coffee.... Tel 312/943–0161 and 800/621-8506, fax 312/944–7241. 20 E. Delaware Place, Chicago, IL 60611. 98 rms, 50 suites. $$$

The Tremont. The efficient staff at this small, understated hotel right off Michigan Avenue treats everyone the same—that is, they treat everyone pretty darn well. The Tudor-style lobby is decked out with burnished brass chandeliers, wingback chairs, a Chinese porcelain bowl of potpourri, and a stack of magazines such as Gourmet, Condé Nast Traveler, and Town & Country; guest rooms are equally posh and Britishy, with VCRs and CD players, even phones in the bathroom.... Tel 312/751–1900 and 800/621–8133. 100 E. Chestnut St., Chicago, IL 60611. 129 rms. $$$$

Westin Hotel. You can't ignore that location—near the northern tip of the Mag Mile, a block from Oak Street Beach, and a crosswalk away from Bloomingdale's. The Westin's been undergoing a badly needed facelift, so by the time you arrive, it should no longer be an embarrassment to its tony neighbors.... Tel 312/943–7200 and 800/228–3000, fax 312/943–9347. 909 N. Michigan Ave., Chicago, IL 60611. 740 rms. $$$

Chicago Accommodations

Knickerbocker Hotel **5**
Lenox Suites **20**
Motel 6 **21**
Ohio House Motel **18**
Omni Ambassador
East **1**
Omni Chicago Hotel **17**
Palmer House Hilton **31**
Park Hyatt **13**
Radisson Hotel and
Suites **15**
Ramada Inn
Lakeshore **39**
The Raphael **11**
Ritz-Carlton **12**
Sheraton Chicago **42**
Stouffer Renaissance
Hotel **27**
Summerfield Suites
Hotel **14**
Sutton Place Hotel **3**
Swissotel **30**
The Talbott **9**
Tremont **10**
Westin Hotel **7**

The old Chicago
stalwarts—deep-
dish pizza at
pizzerias **Uno** and
Due, steaks and
chops "dis thick"
at **Gene &**

Georgetti, and stick-to-your-ribs pierogis at the **Busy Bee**—still exist, but Chicago chefs (and bartenders, for that matter) have moved way beyond the days when that was all that people wanted. Authentic Mexican is hot now, a fact to which the success of **Frontera Grill** can attest, as are tapas as served at **Cafe Iberico**. Thai food made an appearance a decade or so ago and has become one of the city's most reliably consistent cuisines—in fact, it's hard to find lousy Thai these days. (For some reason, though, the Chinese food here isn't all that good, with a few exceptions.) **Harry's Velvet Room** serves five kinds of carpaccio, **Jane's** serves corn pasta, and **Wishbone**'s specialty is hoppin' John (black-eyed peas over rice with cheddar, scallions, and tomatoes). If restaurants' mottoes are any indiciation, they've gotten leaner (Jane's: "vegetarian & clean cuisine"), meaner (**Dick's Last Resort**: "We're the shame o' Chicago"), and kinder (**Chicago Diner**: "Love animals, don't eat them").

How to Dress

Rule of thumb for Chicago restaurants: Wear a jacket to **The Pump Room** and to **Charlie Trotter**, or they won't seat you. (Actually, The Pump Room might lend you an ill-fitting, scratchy blazer.) Though most other places let you wear what you want, scope things out ahead of time, especially at the more expensive restaurants. The listings below warn you whether any dress-code restrictions apply. Chicago isn't a stuffy town, but it's no resort, either; wearing shorts and sunglasses is frowned upon at stylishly chic places like **Ambria**. If in doubt, dress up—you can get away with your Armani tux anywhere if you're dining late after a formal event.

Getting the Right Table

You don't need to worry about greasing the palm of Chicago maître d's—it's not the custom here. And as far as the "right" table goes, the only one to avoid is that near the bathroom or the kitchen (unless, that is, you've reserved the one *in* the kitchen, as you can at **Charlie Trotter**). Of course, certain restaurants have truly prime tables—at **Spiaggia**, they're along the windows overlooking Oak Street Beach; at **Vivo**, they're up a flight of stairs with a view of all the other tables. You can request that seating when you call for reservations, though there's no guarantee you'll get it. At most restaurants that accept reservations you should try to make them at least three days in advance. However, at the city's toniest establishments (such as Charlie Trotter, Ambria, Spiaggia) you should make reservations as soon as you plan your trip, no matter how far in advance, and confirm not once, but twice—say a week before and then the day of your planned meal. If you can, leave a phone number where you can be called to confirm (if they can't reach you, they may drop your reservation).

The Lowdown

Institutions... The really great thing about **Michael Jordan's Restaurant** is just how quickly it became an institution. Of course, it didn't hurt that even the most jaded Chicagoans love Michael Jordan. What's not to love? He's the world's best b-ball player and he actually seems like a pretty nice guy. His sleekly designed restaurant is nice enough, too, even if it's filled mainly with tourists trying to soak up a little Michaelosity before heading to the first-floor gift shop. **The Pump Room** no longer attracts the stars—though black-and-white glossies of former patrons line its walls, from Della Reese to Fred MacMurray—but this historic celebrity haunt still retains something of its old-time glamour. The menu features things like escargot, shrimp bisque, and Caesar salad, just as back in 1938 when it opened. Celebrities—even faux celebrities—don't ever show up at **Ann Sather**, but this north side Swedish restaurant has become an institution anyhow, at least for breakfast. Its gooey cinnamon rolls are famous the world round (okay, maybe just in Chicago's 44th Ward, but that's close enough). Speaking of goo, deep-dish pizza was invented in Chicago more than 50 years ago at **Pizzeria Uno**, a dark, almost seedy, but not-to-be-missed pizza joint (with much more character than the myriad branches of the national chain it spawned) . The pizza here is a culinary marvel—delicious, overflowing with toppings and cheese, and deservedly famous. Rub elbows with the city's bureaucrats, from judges to parole officers, at **The Berghoff**, which holds city liquor license No. 1; established in the 1890s, it's been in the same Loop location since 1905. Bratwurst, sauerbraten, and corned beef are consumed here by a couple-thousand or so hungry businesspeople (and tourists) every day. Last but not least, the **Billy Goat Tavern**, a dive-y newspaper reporters' hangout, achieved immortality by inspiring the famous "cheezeburger, cheezeburger—no Coke, Pepsi" sketches on "Saturday Night Live."

See-and-be-scenes... Of course, it depends on who you want to see and by whom who you want to be seen. For instance, though some say it's yesterday's restaurant, head to **Bice** at lunchtime if you want to see swank p.r. and advertising execs cutting deals, elegant thin-as-a-rail women splitting a salad, and lots of European tourists. (At dinner, Bice feeds Chicago's version of New York Euro-trash, possibly because the mother ship Bice is a trend-setter in oh-so-trendy Milan.) Besides swarms of folks from its Lake View neighborhood, **Mia Francesca** attracts a modelly crowd. But it's not only the crowd that's hot, so is the food—designer pizzas and pastas that never miss. It takes a bit of effort to get to and into the French-inspired bistro **Marché**, which is always crowded yet doesn't take reservations for prime dining hours; but the payoff is a crowd so eye-blindingly fab that it's almost as good as a night at the theater. In Lincoln Park, a bistro called **Un Grand Café** hosts crowds of your basic table-hopping, Powerbook-using lawyers, moguls, and artists, all of whom, it sometimes seem, know one another. There is also a lot of neck-craning at **Gibson's**, a swinging steak house *on* Rush Street but not typical *of* Rush Street; it's filled with middle-aged divorcées, cigar-chomping guys wearing huge pinkie rings, sleek trophy-wife wannabees, visiting celebs, and neighborhood rich people in search of strong drinks from a heavy-handed bartender and steaks the size of Rhode Island. At **Gordon**, things are a bit more refined, but no less frenetic. Filled with everyone from rich young traders to folks celebrating their 50th wedding anniversaries, this upscale spot offers some of the best food in town, including perfectly done fish, artichoke fritters to die for, and a denseless flourless chocolate cake. So popular, in fact, that owner Gordon Sinclair opened the more casual and less expensive **Cafe Gordon** a few blocks away. It fills up with socialites on the cook's night off, pretty young things of all genders, shopping-bag-toting yuppies yakking on their cell phones, and guests from the Tremont Hotel, the Gold Coast hotel where the restaurant is located. At the **Park Avenue Cafe**, the food is good, if a bit highly wrought, yet from almost the first day it opened in 1995 this suave spot off Michigan Avenue has attracted a power crowd.

Deals on meals (under $25)... Neighborhood yuppies and students from nearby DePaul University have discovered **Espial**, a chic little cafe for designer pizzas and pastas; you can eat even lighter here by ordering the coffeehouse choices, such as scones and salads. The most gorgeous people in town continue to eat at **Mia Francesca**, not only because gorgeous people like to stick together (though there's that, too), but because of moderate prices and consistently good trattoria food. If the line here is too long—a nightly problem, since Mia Francesca does not take reservations—and you're set on Italian, try **Scoozi!**, a warehouse-sized River North restaurant with storefront prices. It, too, attracts a great-looking crowd, albeit a bit on the suburban side. Okay, so the gang at **Dick's Last Resort** hasn't just stepped out of *GQ* or *Vogue*, but they know a good thing when they eat it, even if the surroundings at this lowbrow North Pier restaurant are loud, obnoxious, messy, crass, crude, and piggy. The seafood and BBQ is really good, and the price is right. Stay away from the killer margaritas at the **Frontera Grill** and you won't end up spending too much, either—though what you will get is not only the best authentic Mexican food in Chicago, but, according to all the national press attention this place gets, some of the best in these here United States. One of the best-kept dining secrets in town is simple little **Daniel J**, where the husband-and-wife team that owns the place put a high premium on serving terrific, eclectic food—and just wait until you see how they fold their napkins. The word is out, however, about the way-hip **Club Lucky**, where the wait can go on forever. It looks a little like a Forties diner, with plenty of Naugahyde banquettes and an uninspired Italian menu, but the atmosphere and the Wicker Park location are definitely "now." The sprawling space has good sight lines that make it possible to see who's cutting deals with whom, who's sending drinks to whom, and who's basically doing whom. There's no wait, really, at **foodlife**, an upscale mall food court in Water Tower Place, with a healthy, New Age bent. You walk in, get a "credit card," and then hand it to each server as you build your meal, wandering from food booth to food booth. At the end they add it up and, boom, you're spending twice as much as you thought you would (though not as much as in a restaurant with waiters). You really can't spend too much at **Wishbone**, a sprawling Southern-style place in an out-of-the-way location west of the Loop; half the joint is a regular restaurant with waiter service, the other half a cafeteria (at lunch, at least; there's table service at dinner), but both sell hearty country food at country prices. **Jane's** is a casual, moderately priced Bucktown cafe serving inventive food, with many dishes based on health-food ingredients that start out hippie and end up hip. Grungy **Leo's Luncheonette** wears its lack of pretentiousness like a badge of honor (have a pierced nose and you'll fit right in), but, despite the shabby atmosphere, the food's terrific and inventive, with some really creative fish and chicken dishes.

Steak your life on it... While the steaks (as well as chops) at **Gibson's** and **The Palm** are equally good—and enormous and expensive—the former attracts a swinging singles crowd, while the latter, though so loud you'll have trouble hearing yourself talk, is more a neighborhood place (albeit in a very high-rent neighborhood—the Gold Coast locals may be the only ones who can easily afford it). It's a far less chic crowd herding into old-fashioned **Gene & Georgetti** in River North, but judging by the line of big limos with politicos' official license plates, not to mention the chauffeurs loitering out front, it's a no less affluent crowd. The steaks are no less thick and tender, too.

Decor to die for... Though there are easier restaurants to get to than **Marché**, this très chic, grandly decorated grand bistro, located in the up-and-coming River West neighborhood, is well worth the cab fare. Wrought metal and lush swathes of velvet fabric make the room look special; it doesn't hurt, either, that it's filled with the city's beautiful crowd. In the art nouveau dining room of **Ambria**, across from Lincoln Park, the aesthetics are just right—exquisite flowers, dark panellng, stiff white tablecloths, sparkling china and silver, and fine French food presented as if it were art. It's not the black-and-white glossies of Hollywood's stars of yore that make **The Pump Room** such a lovely space, though their old-fashioned glamour certainly doesn't hurt. Its true glitz comes in the form of gigantic chandeliers, lots of big, round tables sparkling with crystal, cutlery, and flowers, and a celebratory feeling. At **The Eccentric** in River North, co-owner Oprah Winfrey's passion for art is shared with her guests—the walls are plastered with an eclectic selection of art, all of it by Chicago artists. It's not only inventive, but beautiful.

The sporting life... Eating burgers at **Michael Jordan's** isn't exactly the same as being courtside at a game, but at least you're in like-minded sports-crazy company. Jordan's sleek River North restaurant is filled mainly with tourists staring at the huge video screen in the first-floor bar waiting for a table in the dining room upstairs. "They" say Michael eats here, too, in a specially-designed-for-him dining room, but don't count on seeing him. If you're in the mood to watch the big game with like-minded yuppies, then you couldn't do better than heading for **Bigsby's Bar and Grill**, a subterranean Lincoln Park hangout where you won't be out of place cheering and jeering at your favorite teams. The bar at **Harry Caray's** is 60.5 feet long—the same as the distance between home plate and the pitcher's mound. It isn't unusual for the waiters, as well as the patrons, to break into "Take Me Out to the Ball Game" at midnight—if Harry, the beloved Cubs' beloved announcer, is around, he even leads the singing. The Italian food is pretty good, but the collection of memorabilia is what's really impressive.

Ethnic eating... **Penny's Noodle Shop**, a popular little place up in Lake View, is the best of the pan-Asian (i.e., Japanese, Chinese, Vietnamese, Thai) noodle shops that have sprouted all over town in recent years. If only the actual countries could get along as well. There's no strife at **Moti Mahal Indian Restaurant**, either, except occasionally between the surly waitstaff and the patrons. But keep your karma cool and this storefront restaurant in Lake View will reward you with the best cheap Indian food in a city filled with cheap Indian food. Also in Lake View, upscale **Mars** serves some of the best Szechuan-style Chinese food in the city (but skip the fried rice—it tastes like Rice-a-roni). It's Cantonese style at **Hong Min**, where the quality of the food rivals Mars, though the surroundings—in a seedy Chinatown storefront—are barely tolerable. Up near Wrigley Field, **The Bangkok** is one of the prettier Thai restaurants in town, and the food is so good that it's a double pleasure to eat here (try the vegetarian "fire spinach"). Forget virtually everything else that's called "Mexican"—River North's **Frontera Grill** is the real thing, with dishes such as *verdras motuleñas* (tostada of grilled portobello mushroom, zucchini, black beans, oranges, and plantains), *caldo de siete mares* (scallop, shrimp, mussel, and snapper soup), and tacos filled with duck, steak, and even catfish. Cheap is the operative word, garlicky the operative flavor at **Cafe Iberico**, an authentic, smoky, raucous River North tapas bar. Actual Spanish people eat here, which is a good sign. It's mostly tourists and people on dates at Lincoln Park's **Cafe Ba-Ba-Reeba!**, which also serves tapas, though at considerably higher prices. At the **Busy Bee**, probably the city's best-known Polish restaurant, tourists mix 'n' mingle with local Poles and artists from its funky Bucktown neighborhood, all chowing down on the fat pierogis. Wild game, such as elk, duck, and venison are the specialties at **The Berghoff**, a hearty wood-panelled German restaurant that's been around for more than a century. Their own beer, called (naturally) Berghoff, is surprisingly good.

Caffeine scenes... **Urbus Orbis** in Bucktown is Chicago's version of a 1950s beatnik coffeehouse—like, copacetic, man. If the high-backed chairs weren't so uncomfortable, you could spend the day here with a cup of joe. The seating is more comfortable over at Clark Street's **Scenes Coffeehouse and Dramatists Bookstore**, and the food is better, though the coffee is, well, can you spell b-i-t-t-e-r? The arty regulars at the **Third Coast Cafe,** just off Michigan Avenue, mix well with the place's other habitués: guys wearing chinos and loafers with no socks, women in Jackie O. wraparound sunglasses who only speak Italian. The best coffee in town, though—called Elaine's Brew—is at **Ina's Kitchen and Elaine's Garden**, a Lincoln Park breakfast place beloved by yuppies. The pastries are the thing at **Lutz Continental Cafe and Pastry Shop**, an old-fashioned German coffeeshop with starched tablecloths. The **Medici**, near the University of Chicago in Hyde Park, serves all sorts of coffee concoctions in a really cozy woodsy setting.

If al fresco's your style... Stylish **Bistro 110** has an outdoor cafe where you won't be overcome by the French food's garlicky aroma; you'll have a postcard-perfect view of the Water Tower and Michigan Avenue, not to mention a parade of crazed shoppers schlepping from one store to the next. **Un Grand Café**'s outdoor space over-looks the Lincoln Park Conservatory, lending this bois-terous bistro one of the more contemplative outdoor views in town. At the **Heartland Cafe**, a mellow health-food-y place stuck in a 1960s timewarp, the front patio tables overlook a sleepy tree-shaded side street in Rogers Park. Competition for seats outdoors at the **Third Coast Cafe** is totally cutthroat, given that most people who do get a streetside seat linger a long time. It's no wonder, though, considering this inexpensive cafe's hot location a block off Michigan Avenue. Eating on the outdoor patio at **Carlucci**, an Italian winner on North Halsted, is like eat-ing in some beautiful, private garden.

We never close... When the host at **Cafe Iberico** says the wait for a table is "twenty minutes," it can translate into five or 50, depending. Still, it's open late, it's in trendy River North, it's cheap, and it's just the kind of food—tapas—you want at the end of the evening. The hepcats who jam into Wicker Park's **Club Lucky** till the wee hours every night (except Sunday) know that the Italian food takes the proverbial back seat to the stylish scene, complete with a great front bar specializing in the best martinis in town. Within spitting distance up North Clark Street, there's **Harry's Velvet Room**, a decadently swanky joint that's dark enough to let you get away with not looking too hot by the end of the evening. It attracts a weird congregation of beautiful people, club kids, bikers, and too-rich-for-their-own-good traders. Lots of good booze, too, particularly the creative martinis. Chinese food has a way of satisfying those late-night hunger pangs like no other cuisine, and though most of Chinatown goes pretty dead late at night, dingy-looking little **Hong Min** serves top-notch Cantonese food until the wee hours. But sometimes there is no better late-night bite than good greasy hand-cut fries and a burger, both of which are served at **Muskie's** amidst the cacophony of Chicago per-sonalities—yuppies, club kids, old ladies, cops on the beat, jocks, and swinging singles shuttling between the clubs and trendy Lake View area restaurants. At **Wiener Circle** in Lincoln Park, the short-order cooks behind the counter may scream at you, but it's generally well-meaning: "WHAT DO YOU WANT? FRIES WITH THAT? COME ON, COME ON, FRIES?" The answer should always be yes, no matter what they ask. Everything on that? Yes. Extra salt? Yes, Yes, Yes. These guys are hot dog and hamburger professionals, and if they can't satisfy your late-night hunger, nobody can.

Pizza classics... Chicago is known for its deep-dish pizzas—artery-clogging globs of cheese, rich and chunky tomato sauce, thick crust, and traditional toppings from sausage to olives to onions, etc. Order extra tomatoes and cheese—it's amazingly good. The wait at most of the best pizzerias is long, but you can generally order way before you're seated, so the food will be delivered not long after you hit the table. (That way they can get you in and out as fast as possible.) Try **Pizzeria Uno** or **Pizzeria Due**, around the corner from each other in River North. You can't go wrong at either venue. Another favorite, if only because of its location just off Michigan Avenue, is **Gino's East**—perhaps the only restaurant in town where people will be lined up outside in the dead of winter.

Designer pizza... At River North's **Scoozi!** the thin, oven-roasted pizzas are deliciously huge oblong things that the waiters present at the table as if they were diamonds from Cartier. They come in two sizes and usually there are six from which to choose, such as the simple margherita (tomato, pesto, and mozzarella), sofisticata (arugula, bacon, and red onion), and forestiera (wild mushrooms, roasted garlic, and fontina cheese). In the same neighborhood, **Harry's Velvet Room** is a way-hip addition in the designer pizza sweepstakes, offering 'zas made with an unusual honey-wheat crust topped with anything from goat cheese to artichokes to mustardy chicken to wild mushrooms. The char-crusted pizzas at **Mia Francesca** are really good, too, though the wait to get into this hot, hot, hot Lake View restaurant can be so long you might as well fly to Roma and back for the real thing. If you do stick around, though, the pizza with mussels and calamari is worth it. The **Quixotic Cafe**, in the Lincoln Park area, is mainly frequented by neighborhood types, but the pizzas are up-to-date; all of them are available with soy cheese, in keeping with the general health-food karma of the place.

The Italian battalion... There was a period a few years ago when every other restaurant that opened in Chicago was a trattoria. Bowls of gnocchi, chicken Vesuvio, and Caesar salads were becoming as common as a burger and fries. A few places, though, stood out from the crowd, and still do, and they're not necessarily all located along Taylor Street in Chicago's tiny Little Italy (the operative word is "little"). In fact, **Spiaggia**, in its coolly upscale space overlooking Michigan Avenue and the lake, is considered by some folks the best Italian restaurant in town. At bustling, elegant **Carlucci** in Lincoln Park, the wait can be long with or without a reservation, but either way, it's definitely worth it to sample its fine, authentic regional Italian cuisine. Indulge in mounds of delicious pastas and creamy cannoli at **Maggiano's Little Italy**, a River North red-sauce classic right down to the checked tablecloths. Two other River North standouts on the tonier end of the trend-o-meter are **Centro** and upscale Tuscan **Coco Pazzo**. Full of Gold Coast glamour-pusses with face lifts and tummy tucks, **Pane Caldo** has an Upper-East-Side-of-Manhattan feel unlike any other Chicago restaurant—the din of foreign languages, well-lit sprays of flowers, decorous waiters, the whole bit. (Another New Yorky thing—it helps to make nice-nice to the host). The bilevel dining room at Lincoln Park's **La Risotteria Nord** is nothing special, but if you like risotto, there's no better place in town. Down in the Loop, there's Tuscan-flavored **Trattoria No. 10** and the long-running **Italian Village**, which is really three restaurants in one (take your pick: upscale, seafood, or country Italian). If you insist upon going to Little Italy, you won't be disappointed at **Rosebud**, which is usually jammed, and which you'll probably leave with a very full doggie-bag in hand.

French toast... **Ambria** is arguably the city's premier French restaurant—rich, classic dishes, game, truffles, the whole haute thing. It's in the Belden Hotel, just across the street from the Lincoln Park Conservatory; across the lobby is **Un Grand Café**, a boisterous and far more casual (and inexpensive) counterpoint serving updated bistro fare. Expect a chic crowd, waitrons scurrying about in starched aprons and black bow ties, and enough Chanel No. 5 in the air that you'll think you're in gay Paree. Far less boisterous but no less authentic is **Le Bouchon**, a tiny Bucktown hole-in-the-wall with simple framed pictures of France on the walls and a tin ceiling above. The maître d' has never quite gotten the fact that here in America reservations actually have meaning, but the inevitable wait is worth it—you'll get authentic bistro food at reasonable prices. Up on North Halsted, romantic-looking **Oo-La-La!** is bipartisan—French and Italian, both very good, all moderately priced. In December, you'll be subjected to really bad holiday music, but otherwise its Edith Piaf on the Muzak and great French fare on your plate at **Bistro 110**, a handsome, busy Mag Miler. And if the exchange rate doesn't worry you, you can spend plenty of francs at River West's trendy **Marché** for French bistro flair, or at **Everest**, a more traditional French dining room in the Loop where the prix-fixe meals are *incroyable*.

Isn't it romantic?... It's candlelit and chic at **Espial**, where the distressed, muralled walls put everyone in just the right mood, and the low-priced Italian food goes down very easy. And for Latin lovers, **La Paella**, an old-world Spanish restaurant that looks as if it hasn't been redecorated since Franco's heyday, is one of the sweetest spots in town. The owners, Mr. and Mrs. Sanchez, divide the room—he acts as host on one side, she on the other—and they make you feel so special, you and your honey may start treating each other that way, too. Up on North Halsted, **Oo-La-La!** is invitingly dark—the individual votives on each table cast a romantic glow on everyone's face—and the satisfying pastas leave you with a well-fed glow.

Eating solo... The long counter or a cozy table in the back room at **Ann Sather** is a great place to settle in with a book or to just watch the passing crowd of locals, which ranges from funky old guys to leather-clad lesbians. You don't have to like Swedish food—most folks come for the breakfasts, anyway. The loquacious bartenders at stylish French **Bistro 110** are great company when dining alone at the copper-topped bar, ideal for a stop-off during a Mag Mile shopping spree. Everything at River North's smart little **Big Bowl Cafe** is served in a big bowl—get the gimmick?—stuff like soups, Asian-style noodles, and other quick and casual solo meals. (The tables are small and close together, so eavesdropping on your neighbors is really easy, too.) Mag Mile people-watching both inside and out the windows make the **Third Coast Cafe** a great, inexpensive eating-alone place, along with piles of newspapers and magazines if you want to read. The arty atmosphere and crowd at **Wishbone** makes eating alone easy too: you can read, just look around, appear depressed and brooding and in need of Prozac—no one cares. What the place does care about, though, is serving as-authentic-as-possible-in-Chicago Southern home cookin'.

Noshing between galleries... River North's gallery scene can be exhausting. Fortunately there are a bunch of nearby places to rest those weary bones. If you've been searching for that perfect little Old Master drawing, a plate of homemade pasta at **Scoozi!** may be called for (and at lunch, there's generally no wait at this huge, pretty restaurant). Three other Italian places are nearby: **Centro**, with large portions and sophisticated patrons; **Coco Pazzo**, an airy restaurant with delicious food and pokey service; and **Maggiano's Little Italy**, a charming spot that helped spark the family-style serving trend in the city. The vaguely pan-Asian **Big Bowl Cafe** is a great lunch stop, too: cheap, stylish, flavorful. There's always the chic Mexican favorite, the **Frontera Grill**; or sprawling **Papagus Greek Taverna**, where the best deal is to sample the long list of hot and cold appetizers.

Near Mag Mile shopping... When schlepping those Crate & Barrel, Marshall Field's, and Cartier bags gets tiring, stop into **Bistro 110**, where the lively atmosphere—not to mention the incredibly garlicky food—will regenerate you. If you're doing that Water Tower Place thing, you really can't go too wrong at **foodlife**, an upscale mall food court with a health-food-y twist. **Cafe Gordon** is an easy stroll off Michigan Avenue (and not all that far from Oak Street's boutiques, either), so no wonder it's a favorite of the ladies-who-lunch. Dangle your shopping bag over your chair so everyone knows where you've been blowing your wad. **Spiaggia**, at the northern tip of the Magnificent Mile, is an elegant bet for top-notch (and top-priced) Italian food. It's not easy to find an inexpensive place to eat around here, so no wonder **Johnny Rockets**—a pastiche of a 1950s diner, transplanted from L.A.—is usually crowded. It's a good choice if you've got kids in tow, as is **Gino's East**, for pizza that'll keep them happy for a few more hours.

Morning glories... With a fire roaring all winter and beautiful murals covering the walls—not to mention snappy waitresses who barely let you swallow a sip of coffee before they're there topping it off—it's no wonder that **Ann Sather** has a line for weekend breakfasts snaking down Belmont Avenue. In Lake View, **Ina's Kitchen and Elaine's Garden** is a more expensive place for breakfast, but the long lines of Cherokee-driving, cellular-phone-using, Banana Republic-outfitted patrons that come here every weekend for pancakes and designer scrapple don't seem to mind. Concerned that your cholesterol is too low? Are your arteries too free-flowing? Could you use a little meat on them there bones? If you answered yes to even one of the above, head on over to **Lou Mitchell's**, which has been around since 1935, for over-the-top hearty breakfasts—omelettes, French toast, all the classics. For a quick bite before Saturday gallery-hopping or shopping, plop down at a table sporting a red-and-white-checked tablecloth at River North's **The Corner Bakery** for some of the best baked goods in the city. The smell alone will thrill you. If you're sick and tired of plain ole eggs, try the *machacado con huevo* (scrambled eggs with shredded jerky, serrano chile, and salsa verde and black beans), *huevos motuleños* (fried eggs on a tostada with tomatoes, ham, fried plantains, and black beans), or *huevos ahogados* (poached eggs with tomatillo-chile sauce and Swiss chard) at River North's **Frontera Grill**, all served in this casual Mexican restaurant's comfy, colorful dining room. At River West's **Wishbone**, folks happily chow down the Southern-style breakfasts (have some grits with them eggs). The gay-as-a-goose freebie magazine *Babble* calls **Oo-La-La!**'s weekend breakfast the "diva brunch," and are they ever right. The guys look awfully good for this early in the day, sating themselves with the strong bloody Marys, great eggs Benedict, or banana-stuffed French toast.

Absolutely fabulous... Don't let the understated decor of this chic townhouse restaurant fool you—suave **Charlie Trotter** pampers its guests in grand style. There's nothing to distract you from the task at hand: being wowed by the food and the service. The international menu's always changing, always fabulous. **Spiaggia**'s floor-to-ceiling windows overlooking Lake Michigan add the perfect sparkle to the city's best Italian restaurant. With its elegant art nouveau decor, **Ambria** (across from Lincoln Park) is where you want to go for classic French, especially if someone else is paying. If fancy to you means being forced to wear a coat (and a tie, please), then eat at **The Pump Room**, under the huge glittering chandeliers, where celebrities have ordered their steaks medium-rare for years. **Everest**, with its panoramic view of the city and its intriguing French-plus cuisine, makes for a luxurious night out.

Off the eaten track... Daniel J isn't really anywhere to speak of other than on a drab street in a drab part of town west of Lake View, but oh the food! Family-run—he's the chef, she's the hostess—it places its priorities on inventive but not outlandish recipes, perfectly executed. Try the oven-baked crab cakes. Don't ask why **Reza's**, a terrific Persian restaurant, is in Andersonville, the Swedish part of town, but it is. The mostly vegetarian **Heartland Cafe** is in a far-north section of the city, but if you're in the mood for a relaxing time (hippie-style, that is), it's the place to go. Do whatever it takes to get to **Lutz Continental Cafe and Pastry Shop**, on the north side, if for no other reason than to bury your face in a huge linzer torte while sipping a teeny-tiny espresso. Cheaper neighborhood rents translate into lower meal checks than you'd expect at **Le Bouchon**, for French bistro fare in Bucktown; and **Club Lucky**, for hip Italian in Wicker Park. Inexpensive Southern home-cooking, served in a casual cavernous space with big paintings of chickens lining the walls, is all that's needed to attract the hipoisie to **Wishbone's** seriously out-of-the-way location (out-of—the-way unless you work for the "Oprah Winfrey Show," since her studios are across the street). It's worth a schlepp to Bucktown to the renowned Polish diner the **Busy Bee**, just for the fat pierogis.

Out in left field... "Take me out to the ball game" is a nice sentiment, but if you've ever eaten the food at Wrigley you'll understand why it's important to find a good restaurant nearby. The area's lined with fast-food joints, but skip them, and head instead to: tiny **Penny's Noodle Shop**, which serves all kinds of Asian noodles; **The Bangkok**, a pretty, second-floor Thai spot with great *pad thai* and satays; or **Angelina**, a warm little Italian trattoria where the food is better than the moderate prices would lead you to expect. **El Jardin**'s stucco-walled outdoor area (clichéd Mexican, just like the food) has one of the most festive atmospheres in the city—especially if the Cubs just won, and everyone's schnockered on frozen margaritas.

CHICAGO | DINING

The children's hour... Ann Sather is casual enough for the kids, but homey-chic enough for the adults. It's located in a former funeral home, which kids find hilarious. There aren't many kid-friendly places convenient for Michigan Avenue shopping, but **Bistro 110** has great French baguettes, and it's loud enough that the kids don't have to suppress their natural, uh, shall we say, effervescence. There's also Fifties-themed **Johnny Rockets**, a fun burger joint near the Mag Mile. It takes a certain tastelessness to really like **Dick's Last Resort**, a loud, obnoxious, messy eatery at the North Pier. But loud can be a plus when you're out with kids. Let your hair down and you and the kids just might have a little quality time, snarfing down great BBQ while listening to live music, usually Dixieland jazz or the blues. You can also get barbecue at the faux-ramshackle **Bub City Crabshack & BBQ** in the Lincoln Park area, but order the kids to order crab: they get a mallet, then a bib, then a hot steamin' plate of what the menu calls a "mess o' crabs" (Dungeness crab, snow crab, and crab claws). River North, as you'd expect, is jam-packed with child-pleasers. **Michael Jordan's Restaurant** is so kid-friendly it has a separate menu for the little ones. And it's soooo cute it'll make you want to throw up, but the kids won't know. Serving "Fastbreak Fingers" (chicken fingers), "Center Court Cheese" (grilled cheese sandwich), "Bankshot Cole Slaw," and "Courtside Cookies," it's fun for the very short and young. Older kids probably will be more than happy with a meal at **Planet Hollywood** or the **Hard Rock Cafe**, even if the thought of those places makes you lose your appetite. A happy compromise might be **Maggiano's Little Italy**, a festive place where favorites like spaghetti-and-meatballs are served family-style, or **Ed Debevic's**, a 1950s-themed eatery that's like one long "Happy Days" re-run.

Veg-o-rama... Die-hard vegetarian Linda McCartney (wife of Paul) would feel right at home at the **Chicago Diner**, a North Halsted vegetarian restaurant where the motto is "Love animals, don't eat them." Sounds a bit retro, but then that's the point. In the high-gloss Nineties it seems almost quaint to order a tempeh burger and carrot juice, and even more quaint to enjoy it, but here the vaguely preppie crowd does. The agonizingly slow service will give you time to reminisce about the Sixties. The **Heartland Cafe** is a touch of Santa Cruz in Rogers Park—lots of tofu on the menu, most of it so delicious it could convert you. Peace, love, and live music abound, though the waitstaff could go a little lighter on the patchouli oil. While the **Big Bowl Cafe**, a stylish restaurant in River North, isn't strictly vegetarian, there are enough interesting veggie choices to satisfy any non-meat-eater, including delicious no–fat (baked) spring rolls. Mellow **Jane's** in Bucktown isn't strictly vegetarian either, but its motto—"vegetarian & clean cuisine"—pretty much sums it up: whole-food ingredients, put together with flair. The grilled veggie quesadilla is to die for. At **Quixotic Cafe**, in the Lincoln Park area, all the veggies used are organic and the selection of meatless dishes is vast.

Retromania... In the mood for the type of swank 1940s supperclub that Bogey himself might have frequented? Try **Club Lucky**, where the hepcat crowd hangs, sipping the best martinis in town (and giving the forgettable Italian food a miss). If Frankie Valli and the Big Bopper are more your style, go for burgers and shakes to **Ed Debevic's**, a snappy Fifties-memorabilia-jammed diner in River North; or **Johnny Rockets**, a cartoonish diner where *American Graffiti* meets the Magnificent Mile. Far out, literally and figuratively, is the **Heartland Cafe** in Rogers Park—so 1960s, so mellow, so much tofu. Chicago restaurateurs have mercifully skipped the urge to create a 1970s-style dining experience, but the go-go Eighties are alive at brassy **Bice**, an offshoot of the high-glam Milanese original, which attracts the sort of people who make sure that the next table hears them order "two bottles of Dom."

The Index

$$$$$	over $50
$$$$	$40–$50
$$$	$30–$40
$$	$20–$30
$	under $20

Price categories reflect the cost of a three-course meal, not including drinks, taxes, and tip.

Ambria. Arguably the city's premier French restaurant, with an ever-changing menu that may include melt-in-your-mouth sweetbreads with portobello and endive; Beluga caviar; pomegranate-glazed squab; or a host of other delicacies, from rabbit to truffles. Impeccable service and prices to match, but you get what you pay for. Comme il faut, eh?... *Tel 312/472–5959. 2300 N. Lincoln Park West. Reservations required. Jackets required. $$$$$*

Angelina. Serving simple but tasty pastas, chicken, and fish dishes, this hip, two-room Italian restaurant is a neighborhood fave, but deserves a visit from outsiders as well, especially before hitting the nearby clubs.... *Tel 312/935–5933. 3561 N. Broadway. $$*

Ann Sather. Homey, yes; cozy, not. But while this is supposed to be a Swedish restaurant, with Swedish potato sausage, Swedish meatballs, and sandwiches on limpa bread on the menu to prove it, it's the breakfasts-like-Mom-would-make that stand out. To some, the huge gooey cinnamon rolls are the object of worship.... *Tel 312/348–2378. 929 W. Belmont Ave. (also at 5207 N. Clark St., tel 312/271–6677). AE not accepted. $*

The Bangkok. Up a narrow flight of stairs you'll find this pretty Thai restaurant, complete with a bar to hang out at if you have to wait. And you probably will, since its location near a lot of nightclubs and Wrigley Field almost ensures huge crowds. But persevere and you'll be rewarded with great noodle dishes, especially *pad Thai* and *pad se ue*, the usual chicken satay, and more than a dozen unusual curry dishes.... *Tel 312/327–2870. 3542 N. Halsted St. $*

The Berghoff. This old-timey oak-panelled German restaurant decorated with murals and stained glass attracts hordes at lunchtime, chowing down on hand-carved roast beef, turkey, and corned beef sandwiches in the stand-up bar. Classic wiener schnitzel, sauerbraten, and apple strudel in the vast dining room are your best bets.... *Tel 312/427–3170. 17 W. Adams St. $$*

Bice Ristorante. Despite the pretension and high prices, this just-off-Michigan-Avenue restaurant, the original of which is in Milan, has it all—including the regular Italian dishes you'd expect and some you wouldn't, like pasta in pesto with green beans and potatoes.... *Tel 312/664–1474. 158 E. Ontario St. Reservations required. $$$$*

Big Bowl Cafe. You'll be (excuse the pun) bowled over by the terrific dishes here, from the grilled-vegetable soup with angel hair noodles to the ginger chicken, vegetable, and shrimp with roasted garlic. Various combo plates include the "Natural" (the above soup, veggie rice, and veggie potstickers) and the "Szech-Mex" (Thai-chili quesadilla, roasted corn tortilla soup, and salsa).... *Tel 312/787–8279. 159 1/2 W. Erie St. $*

Bigsby's Bar and Grill. Here you'll find great burgers and fries served by a perky waitstaff. Big selection of beer, too, and enough video monitors that you won't miss a second of the game, no matter how hard you try. Most of the patrons are wearing their college sweatshirts.... *Tel 312/642–5200. 1750 N. Clark St. $$*

Billy Goat Tavern. Within a block of both the *Sun-Times* and the *Chicago Tribune*, this dive—and that's a charitable description—is a media hangout, its walls covered with scores of sepia-tinted newspaper clippings. Greasy but delicious burgers are about the only thing worth eating.... *Tel 312/222–1525. 430 N. Michigan Ave. No reservations. No credit cards. $*

Bistro 110. A stylish bistro with a garden room, great bar, and energetic dining room, just off the Mag Mile. Meals start with a hot 'n' crusty baguette, ramekin of butter, and head of roasted elephant garlic—it's heaven on earth. Segue into great roasted red snapper, if they have it, or one of the wonderful pastas or the half-chicken. Most everything is very garlicky—except, fortunately, the desserts.... *Tel 312/266–3110. 110 E. Pearson St. Reservations advised. $$$*

Le Bouchon. Zis is really one of ze best (cheap-ish) Frunch bistros in town. While there's a tin ceiling, there's no tin ear for cooking out back: delicious steak frites, cassoulet, great onion tart, d'accord, and chicken dishes.... *Tel 312/862–6600. 1958 N. Damen Ave. Reservations advised. $$*

Bub City Crabshack & BBQ. A big messy ol' restaurant serving the obvious: crab, as well as great big ol' sloppy dishes of BBQ brisket, chicken, pork, and terrific gumbo. For a real hot time—literally—try the fried jalapeños. In truth, the atmosphere is about as crabshacky as a Disney exhibit, but the friendly buzz, loud country music, and good-time feeling are infectious, even if they're fake.... *Tel 312/266–1200. 901 W. Weed St. $$$*

Busy Bee. *The* Polish diner. All the dishes you'd expect—delish pierogis made with meat, potato, and cheese, stick-to-your-ribs Polish sausage, potato pancakes, and boiled beef (always a crowd pleaser)—at seriously low prices.... *Tel 312/772–4433. 1546 N. Damen Ave. AE not accepted. $*

Cafe Ba-Ba-Reeba! One of the first restaurants in the city to tap into the tapas trend, it's still one of the most popular—or is that just crowded? The boisterous, jammed-with-yuppies atmosphere is a lot of fun, and the food on the ever-evolving menu—from the tortilla española to the marinated octopus to the full meals (such as paella)—is nearly as good as a trip to the Costa del Sol. Wash it all down with wine or a sherry.... *Tel 312/935–5000. 2024 N. Halsted St. Reservations advised. $$*

Cafe Gordon. Located just off Michigan Avenue in the Tremont Hotel, this is the perfect people-watching spot after a long day of shopping. The food's creative without being intimidating—delicious flatbread designer-pizzas, grilled halibut with couscous and mango, and the ubiquitous grilled portobello mushrooms. Really great bathrooms upstairs with the biggest stalls you've ever seen.... *Tel 312/280–2100. 100 E. Chestnut St. $$*

Cafe Iberico. A real tapas bar—sprawling, raucous, loud, crowded, smoky. Great shrimp dishes, tortilla española, baked goat cheese, and terrific pitchers of sangria add to the party atmosphere.... *Tel 312/573–1510. 739 N. LaSalle St. AE not accepted. $$*

Carlucci. Rambling, with murals, huge sprays of flowers, and a staff that assumes you already know the difference between mafaldine and tagliolini, so don't expect a lot of complicated descriptions. Do expect, though, a wide choice of wonderful pastas, salads, designer pizzas, and chicken and fish dishes. The charcoal-grilled giant portobello mushrooms are a real stand-out, as are the risottos.... *Tel 312/281–1220. 2215 N. Halsted St. $$$*

Centro. The patrons all reach for their pockets when a cell phone rings, but at least they know good northern Italian food. Try the garlic-bathed chicken Vesuvio. The long narrow dining room is a modern little slice of Milan in River North.... *Tel 312/988–7775. 710 N. Wells St. Reservations advised. $$$*

Charlie Trotter. If not the best restaurant in Chicago, this is certainly the one that gets called the best most often. No regular menus, but an $85-a-person "degustation," which might include Maine lobster with preserved papaya, Olympian oysters and Tahitian vanilla bean vinaigrette, scallops and foie gras, white asparagus soup, California pigeon breast with spring vegetable, sweetbreads, and on and on. Try to reserve the one table in the kitchen, where you can watch the chefs at work.... *Tel 312/248–6228. 816 W. Armitage Ave. Reservations required. Jacket and tie required. $$$$$*

Chicago Diner. Popular vegetarian diner with uncomfortable wooden booths, service so slow you may think there's no waitstaff at all, and food that... well, if you like tempeh, then it's actually quite good, and if you don't like tempeh, then it's not. (Because everything here, including the desserts, tastes suspiciously like tempeh.) Organic everything, including wine.... *Tel 312/935–6696. 3411 N. Halsted St. $*

Club Lucky. The Italian food here—all the basics from fettucine alfredo to chicken Vesuvio to cannoli—takes the proverbial back seat to the oh-so-swank scene. Low prices lure an artsy crowd.... *Tel 312/227–2300. 1824 W. Wabansia Ave. Reservations advised. $$*

Coco Pazzo. In River North, this very tony Italian eatery has large windows and an airy, loft-like space. A sister restaurant to New York's Coco Pazzo, it serves great food, from the breads all the way to the desserts, and attracts a cosmopolitan crowd....*Tel 312/836-0900. 300 W. Hubbard St. Reservations advised. $$$$*

The Corner Bakery. Cappuccino, espresso, latte, exceptional muffins, blondies, sticky buns, and apricot or chocolate babka, all baked right on the premises. Fierce competition, especially at breakfast, for one of the few tables available is the only drawback.... *Tel 312/644–7700. 516 N. Clark St. $*

Daniel J. Just a simply decorated, family-run storefront in a not-very-convenient part of town—but what good food! From the oven-baked crab cakes, to the mahi mahi with toasted coconut, pineapple, and macadamia nuts, to the stone-baked thin-crust pizzas, there isn't a loser in the bunch. Don't tell anyone.... *Tel 312/404–7772. 3811 N. Ashland Ave. $$$*

Dick's Last Resort. Eat here and you'll be transported back to frat living at its best (or worst, depending on your outlook): loud, raucous, everything chugged down with beer. You get to slobber over slabs o' ribs, messy chicken, and what they themselves call "squirty" crab's legs; live music, usually Dixieland jazz or the blues, is usually on tap too. You'll stomp your feet, even if you're not the stomping kind.... *Tel 312/ 836–7870. 435 E. Illinois St. $$*

The Eccentric. Quite possibly the best mashed potatoes (whipped with horseradish) in town are served at this restaurant co-owned by restaurateur Rich Melman and Oprah Winfrey. (They're supposedly from her grandmother's recipe.) Otherwise, the American food here doesn't live up to the beautiful surroundings.... *Tel 312/787–8390. 159 W. Erie St. $$*

Ed Debevic's. This homage to the 1950s must've taken a dozen high-priced creative directors to dream up, but what a good job they've done. Oh, the food—everything you'd find on any diner menu, from meatloaf to burgers to chicken pot pie to creamy malts. It's all delish, and cheapish, and fattening. But hey, who knew from diets in the Fifties, anyhow?.... *Tel 312/664–1707. 640 N. Wells St. $*

Espial. Candlelit and chic, this distressed-walled hole-in-the-wall (in the shadow and rumble of the el) serves mostly Italian fare, from designer pizzas to fettucine primavera, at surprisingly reasonable prices.... *Tel 312/871–8123. 948 W. Armitage Ave. $$*

Everest. Take the elevator 40 stories up from the Chicago Stock Exchange and treat yourself to an exceptional French meal accented with North American ingredients such as Maine lobster and Texas venison. A well-heeled crowd of diners comes to this quietly elegant spot for the $39 pre-theater meal; fixed-price meals start at $69 a head.... *Tel 312/663–8920. 440 S. LaSalle St. Reservations required. $$$$$*

foodlife. The grand pasha of mall "food courts," this 13-station food-o-rama at Water Tower Place is all one restaurant, instead of separately owned ones. Choose whatever you please, from rotisserie chicken, stir fries, pastas, tofu burgers, tacos and burritos, and great desserts, and you pay just once. Beer and wine, as well.... *Tel 312/335–3663. 835 N. Michigan Ave. $*

Frontera Grill. This award-winning Mexican restaurant in River North is about as authentic as it gets, with a weekly changing menu of delightfully non-greasy, non-taco dishes. Colorful artwork, wooden tables, and bright Southwest-inspired walls make the whole experience a pleasure.... *Tel 312/661–1434. 445 N. Clark St. $$*

Gene & Georgetti. In the shadow of the Ravenswood el, this dark, old-fashioned, two-level steak house specializes in aged prime steak. It's an honor to sit on the first floor, but don't count on it, since you've gotta be palsy-walsy with the host for a while before you're granted such a seat. Of course, it helps if you're a judge or local politician, many of whom eat here regularly.... *Tel 312/527–3718. 500 N. Franklin St. Reservations advised. $$$*

Gibson's. Near the Oak Street boutiques, this place is as subdued as the crowd isn't—huge booths, dark panelling, big ferns, good lighting. Try the steaks, of course, from porter-house to T-bone, sirloin to filet mignon, but don't skip well-prepared fish dishes either. Great baked potatoes, slathered in sour cream, naturally.... *Tel 312/266–8999. 1028 N. Rush St. Reservations advised. $$$*

Gino's East. Really good pizza. Really long lines. But don't despair, they'll take your order while you wait for a table or booth in this dark, cave-like subterranean restaurant. Decades of patrons have carved their initials, witticisms, and a few unprintable *bon mots* into the wood tables. Makes for good reading.... *Tel 312/943–1124. 160 E. Superior St. No reservations. $$*

Gordon. Quirky to the max—chic interior decor with swaggering swags, huge plaster fists, and erotic drawings in the bath-rooms. The evolving menu may include grilled squab, bouil-labaisse, or pan-roasted lobster. Entrees are available at half-size for half-price plus a buck. If the cold lemon soufflé in a pool of warm caramel is available, order it. A jazz trio appears on weekends, and there's dancing for the twinkle-toes amongst you.... *Tel 312/467–9780. 500 N. Clark St. Reservations required. $$$$*

Un Grand Café. This big, boisterous Lincoln Park bistro is the perfect place for either a full-fledged dinner or a late-night omelet and a glass of wine. Without reservations, though, you'll be waiting a long time to sample its fine fare, such as steak frites, cassoulet, and bouillabaisse. Très bon.... *Tel 312/348–8886. 2300 N. Lincoln Park West. Reservations advised. $$$*

Hard Rock Cafe. Mediocre burgers-and-fries food, served to gawking masses surrounded by rock mementoes of minimal interest. Excuse me, but I don't think so.... *Tel 312/943–2252. 63 W. Ontario St. $$*

Harry Caray's. A big, loud restaurant like its namesake, the dining rooms are sprawling affairs jammed with people eat-ing better-than-average traditional Italian food. Don't miss the deep-fried calamari or the chicken Vesuvio—you'll real-ly love the garlicky French fries that come as a side. As you'd expect from a restaurant owned by the Cubs' play-by-play announcer, the walls are covered with sports memora-bilia.... *Tel 312/465–9269. 33 W. Kinzie St. $$*

Harry's Velvet Room. Lushly outfitted, like Marrakesh meets Salvador Dali with a little Dean Martin thrown in for good measure. In other words, deep velvet swags, *fauxed* walls, deep booths—the ambience is very Rat Pack, or at least trying to be. Fortunately, this late-nighter is supported by a terrific menu, especially the salad niçoise, designer pizzas, and five—count 'em, five—kinds of carpaccio.... *Tel 312/828–0770. 534 N. Clark St. Reservations advised. $$*

Heartland Cafe. Terrific semi-vegetarian restaurant with omelets and stir-frys, okay pasta, and, surprise, surprise, everything with tofu is a standout. The burgers are made from buffalo meat—not just any buffalo meat, but farm-raised buffalo meat. Live music most nights; there's a health food store attached, too.... *Tel 312/465–8005. 7000 N. Glenwood Ave. No credit cards. $*

Hong Min. Located in a bordering-on-seedy storefront in Chinatown, this is, nevertheless, one of the best Chinese restaurants in town. The service can be abrupt, but worth it to taste such great Cantonese and Mandarin dishes as steamed fish or barbecued pork in black bean and garlic sauce, or chow foon noodles. BYOB.... *Tel 312/842–5026. 221 W. Cermak Rd. AE not accepted. $$*

Ina's Kitchen and Elaine's Garden. Long lines of prototypical yuppie families line the block every weekend morning, mouths watering in anticipation of corn–black-bean–cheese scrapple, and sour cream pancakes that are so good you'll forget how fattening everything is. Dieters should stick to the better-than-you'd-think hearty oatmeal.... *Tel 312/525–1116. 934 W. Webster St. No dinner. No credit cards. $*

Italian Village. Actually composed of three Italian restaurants under one roof, the Italian Village has been here in the Loop since 1927. Busy at weekday lunch and during the pre-theater rush. Take your choice of chi-chi (Viviere), seafood (La Cantina), or traditional small-town Italy (The Village). You can't lose.... *Tel 312/332–7005. 77 W. Monroe St. Reservations required. $$–$$$*

Jane's. Whadyya know—an artsy Bucktown restaurant that isn't pretentious! Brick walls, a high, high, high exposed-beam ceiling, good lighting, and pictures on the walls by local

CHICAGO | DINING

artists all create a simple, calming atmosphere, even if the food is anything but. The inventive menu changes, but may include great corn spaghetti with calamari, shrimp, and scallops; an unbelievably filling tofu-stuffed burrito; and brown rice risotto. (Sounds too, too mellow, but it really works.)…. *Tel 312/862–5263. 1655 W. Cortland St. $$*

El Jardin. If it weren't for the fact that this Mexican restaurant is just a couple of blocks south of Wrigley Field, it would have little to offer. But it is located there, and it's constantly jammed. The food is your typical oozing-cheese, glopped-guacamole Mexican, but it's satisfying in a way because it's just so bad for you…. *Tel 312/528–6775. 3335 N. Clark St. $$*

Johnny Rockets. Red and black and white all over, with mini-jukeboxes at each booth—you get the picture. Don't stray much beyond burgers, fries, and shakes at this transplant from L.A.'s Melrose Boulevard, and you'll do fine. Kids love it here, and the corner windows make for good people-watching…. *Tel 312/337–3900. 901 N. Rush St. No credit cards. $*

Leo's Luncheonette. Don't be fooled by the dive-like looks of this tiny storefront restaurant. It's not only as if a trained chef just happens to be in the kitchen of a greasy spoon—there is a trained chef here, turning out imaginative, eclectic cuisine. Pretty incongruous, but don't think, just eat. BYOB…. *Tel 312/276–6509. 1809 W. Division St. No reservations. No credit cards. $$*

Lou Mitchell's. A Chicago breakfast institution, this place serves the definitive "hearty" breakfast, with homemade breads and cakes, omelets oozing butter and cheese, and great stacks of pancakes and French toast. And you'll need the nourishment after waiting in the long line…. *Tel 312/939–3111. 625 W. Jackson Blvd. No credit cards. No dinner; closed Sun. $*

Lutz Continental Cafe and Pastry Shop. Ageless and quaint, this cozy German pastry shop located on the north side, far from the madding crowd, serves lush pastries, cakes, and tortes, as well as espresso, cappuccino, and American coffee. Starched tablecloths, real china cups and dishes, and polite service add to the overall loveliness. Try the petit fours.... *Tel 312/478–7785. 2458 W. Montrose Ave. AE not accepted. $*

Maggiano's Little Italy. Red-and-white-checked tablecloths, sepia-tinted pictures of the Old Country, and enormous platters of traditional pastas, like red-sauced mostaccioli, fettucine alfredo, and spaghetti and meatballs, make this one of the most enjoyable Italian restaurants around. Family-style service keeps the prices down, too.... *Tel 312/644–7700. 516 N. Clark St. $$*

Marché. Yes, there's paillard of this and grantinée of that on the menu at this grandly decorated bistro, but the chef here uses French cuisine merely as inspiration. Try the aromatic couscous with grilled vegetables, the haricots verts with fennel and tomato, or any of the spectacular desserts, such as toasted walnut banana cake, profiteroles, or orange and coconut crème brûlée. Large selection of cognacs, single malt scotches, and other liqueurs to finish off the evening.... *Tel 312/226–8399. 833 W. Randolph St. Reservations advised. $$$$*

Mars. Black lacquer chairs, pretty tablecloths, and waiters and waitresses in starched white shirts are the hallmarks of this upscale, gracious Szechuan Chinese restaurant. The vegetarian potstickers are really good, and an unusual find in Chicago; the crispy family-style tofu is another winner.... *Tel 312/404–1600. 3124 N. Broadway. $$*

Medici. A short distance from the University of Chicago, this college and neighborhood hangout serves great burgers, natch, as well as salads, pizzas, and beer.... *Tel 312/667–7394. 1327 E. 57th St. $*

Mia Francesca. About as sizzling as sizzling restaurants in Chicago get, this trattoria has managed to stay hot thanks to moderate prices and consistently good food. The menu changes daily, but may include portobello-mushroom pizza, roasted red snapper, and a mélange of great pastas—there isn't a bad dish to be had. The room, sparely adorned with black-and-white photographs on clean white walls, is the perfect setting for the crowd's bounteous beauty. Oprah occasionally eats here.... *Tel 312/281–3310. 3311 N. Clark St. AE not accepted. $$*

CHICAGO | DINING

Michael Jordan's Restaurant. Surprisingly good food at this good-looking celebrity restaurant (warm, woody, lots of video screens) that doesn't try to rip off its patrons with obscenely high prices. If you're not dieting, try the cornmeal-fried catfish; the rotisserie chicken with scallion whipped taters is terrific, too. "The Big Mike" is two all-beef patties with a "special sauce," which sounds suspiciously like McDonald's but doesn't taste it. Juanita's macaroni and cheese is another great choice.... *Tel 312/644–DUNK. 500 N. LaSalle St. $$$*

Moti Mahal Indian Restaurant. The crowds crowding into Moti Mahal's storefront space say it all. Tandooris excel; so do vegetarian dishes like aloo gabhi (potato and cauliflower in a gingery sauce) and sag paneer (spinach and homemade cheese). In exchange for low prices, however, you also get service with a sneer. Even so, this modest place would make the Mahatma proud. BYOB.... *Tel 312/348–4392. 1031 W. Belmont Ave. $*

Muskie's. Competing (with Wiener Circle, see below) in the "Best Fries" category is this char-grilled ur-burger joint, but here at least there's plenty of indoor seating. Chow down on great burgers, the aforementioned fries, mozzarella sticks, char-chicken sandwiches, and veggie sandwiches.... *Tel 312/477–1880. 963 W. Belmont Ave. No credit cards. $*

Oo-La-La!. Great looking place, with its hand-painted dark booths, sexy lighting, and heavy draperies. The food at times is terrific and at other times merely okay. The pastas are your best bet, from the plain-as-day pasta pomodoro, which is too simple to screw up, to the *fettucine al sapori forti* (pasta with pine nuts, raisins, and garlic), which when it's good is really good. Fish is sometimes way overcooked.... *Tel 312/935–7708. 3335 N. Halsted St. $$*

La Paella. Duck, rabbit, and veal are on the menu, too, but the main attraction at this old-fashioned, family-owned restaurant is paella, with offerings running from paella Marinera (seafood paella) to paella Valenciana (chicken, pork, and chorizo). One night the solicitous hostess insisted I eat fish cheeks as an appetizer—yes, the CHEEKS OF FISH—and they were delicious. If you claim you're too full for dessert, they bring you oranges soaked in Cointreau anyhow.... *Tel 312/528–0757. 2920 N. Clark St. Reservations required. $$$*

The Palm. Celebrity caricatures, sawdust on the floor, and whirling ceiling fans lend a casual feel to this very expensive steakhouse. The lobsters are huge and beautifully cooked, as well, and the cottage fries are so good you'll eat the entire mountain they serve. The cheesecake is flown in daily from New York.... *Tel 312/944–0135. 181 E. Lake Shore Dr. $$$$*

Pane Caldo. Though you might be tempted to fill up on the great before-the-meal bread basket and perfect tapenade at this sophisticated Italian restaurant, don't—the pastas are terrific, and so's the salmon. Desserts are so-so; the between-course sorbets and after-dinner cookies and candied jellies are a nice touch.... *Tel 312/649–0055. 72 E. Walton St. Reservations advised. $$$*

Papagus Greek Taverna. The Greek decorations may be slightly on the kitschy side, but the food is pretty good—your basic moussaka, spanakopita, and baklava. Busy, noisy, dimly lit, and convenient to River North (in the Embassy Suites hotel).... *Tel 312/642–8450. 620 N. State St. Reservations advised. $$*

Park Avenue Cafe. From the onion-crusted roast chicken to the steamed red snapper with crab-meat-and-artichoke strudel, all the dishes on the frequently changing menu here are presented as handsomely as anything at the Art Institute, and there's hardly ever a miss. Desserts are especially terrific—mango sorbet with caramelized banana, carrot cheesecake soufflé—oy! The decor is as smoothly sophisticated as the well-heeled patrons.... *Tel 312/664–1100. 199 E. Walton St. Reservations advised. $$$$*

Penny's Noodle Shop. This 30-odd-seat sliver of a place beneath the Chicago el tracks attracts a neighborhood crowd, but it's worth a special trip for outsiders. From delicious Thai dishes like peppery *pad se ue*, to great *lad nar*, to crisp and savory Chinese greens with oyster sauce, to Vietnamese spring rolls, to Japanese *udon* with fish cakes, it all works. BYOB.... *Tel 312/281–8222. 3400 N. Sheffield Ave. (also at 950 W. Diversey Pkwy., tel 312/281–8448). No credit cards. $*

Pizzeria Due. An old reliable in an old brownstone—thick deep-dish 'zas oozing cheese, sausage, and virtually every vegetable imaginable, just like you like 'em. Long waits.... *Tel 312/943–2400. 610 N. Wabash St. $*

CHICAGO | DINING

Pizzeria Uno. Basically the same as above.... *Tel 312/321–1000. 29 E. Ohio St. $*

Planet Hollywood. A clone of Hard Rock Cafe (see above), only with movie memorabilia. Not that it makes much difference.... *Tel 312/266–9850. 633 N. Wells St. $$*

The Pump Room. Glitz galore in a chandeliered dining room with big booths, bigger tables, and biggest portions. Mostly steaks and chops traditionally prepared and all well-done, literally and figuratively. Neat little bar, too, and dancing to a trio on weekends. Do the cha-cha, drink a Manhattan, have a good time.... *Tel 312/266–0360. 1301 N. State St. Reservations required, jacket required. $$$$*

Quixotic Cafe. Up a flight of stairs from and overlooking the luxurious Whole Foods grocery store, this cafe serves some of the healthiest food in town: a BLT with nitrate-free bacon, a grilled chicken sandwich with "naturally-raised" chicken, organic wild greens, whole-wheat pizza crusts, and, of course, a selection of tofu, tempeh, and veggie burgers. The service generally stinks, though, and some of the waiters are pierced in places you'd never dream of piercing.... *Tel 312/587–0648. 1000 W. North Ave. $*

Reza's. Huge and boisterous, this Persian restaurant is a great place to eat if you're with a large crowd, or at least have a large appetite—there are more than 100 choices on the menu, from lamb kabob to *kashkeh bodemjan* (eggplant, curds, and whey) to quail to grilled duck breast in pomegranate sauce. And nothing costs more than $12.95. The service can be about as pleasant as wearing a chador in summertime Teheran, but the food makes it worth it.... *Tel 312/561–1898. 5225 N. Clark St. AE not accepted. $$*

La Risotteria Nord. While pastas, veal, and chicken dishes are available at this bilevel restaurant (sitting upstairs is nicer), come here for what the name promises—delicious, velvety risotto, of which there are more than two dozen choices nightly.... *Tel 312/348–2450. 2324 N. Clark St. $$$*

Rosebud. Everything served in this rambling, bustling Little Italy restaurant is big, bigger, biggest: heaping servings of pastas, a garlicky chicken Vesuvio as big as Vesuvius itself, and overwhelming Caesar salads. Bring your appetite, but don't expect it to be sated quickly—even with a reservation you're bound to wait. At least the huge mahogany bar is a great place to hang out.... *Tel 312/942–1117. 1500 W. Taylor St. $$$*

Scenes Coffeehouse and Dramatist Bookstore. If you can wade through all the smoke and pseudo-beat generation pretension, this oddly shaped, odd, and popular coffeehouse and bookstore can be a hoot. Don't expect service— the pierced-nosed (and more) waitrons are usually doing something else. Still, the windows overlook the passing Clark Street parade, and the soups, scones, and espresso eggs (steamed instead of scrambled) are fabulous.... *Tel 312/525–1007. 3168 N. Clark St. No credit cards. $*

Scoozi!. It's warehouse-sized and should be impersonal, but it's not—the service is fast and fine. And it's a feast for the eyes, with purposely decrepit walls, immense sprays of flowers, mirrors, and golden-glow lighting. The food doesn't taste as if it had rolled off a conveyor belt, either—the pastas, especially the homemade ravioli, are delish (though the portions are small), and the fish and chicken dishes are all top-notch. Tart gelati are perfect endings.... *Tel 312/943–5900. 410 W. Huron St. Reservations advised at lunch. $$*

Spiaggia. Soaring ceilings, pastel colors, views of the lake, and enough waitstaff scurrying around to make you feel as if you're at some modern-day palazzo. Often filled with Chicago's power elite, this exquisite Italian restaurant offers an equally powerful choice of dishes from a frequently changing menu, ranging from pastas to fish to game.... *Tel 312/280–2750. 980 N. Michigan Ave. Reservations required. $$$$$*

Third Coast Cafe. Hot location a block off Michigan Avenue and good inexpensive food that people actually want to eat (home-baked scones oozing raspberries, fresh-tasting eggs, really good salad niçoise, and, hallelujah, perfectly fine coffee—espresso, etc.). No wonder it's one of the neighborhood's most popular hangouts.... *Tel 312/664–7225. 888 N. Wabash St. $*

Trattoria No. 10. If you're searching for a great Italian meal in the Loop, head to Trattoria No. 10. A favorite of the busi-

CHICAGO | DINING

ness-lunch crowd, it has a burnt-orange ambience straight out of Tuscany, and food—particularly the ravioli—to match.... *Tel 312/984–1718. 10 N. Dearborn St. Reservations advised. $$$*

Urbus Orbis. With its high ceilings, high-back chairs, and anything but high prices, this artsy coffeehouse is a great rainy-day hangout. While the coffee and food, including sandwiches and scones, are only passable, watching the passing crowd of students and struggling artists more than makes up for it.... *Tel 312/252–4446. 1934 W. North Ave. No credit cards. $*

Vivo. The first to conquer the obscure Market West area (west of the Loop) was the self-consciously hip Vivo, with its exposed brick walls and ducts and pipes. The Italian food is nothing special, and the scene here by now is really passé. You're better off at its sister restaurant, the oh-so-trendy Marché (see above).... *Tel 312/226–2555. 838 W. Randolph St. Reservations advised. $$$*

Wiener Circle. Burgers are better than the dogs here, and the fries are some of the best in town. There's really nowhere to eat except at the few icky wood picnic tables out front, where you can sit in the wake of the carbon monoxide spewed from passing buses. That said, though, the place does have a certain urban charm.... *Tel 312/477–7444. 2622 N. Clark St. No credit cards. $*

Wishbone. At this hip, casual restaurant, Southern home-cooking, such as pan-fried chicken or the house specialty—hoppin' John (black-eyed peas over rice with cheddar, scallions, and tomatoes)—comes with two sides—the yams and spinach are the best. Of course, they also serve great pecan pie and pretty good grits (that is, if you're disposed to even like grits).... *Tel 312/850–2663. 1001 W. Washington St. $$*

North Side Dining

Ambria **21**
Angelina **5**
Ann Sather's **13**
Carlucci **19**
Charlie Trotter's **24**
Chicago Diner **7**
Daniel J. **3**
El Jardin **9**
Espial **23**

Ina's Kitchen and
  Elaine's Garden **18**
La Paella **16**
La Risotteria Nord **17**
Lutz Continental Cafe
  and Pastry Shop **1**
Mars **15**
Mia Francesca **10**
Moti Mahal Indian
  Restaurant **11**

Muskie's **12**
Oo La La! **8**
Penny's Noodle Shop **6**
PS Bangkok **4**
Reza's **2**
Scenes Coffeehouse and
  Dramatist Bookstore **14**
Un Grand Cafe **21**
Wiener Circle **20**

© 1995 GeoSystems Global Corp.

Chicago Dining

Berhoff **49**
Bice Ristorante **30**
Big Bowl Cafe **24**
Bigsby's Bar and Grill **8**
Billy Goat Tavern **42**
Bistro **18**
Le Bouchon **1**
Bub City Crabshack & BBQ **7**
Busy Bee **9**
Cafe Ba-Ba-Reeba **4**
Cafe Gordon **17A**
Cafe Iberico **12**
Centro **23**
Club Lucky **2**
Coco Pazzo **34**
The Corner Bakery **38**
Dick's Last Resort **41**
The Eccentric **53**
Ed Debevics **25**
Everest **51**
foodlife **19**
Frontera Grill **39**
Gene & Georgetti **33**
Gibson's **54**
Gino's East **20A**
Gordon **36**
Hard Rock Cafe **27**
Harry Caray's **40**
Harry's Velvet Room **31**
Hong Min **21**
Italian Village **48**
Jane's **3**

Johnny Rocket's **15**
Leo's Luncheonette **10**
Lou Mitchell's **47**
Maggiano's Little Italy **37**
Marché **46**
Medici **52**
Michael Jordan's **35**
The Palm **43**
Pane Caldo **14**
Papagus Greek Taverna **28**
Park Avenue Cafe **20**
Pizzeria Due **29**
Pizzeria Uno **32**
Planet Hollywood **26**
The Pump Room **13**
Quixotic Cafe **5**
Rosebud **50**
Scoozi! **22**
Spiaggia **16**
Third Coast Cafe **17**
Trattoria No. 10 **44**
Urbus Orbis **6**
Vivo **45**
Wishbone **11**

3

sions

Chicago is a hard
city in which
to stick to an
itinerary. Sure,
you may think
you're going to
walk from your

hotel to the Art Institute of Chicago, but you find yourself passing through **Lincoln Park** and instead decide to sit in the shadow of the bronze statue of William Shakespeare and read a detective novel. Or you plan to lounge on **Oak Street Beach** and work on your tan, but wind up renting roller-blades at the concession stand and hotdogging it up and down the boardwalk until the sun sinks beneath the horizon. Day after day your plans don't quite get fulfilled, there are fewer and fewer activities checked off on your "to do" list. And yet you've done so much.

It's not merely that Chicago is a big city—after all, Detroit is a big place, too—but it's a big city with an unusually wide array of things to do. It's not a sunny resort area where you either sit on the beach or windsurf, 'nuff said, or a cement canyon where you walk around museums and sample tony restaurants. It's both of those things: windsurfing at **Montrose Beach** in the morning, high tea at the **Ritz-Carlton** in the afternoon one day; the next a brunch at **Spiaggia** and a stroll through the **DuSable Museum of African American History**, with the afternoon spent learning to sail at **Belmont Harbor** and the evening at a first-rate play at the **Steppenwolf Theater**. The only real challenge is apportioning your time so you don't feel cheated in the end.

Getting Your Bearings

Chicago, bless its heart, is about as easy a big city in which to get around as exists. The city is laid out like a grid, with the intersection of north–south **State Street** and east–west **Madison Street** in **the Loop** being its blessed heart. Addresses get incrementally bigger in all directions as you move away from this point, with about 100 numbers per block, 800 per mile. So, at the same place on each perpendicular street you'll more or less find the same address; 3000 North Sheridan Road, for instance, is as far north as that same address on every other north–south street. There are a few diagonal thoroughfares, such as **Lincoln** and **Ridge** avenues, but their number systems by and large are in keeping with the grid streets—2000 Clark Street, for example, is at Armitage, the same way 2000 Lincoln Park West is. The lake is east—always. The most significant street to know is **Lake Shore Drive**, which hugs the coast north–south. The other main north–south drags include **Broadway, Clark Street, Halsted Street, Dearborn Parkway, LaSalle Street**, and **Michigan Avenue**. Six of the Loop's east–west thoroughfares are named after presidents—**Washington, Madison, Monroe, Adams, Jackson**, and **Van**

Buren. Farther north, **North Avenue**, **Fullerton**, **Diversey**, and **Belmont** are zeniths of neighborhood activity. Laid on top of this grid-like scenario are the el and bus routes, which traverse the city in such a way that a car, while helpful, is unnecessary. Getting from the Loop to Wrigley Field for a Cubs game is a one-train deal. You can take a bus from the Lincoln Park Zoo to Marshall Field's and, as you glide down Stockton Drive and then Michigan Avenue, you get a magnificent sight-seeing tour thrown in for free. The **Chicago Transit Authority (CTA)** is one of the few remaining subway systems in the United States that operates most days around the clock (though some stations are closed after traditional work hours and on part or all of the weekends, so it's imperative to check). Generally, the entire system is referred to as the "el" because parts of it are elevated, like a roller coaster. At places it curves from side to side like a roller coaster, too. There are six separate subway routes, denoted in different colors on the maps, copies of which are available at every subway token booth. And then there are buses, which follow various routes illustrated on blue-and-white signs posted at the bus stops (generally every two blocks along the route). The fare on trains and buses is currently $1.50 (plus a 30-cent transfer for use between bus lines, which must be used within two hours of its issuance). For a

The City Architectural

Chicagoans take their architecture very seriously. They argue about it on the el; they discuss it over breakfast reading the Tribune; they take special trips to the Loop to see the latest controversial building. And they have good reason for such passion, for Chicago's a city of hundreds of architectural gems, a living, breathing hothouse of important buildings, controversial construction, and innovation. Chicago is known as the birthplace of modern American architecture. Why? Well, after the Great 1871 Fire singed four densely built square miles of mostly wooden buildings, the 1869 stone **Water Tower** *on Michigan Avenue was one of the few buildings left standing (and it's not much to look at). So the city had to be rebuilt, coincidentally just as new technologies (like the elevator, steel skeletons, and fireproof terra-cotta cladding) were making it possible to build taller, more interesting buildings. The city's building boom attracted the country's greatest architects, from Louis Sullivan to Henry Hobson Richardson to Frank Lloyd Wright. (It's still home to great architects, such as Helmut Jahn, Stanley Tigerman, and Larry Booth.) The boom encouraged them and others to experiment with form and function—and did they ever.*

CHICAGO | DIVERSIONS

map or free advice on how to get from one place to another, call the CTA (tel 312/836–7000). Just remember, Chicago is flat, streets run for the most part straight north–south, east–west, and the lake is always, always, always east. Now go have fun.

The Lowdown

Must-sees... You should not leave the city limits without going to the **Art Institute of Chicago**, even if it's just to stand slack-jawed with the crowd that is usually massed before what may be the museum's most famous holding, Georges Seurat's *Sunday Afternoon on the Island of La Grande Jatte*. The thing is, it's actually an incredible painting; the only one I know of to have a Broadway musical based on it. And no visit to Chicago would be complete without walking around the 72-foot-long apatosaurus at the **Field Museum of Natural History**, the highlight of the museum's grand "DNA to Dinosaur" exhibit. Odds are, once you get home, some neighborhood wisenheimer will ask if you walked through the giant heart at the **Museum of Science and Industry**— and in this case, the wisenheimer knows whereof he speaks. It may sound kitschy, but it's an oddly impressive experience, as is this whole huge hands-on museum where adults are just as enthralled as kids. Graceful, ornate **Buckingham Fountain**, along Lake Shore Drive in Grant Park, is another don't-miss-it, if for no other reason than because over the years it's become a city icon.

Special moments... You must, must, must take a long, lazy drive up (or down) **Lake Shore Drive**. The experience is what they call a two-fer: you see the lake on one side, *and* the **Loop skyline**, **Grant Park**, the **Gold Coast**, and **Lincoln Park** on the other. Day or night, it's a stunning vista. Walk around **the Loop**—better yet, take a guided tour given by the **Chicago Architecture Foundation**—to get a feel for the business that makes this powerful city really tick. As crowds of stockbrokers and lawyers scurry around you, stand still on a corner and crane your neck to study America's most perfect assemblage of classic skyscraper architecture. Speaking of walking, take a jaunt up (or down) **North Michigan Avenue**, the city's prime shopping thoroughfare, with huge stores and malls housing the city's most glamorous places to buy stuff. Whether or not you spend a dime, the dazzling retail display can induce a sense of well-being in all but the most hardened consumer. And if you're in town during baseball season, make time to attend a **Cubs** game at **Wrigley Field**. The ballpark is in the middle of a tight residential neighborhood; parking stinks, so take public transportation if you can.

Only in Chicago... No matter how happy you are to be in Chicago, there's always room for **the blues**. Whether you visit the **Checkerboard Lounge** on the South Side or **Kingston Mines** on the North Side (see Nightlife), you won't regret it. After all, Chicago is the home of the blues. You shouldn't miss **Robie House**, either, perhaps Frank Lloyd Wright's most famous residential building within the city limits (it's in Hyde Park); it may inspire you to trek on out to suburban **Oak Park** to see more of Wright's iconoclastic

Get yer free art right here!
Art should free your mind, not free your wallet of all its money. Given the breadth of Chicago's museums, an inexpensive day is easily had (just stay out of the gift shops). But be warned: Museums are generally most crowded on their free-admission days, when it's often impossible to get close to any of the exhibits and you'll have to wait your turn for the interactive displays; parking can be a hassle, too. Some museums in Chicago are always free: the **DuSable Museum of African American History**, *the* **Oriental Institute**, *and the* **David and Alfred Smart Museum of Art**, *all three in Hyde Park; and the* **Mexican Fine Arts Center Museum**. *Others at least have a free day, to wit: Monday:* **Chicago Historical Society, Chicago Academy of Sciences, International Museum of Surgical Sciences**. *Tuesday:* **Adler Planetarium, Art Institute of Chicago, Museum of Contemporary Art.** *Wednesday:* **Field Museum of Natural History.** *Thursday:* **Chicago Children's Museum** *(tel 312/527–1000, at Navy Pier),* **Museum of Science & Industry.** *Friday:* **Spertus Museum of Judaica.** *See The Index for details.*

CHICAGO | DIVERSIONS

Prairie Style architecture, born and bred here in Chicago. Then go stuff your face with a world-famous **deep-dish pizza** from either **Uno** or **Due**, the city's premier pizza makers (see Dining). Other cities, from New York to London, may claim that they make authentic Chicago pizzas, but none—and I mean none—make them as good as pizza makers in Chicago. There is no room for argument here.

Prowling the Gold Coast... According to a 1994 study by Roosevelt University, Chicago's Gold Coast is second only to Manhattan when it comes to the highest concentration of moolah in the country. From the lake to roughly about LaSalle Street, Chicago to North avenues, this is Chicago's fancy-shmanciest area, incorporating exclusive shopping and tree-shaded residential streets lined with gorgeous townhouses, pre-war apartment buildings, and more than a few very ugly modern towers. Roaming around is a pleasure. The former **Playboy Mansion** (1340 N. State St., at Lake Shore Dr.) is now condos, but you can still try to imagine what Hef was up to all those years. The **Archbishop's Residence** (1555 N. State Pkwy.) is a Queen Anne-style red-brick mansion, typical at least in size of the many ornate palaces, built after the Chicago Fire, that used to line Lake Shore Drive. Other architectural highlights include McKim, Mead & White's 1892 **Patterson-McCormick Mansion** (20 E. Burton Place), originally built for Joseph Medill, who was mayor of Chicago and part owner of the *Chicago Tribune*; the 1914 **Three Arts Club** (1300 N. Dearborn St.), by the architectural firm of Holabird & Roche; the **Louis Sullivan Townhouses** (1826–1834 N. Lincoln Park West), designed by Sullivan himself; and **Charnley House** (1365 N. Astor St.), designed by Adler & Sullivan. In fact, all of **Astor Street**, from Division Street to North Avenue, is a designated national landmark. Check out the **Chicago Historical Society**, at Clark Street and North Avenue. It's a really wonderful museum—not boring or staid like a lot of historical society digs. Alongside memorabilia from the Civil War (including Lincoln's deathbed) and from the Chicago Fire, there's neat stuff like a poster advertising John Wilkes Booth playing Hamlet in a Chicago theater a week before he shot Lincoln, as well as the first copy of *Playboy* magazine. When walking around finally starts to get to you, head over to the **Oak Street Beach**. It's Chicago's most famous, probably, and it's best for people-watching. All the sunbathers, Rollerbladers, walkers, runners, and saunterers provide a good dose of live theater. At the south end of **North Avenue Beach** (or, depending on where you are, the north end of Oak Street Beach), you can rest and play chess at the **Chess Pavilion**, where chess challengers from around the city gather to square off. Beneath a concrete sculpture that looks almost airborne, schmoozers and players alike sit around at all hours, some playing the game, some watching, some just contemplating the passing crowd. Bring your own chess pieces and you too can play on the built-in boards. It's almost always a wonderful Chicago scene. Along **Oak Street** itself is a prime shopping area, one block crammed with world-famous **designer boutiques**, from Armani to Versace, set in exquisite brownstones (see Shopping for details). Once your throat becomes parched, take a load off. Skip all the tacky bars along Division Street unless you get off on wet T-shirt contests or gargantuan bouncers guarding the doors. But do stop in at the **Third Coast Cafe** (see Dining) for a half-caf skim latté and scone, no butter on the side; **P.J. Clarke's** (tel 312/664–1650, 1204 N. State Pkwy.) for a terrific burger and fries and really good Caesar salads; **Albert's Café** (tel 312/751–0666, 52 W. Elm St.) for yet another latté and a frilly French pastry or sandwich; or for some of the best people-watching, the **Brasserie Bellevue** (21 E. Bellevue Place, in the Sutton Place Hotel), a glass-enclosed "sidewalk café" where the food is utterly beside the point.

Museumscapes... There's a velvet rope in front of Seurat's pointillist masterpiece, *Sunday Afternoon on the Island of La Grande Jatte*, perhaps the most beloved picture at the **Art Institute of Chicago**. Everyone wants to get close to it, to be near it, to see it, to remember it. "Hey, remember when we studied that?" visitors ask each other, pointing to the picture. In fact, you hear that sort of thing all over the museum—in front of Claude Monet's *Haystack* series, Edward Hopper's *Nighthawks*, Vincent Van Gogh's *Bedroom at Arles*, and Grant Wood's *American Gothic*. So, if you've only got the stamina to see one museum in the city, this should definitely be it. Though its collection does not have the depth of some other, larger museums, it's many famous holdings make it seem like Art History's Greatest Hits. The museum, which was built in 1892 and sits on a majestic site on Michigan Avenue with the

Loop's lakeside Grant Park as its backyard. Don't miss what's left of the Trading Room of the original **Chicago Stock Exchange**, the rest of which was demolished for stupid reasons in 1972 (to make way for a modern skyscraper); luckily, portions of the beautifully stencilled walls, moulded pilaster capitals, and art glass were preserved and incorporated into the re-creation you'll see here. (The Exchange's two-story entry arch was also saved and re-erected in a nearby garden at the museum.) Also, check out the Rubloff paperweight collection. It sounds dumb—paperweights—but their magnificent sparkling colorings and designs make them as gorgeous as fine jewelry. Also, whether you're a Martha Stewart devotée or not, the Miniature Thorne Rooms—68 tiny but scarily intricate re-creations of spectacular period interiors—is worth a visit to the museum alone. Sometime in 1996 the **Museum of Contemporary Art** will move from its cramped headquarters on Ontario Street to a newly built four-times-as-big limestone home on a very showy spot where the Illinois National Guard Armory used to be, on Chicago Avenue. In the past, this museum was known mostly for its cutting-edge temporary exhibits in all sorts of avant-garde media; the new site's two huge temporary exhibition spaces and numerous other galleries will finally let the museum exhibit some of its extensive permanent collection, and there will be a one-acre sculpture garden facing Lake Michigan. Nearby is the **Terra Museum of American Art**, which displays pictures from the 18th century through today by American masters such as Homer, Cassatt, Hopper, and Audubon. Some people find the Terra pretty staid, but it is a perfect place to bone up on American Art 101, being one of the few museums in this country solely devoted to American artists. In Hyde Park, the **David and Alfred Smart Museum of Art** displays the University of Chicago's eclectic art collection. The best thing here is the original dining room set designed by Frank Lloyd Wright for his now-famous **Robie House**, a few blocks away in Hyde Park. (Robie House is currently used as the University of Chicago's admissions offices).

Ethnic museums... Jewish art and artifacts, from ritual objects to paintings and sculpture, are on display at the **Spertus Museum of Judaica**, which is of limited interest except for the moving Zell Holocaust Memorial and the Children's Artifact Center, a clever hands-on exhibit that lets kids learn through archaeology the history of the Middle East. If you're already heading down to the Hyde Park area, there are two other museums to make the trek worthwhile, and they're both fairly small—you can easily do them in the same day as the Smart Museum. On the University of Chicago campus, the **Oriental Institute Museum** showcases the art and artifacts of the Near East—ancient Persia, Iraq, Egypt, Israel, Syria, and Turkey—from about 9000 B.C. to the tenth century A.D., with many pieces of art, archeological finds, and other things pillaged from other cultures during a time when pillaging wasn't so un-p.c. Highlights include Egyptian mummies and, from an Assyrian palace a 40-ton sculpture of a winged bull. The **DuSable Museum of African American History**, also in Hyde Park, traces the black experience in America through an extensive collection of art, artifacts, and displays. For good luck rub the nose of the bronze bust of Haitian-born Jean Baptiste-Pointe DuSable, a trader born of mixed African and European blood; he was the first known non-Native American settler in Chicago. In Pilsen the **Mexican Fine Arts Center Museum** showcases contemporary Mexican and Mexican-American art with new exhibits every couple of months, while on the Northwest Side the **Polish Museum of America** highlights both traditional and modern Polish and Polish-American art, including the Stations of the Cross from the first Polish church in America. It's one of the largest museums in the country devoted to the art and history of one ethnic group, but given that there are more Poles in Chicago than in any other city in the world other than Warsaw, that shouldn't come as too big a surprise.

Techno-museums... As it happens, Chicago has a whole raft of museums devoted to the sciences, strung out along the shore of Lake Michigan. The starting point has to be down in Hyde Park at the truly great **Museum of Science and Industry**. One of its most beloved exhibits is also one of the simplest: Stand in one spot in the oval-shaped Whispering Gallery and you can murmur to a person standing all the way on the other side—they'll hear you loud and clear. It's an ever-amazing thing to do, and more so because while doing it you realize you've learned a little something, too, about how sound travels. It's like that all over the museum, where visitors learn almost by osmosis as they walk through, pull, touch, explore, and wonder at the more than 2,000 interactive exhibits, including an actual Boeing 727's fuselage, an authentic U-505 Nazi submarine, and a reproduction of a Southern Illinois coal mine. Go north up the lakeshore to Grant Park, and you'll find another of the big kahunas of Chicago's museum world, the **Field Museum of Natural History**, with its mighty dinosaurs, hairy beasts, and permanent and temporary exhibits devoted to all things natural, from anthropology to zoology. Enormous exhibits, such as "Africa," "Oceana," or "Inside Ancient Egypt"—which includes the *masaba* (tomb) of Pharaoh Unis and 23 actual mummies—feature interactive experiences that allow visitors to not only see how other cultures and environments exist, but to feel a visceral connection to them. Across a road from the Field is the **Shedd Aquarium**, a splendid facility that's practically as good as an indoor Sea World. The Shedd got some unwelcome publicity a few years ago when it opened its Oceanarium, which tries to re-create the coast of the Pacific Northwest—lots of people weren't thrilled about the display of the Beluga whales, whom they felt were living in unnatural living quarters (as if most of us aren't). But the Oceanarium is, in fact, a marvel, where you can walk along a trail that mimics the coastal environment, as you encounter whales, dolphins, sea otters, and harbor seals (you can also watch the sea mammals through underwater windows). Once you've checked out the water, look up to see the sky at the nearby **Adler Planetarium** with its high-tech, special-effects-laden 68-foot-high Sky Theater. If you can, go on a Friday night—after the show the Adler uses its incredible 20-inch computerized telescope to instantly project 18-foot by 24-foot live images of outer space to the audience. For those bored by the usual museum displays, head to the oddly fascinating **International Museum of Surgical Sciences**, housed in a couple of great 1917 former residences on Lake Shore Drive, for a tour of medical devices through the ages, as well as a re-creation of a turn-of-the-century drug store (it's not exactly Walgreens).

Talk is cheap... Have you slept with your mother-in-law lately? Or perhaps you are a very confused cross-dressing hermaphrodite. Did your father break up your marriage by running over your spouse with a bulldozer? If you've answered yes to any of these questions, you belong as a guest on one of the three talk shows that tape in Chicago. If you'd just like to be an audience member at one of the tapings, however, call "The Oprah Winfrey Show" (tel 312/591–9595), "The Jerry Springer Show" (tel 312/321–5350), or the infamous "Jenny Jones Show" (tel 312/836–9400) at least a month in advance for tickets. Most shows tape twice a day, three days a week, August through May. Sorry, but none will tell you that day's topic until you get there for the taping.

Kid-pleasers... Be warned, the museums that are particularly kid-friendly, such as the **Field Museum of Natural History**, the **Shedd Aquarium**, and the **Museum of Science and Industry** (see above), are absolute mob scenes on free days, especially in the summer or over holidays when school is out. Still, if that's the only time you're here, brave the crowds—these are not to be missed, even if your kids are only toddlers. The **Spertus Museum of Judaica** has a children's museum and a hands-on archaeology exhibit, which older kids can enjoy. Of the city's two zoos (see "Cruise the zoos," below), the smaller **Lincoln Park Zoo** is better for the under-eights, while older kids will probably prefer the more spread-out **Brookfield Zoo**. A **boat tour** on the lake (see "Tour time," below, or Getting Outside) makes sightseeing pretty palatable for children, and, of course, no thrill-seeking youngster would want to miss the zooming elevator ride to the way-high observatories at the **Sears Tower** or the **John Hancock Center**.

Art al fresco... In front of Chicago's big skyscrapers, there are a lot of big sculptures. Here are my favorites: The highest density of outdoor art is in the Loop, where approximately 65 pieces are within easy walking distance of one another. The most famous, and probably the only one you should go out of your way to see, is the great untitled 1967 **Picasso sculpture at the Daley Plaza** (Dearborn and Randolph streets). It's become a virtual icon of the city, as much so as the Hancock building or Wrigley Field. There's a miniature version there, too, for the visually-impaired and/or touchy–feely. **Flamingo**, Alexander Calder's bright-red, spidery-looking 1974 sta-

CHICAGO | DIVERSIONS

bile, soars 53 feet into the air in the shadow of the sullen-looking **Federal Center** (219 S. Dearborn St.). Touted as vandal-proof, it does look like it's still in perfect condition, so the boast must be true. *Les Quatre Saisons* is a fancy way of referring to Marc Chagall's 1967 *Four Seasons* at One First National Plaza (Dearborn and Monroe streets): an extraordinary piece, it's a 70-foot-long, 14-foot-high, four-sided colorful mosaic. Jean Dubuffet's *Monument with Standing Beast* at the State of Illinois Building (100 W. Randolph St.) is an exuberant 10-ton black-and-white fiberglass gift from the artist himself. At more than 100 feet high, they say it's a bat, but Claes Oldenberg's 1977 *Batcolumn* at the Social Security Administration Building (600 W. Madison St.) just looks like a big phallic symbol to many. Check out Louise Nevelson's 1983 *Dawn Shadow* from the street at Madison Plaza (Madison and Wells streets) if you must, but the view from the nearby el platform is better. The last of the best is Joan Miro's 1981 *Chicago* near the Chicago Temple (69 W. Washington St.), a bronze, concrete, and ceramic structure that mostly resembles a totem pole gone haywire.

Cruising the zoos... Chicago is lucky to have two world-class zoos. Even for those who find zoos slightly depressing—after all, would most of these animals really choose to be in Chicago if they had their druthers?—both the **Lincoln Park Zoo** and the **Brookfield Zoo** can be terrifically fun. The **Brookfield**, spread out over 200 acres 14 miles due west of the Loop, is by far the bigger of the two. Its 2,000 animals (representing 425 species) are housed in more naturalistic settings than those in the Lincoln Park Zoo, and somehow the animals just seem, well, happier there. Tropic World, for instance, is a football-field-sized indoor rain forest, complete with three different ecosystems, one each for South America, Asia, and Africa. While the trees, rocks, lush foliage, phony-but-fun-anyhow thunderstorm, and 50-foot waterfall won't fool you, it apparently does fool the myriad birds, apes, and other critters that live there. There's more, including a five-acre "Habitat Africa," the mandatory synchronized-swimming dolphin show in the Seven Seas Panorama and Dolphinarium (there's a really bad word for you), a reptile house, a pachyderm house, a baboon "island," bear grottos, zebra and camel areas, and a separate children's zoo. The Motor Safari Tram tours the zoo and allows you to get on and off at various points. Now, it's heresy in Chicago to whine about the **Lincoln Park Zoo**, the most visited zoo in the entire country; but, truthfully, it's a bit harder to love than Brookfield. However, it's one of the last zoos in the country that doesn't charge admission, and it's a neighborhood zoo, where kids can come after school and families can stroll over on a summer evening or on weekends. Set on 35 urban acres smack dab in the middle of Lincoln Park, it has a certain sophisticated allure, like the zoo in New York's Central Park, and it's the obvious choice for quick visits—it does manage to be both fun for families and sort of romantic for couples. But many of the animals are still housed in long brick animal houses, reminiscent of 19th-century orphanages, which casts a depressing pall. If you can hold your nose—both literally and figuratively— about all that, the rest of the zoo is really great. And zoo officials are trying to make the animals' living conditions better by modernizing and upgrading the spaces and creating a few naturalistic outdoor habitats. Considering its comparatively petite size, the zoo has a lot to offer, including the Farm-in-a-Zoo and a small children's zoo, inhabited mainly by babies of all manner of species; a trainer is often on hand to let kids pet one thing or another.

Strolling around Old Town... Old Town, the area roughly from Division Street north to Wisconsin Street, and LaSalle Street west to Larrabee Street, used to be funky; now it's rehabbed and refurbished. Its narrow side-streets are jammed with both huge new-money houses and tiny renovated jobs (there's hardly anything rundown anymore). For strolling and strollers (the baby kind), the neighborhood is a perfect place to spend a lazy afternoon, gazing around the not-always-beautiful but definitely always-interesting residential streetscapes. Check out **Crilly Court** (covering about five blocks east of Eugenie Street, bounded by Eugenie, West St. Paul Street, North Wells Street, and North Park Avenue), built in the 1880s by Daniel Crilly, a local developer, and rehabilitated in the 1940s, which touched off Old Town's renaissance. It's lined with townhouses and apartment buildings that have magnificent gardens behind them, though you can't see them unless you know someone. You can, however, look above some of the apartment buildings' doors to find the names of Crilly's children carved there—Edgar, Oliver, Isabelle, and Erminie. Other beautiful buildings worth a look-see include the Romanesque-style **St. Michael's Church** (458 W. Eugenie St.), part of which actually lived through the 1871 fire. Legend has it that its church bells define the area because, supposedly, you're only really in Old Town if you can hear them. (What that means for the whereabouts of the hearing-impaired is unclear.) On Wells Street, which was to Chicago in the 1960s what Haight-Ashbury was to San Francisco, a few small, funky boutiques remain, but mostly it's upscale Italian restaurants and a couple of nice clothing stores. There's also one terrific bookstore, **Barbara's Bookstore** (see Shopping), where you can browse endlessly. It's actually sort of sad to see **Piper's Alley**, which used to be filled with psychedelic stores catering to Chicago hippies and hippie-wannabes and is today an antiseptic hallway with a huge four-screen movie theater attached. **Trattoria Roma** (tel 312/664–7907, 1535 N. Wells St.) and **Topo Gigio** (tel 312/266–9355, 1437 N. Wells St.; and tel 312/751–8070, 1800 N. Wells St.) are two of the better restaurants along the strip. If you just want a fast, inexpensive bite, try **Old Jerusalem** (tel 312/944–0459, 1411 N. Wells St.), a storefront restaurant serving great falafel, fresh tabbouleh, and other Middle Eastern dishes. And something has to be said here about **Second City** (tel 312/337–3992, 1616 N. Wells St.; see Entertainment), the world-famous improvisational comedy club that has spawned such hilarious luminaries as Elaine May, John Belushi, Shelley Long, John Candy, and Gilda Radner. Mainly tourists go there, and while they usually have a laugh-riot, it's not as funny as it used to be, and it can be expensive. A less expensive alternative is to go after the main show for improv only.

Gallery hopping... Gallery-hopping is a major Chicago pastime, with dozens of galleries from which to choose. Chicago's art scene, mind you, is devoted mostly to contemporary art, and unlike galleries in some, ah-hem, eastern cities, Chicago gallery owners actually welcome browsers. New places open (and close) constantly; pick up a copy of *The Reader*, Chicago's free weekly, or the quarterly *Chicago Gallery News* at almost any gallery, for the latest listing of exhibits. Keep in mind that most galleries are open Tuesday through Saturday, 10–5, with shorter summer hours—call ahead if there's one show you want to make sure you see. Though there are galleries throughout the city, the highest concentration is still in **River North**, west of the Michigan Avenue area, a neighborhood of warehouses-turned-lofts, oh-so-chic boutiques, and a few good restaurants. Start at **Carl Hammer** (tel 312/266–8512, 200 W. Superior St.), a gallery dealing in contemporary art and outsider art, or art created by "self-taught artists." Hammer started out as a school teacher and is usually on hand to help educate browsers in the kind of art he sells. In a smilar vein, the owner of the **Catherine Edelman Gallery** (tel 312/266–2350, 300 W. Superior St.) showcases both established photographers such as Jock Sturges and Joel Ziolkowski and emerging photographers like Zeke Berman and Albert Chong. Just down the block and up a few steps, the **Struve Gallery** (tel 312/787–0563, 309 W. Superior St.) presents superior 20th-century paintings and objects, many of which have an architectural bent or an Eastern European influence. Some of the biggest names in contemporary art, from Ed Pashke to Roger Brown to Karl Wirsum, are exhibited at the **Phyllis Kind Gallery** (tel 312/642–6302, 313 W. Superior St.), while at nearby **Rhona Hoffman** (tel 312/951–8828, 325 W. Superior St.) you'll find contemporary masters such as Sol Lewitt and Bruce Nauman. One of the first, and still one of the finest, galleries in the area is the **Zolla/Lieberman Gallery** (tel 312/944–1990, 325 W. Superior St.), a beautiful light-filled space showcasing avant-garde painting and sculpture from around the world.

T.G.I.F. in River North... Unlike New York (where art gallery openings are exclusive, invitation-only affairs), galleries in Chicago's River North and River West sections hold their **openings just about every Friday evening** and are open to anyone who happens to cruise by. In River North particularly, where dozens of galleries are concentrated in a six-block area, an entire evening can be spent meandering around, sipping free wine from small plastic cups (even getting some chocolate-covered raisins from the Carl Hammer Gallery), and checking out the art and your fellow artlovers. Sometimes there may be as few as two or three openings, but usually there are at least five. Once a year, on the Friday after Labor Day, the galleries in the area coordinate their openings, turning things into a huge block party.

Mayhem on the trading floors... Millions of dollars, tons of pork bellies, and tankers full of oil exchange hands every day in Chicago's money pits, one of the best and cheapest shows in town. You'll be amazed at the feral behavior of the traders as they scream, bellow, make what look to be obscene gestures, and just generally behave like pigs at the **Chicago Board of Trade**, the **Chicago Mercantile Exchange**, and the **Chicago Board Options Exchange**. You'll be relieved that there is a glass partition separating the visitors gallery from them. The scene is pretty much the same at each of them—toss a coin to decide which to visit (taking in all three would definitely be overkill).

One good read deserves another... Sometimes you just vant to be alone, to sit, and to read a good book. So head for the **Harold Washington Library Center**. Going to the library to read a book may sound like an obvious choice, but in Chicago the building in itself is a pretty wonderful civic monument, opened in 1991 after years of political infighting (the usual Chicago thing). The collection, having long ago outgrown its original Michigan Avenue home, had been dispersed among several buildings, while plans to replace the main library ran the gamut from rehabbing the former Goldblatts department store to erecting a new building altogether. The latter won out, resulting in this 10-story red granite-and-brick neoclassical edifice holding about a zillion books, all in open-stack shelving. In good weather (admittedly always iffy in Chicago), another good place to lounge and read just off the Magnificent Mile is **Washington Square** (Walton St. at Dearborn), a patch of green unofficially known as "Bughouse Square." Chicago's first public park, it earned that nickname in the 1920s, when people would gather to hear radicals scream and yell about the ills of the world, a nutty open-air forum much like London's Speaker's Corner. It's across from the magnificent **Newberry Library**, a private research library specializing in Western civilization and the humanities;

though you have to get permission to read here, check to see if any special events, for adults or kids, are on tap that day. Or, with book in hand, head up to **Lincoln Park**— either to the formal gardens in front of the Lincoln Park Conservatory or to lounge in the shadow of the fake totem pole, a replica of the original that stood here (until some carvers noted its historical significance to the Kwakiutl Indians of British Columbia and had it shipped off to a Canadian museum). Other good outdoor reading spots are the concrete boardwalk and lawn along the lake, just south of Diversey Parkway; almost any bench on the **University of Chicago** campus; or the Gold Coast's **Goudy Square Park** (Astor and Goethe streets), if you don't mind the sound of neighborhood rich kids playing in the background.

Cool views... There's a difference between most comprehensive and "best." Most people think the best view is the most extensive panorama, where they can gawk at the most square mileage—"Look, it's Indiana! How divine!" But the truly breathtaking views, the ones that still make Chicagoans catch their breaths, are actually lower to the ground, if not on it, and sometimes from a moving vantage point. For instance, drive (or take a cab) north along **Lake Shore Drive from Congress Parkway**. On your left you'll see the city skyline at its most gorgeous advantage; on your right, the lake will spread out like an ocean. As you round the bend at **Oak Street Beach**, majestic residential buildings begin to line the drive. Another possibility is to get on **the el** almost anywhere in the Loop—the views from either side as you circle the neighborhood bring you face to face with some of the city's best architecture, from the Monadnock Building to the Harold Washington Library Center. Other low-to-the-ground great views include standing on the **Michigan Avenue Bridge**, which crosses the Chicago River and neatly divides the city. It's a picture-postcard-perfect view of downtown, looking towards the south; of the Magnificent Mile to your north; and of the river both east and west. Picnic at the tip of **Belmont Harbor**, where the view of downtown and the lake is one of the best; or stand in front of **Buckingham Fountain**, with your back to the lake—before you, the downtown skyline looms like a Hollywood movie set, so gorgeous it almost looks fake. You can see much more than the stars and skies from the **Adler Planetarium** if you know where to look, such as north across Monroe Harbor from Solidarity Drive. In addition to the harbor itself, which in summer is jammed with sailboats and yachts, in the distance you'll get a spectacularly panoramic view of Navy Pier, Lake Point Towers, and the Michigan Avenue skyline. Another great but little-known view spot is from the **fourth-floor balcony at Crate & Barrel** overlooking Michigan Avenue (see Shopping), where you'll see the Magnificent Mile in all its glory from a unique angle.

Tried-and-true views... If you must see the city from the sky, there's nothing like the view from either the **Sears Tower Skydeck** on the 103rd floor of the 110-story building—at 1,450 feet, the world's tallest—or from the 94th-floor **John Hancock Center Observation Deck**. Nonstop, ear-popping express elevators zoom you to both observation decks in less than a minute, and what awaits is a breathtaking 360-degree panorama. On a clear day they say you can see up to 60 miles and four states— it *is* Indiana! From the Sears Tower you'll get a better sense of downtown Chicago; from the Hancock, fondly known to locals as "Big John," you'll see the entire lake and the north side, on up all the way to Wisconsin.

Architectural masterpieces... The American Institute of Architecture publishes the *AIA Guide to Chicago*, a detailed guidebook to the city's scores of important buildings; the following are just the top stars. The **Rookery Building** (209 S. LaSalle St.), designed by the firm of Burnham and Root in 1886, is a monumental office tower of scarlet stone in the south Loop; its lobby, designed by Frank Lloyd Wright in 1905, was restored in 1991 to its 1910 appearance. The north half of the **Monadnock Building** around the corner (53 W. Jackson Blvd.) was designed in 1891 by Burnham and Root as well, while the south half is the work of the firm of Holabird and Roche. It's literally a transitional building: Burnham and Root's half has the distinction of being the tallest masonry building in the city, with six-feet-thick walls at its base (to hold the whole thing up!), while the other half, built two years later, is of steel-frame construction. A few blocks north, large expanses of glass lend Daniel Burnham's 1890 **Reliance Building** (32 N. State St.) an elegant profile, which is today mainly significant as a fine example of just how far early architects were able to go in creating glass walls. The building, unfortunately, has seen better times.

Six buildings that scream "Chicago"... The fact that the yellow stone **Water Tower** (800 N. Michigan Ave.) is still standing at all lends it a modicum of significance— it's just so old and, like Chicago itself, a survivor. It doesn't hurt, either, that it's the focal point of the city's most traveled street, or that Oscar Wilde notoriously labelled it a "monstrosity" during his 1882 visit to Chicago. For all its fame, it's really just a cover for a 38-foot-high standpipe. Ungainly and sinister looking and just a block north, Skidmore, Owings & Merrill's 1970 **John Hancock Center** (875 N. Michigan Ave.) sticks out like a sore thumb on the city's skyline, but it's one of its best-known buildings. You couldn't miss it if you tried. A few blocks south, the white terra-cotta-clad **Wrigley Building** (400 N. Michigan Ave.) is an ode to the chewing-gum empire of the building's namesake. Lit like a birthday cake (which many say it resembles) at night, the building sits at the foot of the Magnificent Mile. Known as the "corncob buildings," the 62-story **Marina City** (300 N. State St.), built by Bertrand Goldberg in the early 1960s and just west of the Wrigley Building, is perhaps Chicago's best-known silhouette. That galls some people, since the two round buildings (filled with pie-shaped apartments) aren't very architecturally significant, and worse, they're not in such pristine shape, inside or out. Still, it's their exterior shape, which most people only see from afar, that locals love. Owned today by the Kennedys (yes, those Kennedys) but originally built in 1931 by Marshall Field, the elephantine **Merchandise Mart** (350 N. Wells St.) is still, at 4 million square feet, one of the world's largest wholesale markets, its enormous floors lined with furniture, knickknack, and fabric showrooms open to the trade only (the first two floors are a bland retail shopping mall, with a branch of Carson Pirie Scott, the usual chain stores, and a food court—see Shopping). It sits along the Chicago River west of Marina City, dominating the neighborhood like a Buddha. **Wrigley Field** (Clark and Addison streets) may not be the most up-to-date ball park in the nation—it was built in 1914—but like the Chicago Cubs, it's much beloved. Its location in the middle of a north side neighborhood and grass field are almost unique in professional baseball nowadays.

CHICAGO | DIVERSIONS

Architecturally significant *and* they scream "Chicago"... While **Carson, Pirie, Scott & Co.** (1 S. State St.) may be merely a place in the Loop to buy socks and underwear to some, to others it is Louis Sullivan's masterpiece. Built between 1899 and 1904, the steel-frame building was originally the Schlesinger & Meyer Company Store. But its retailing history takes second place to its architectural importance, which lies in its extraordinary use of ornamentation on the ground floor—especially the world-famous front door—topped by floor after floor of sleek terra-cotta clad walls punctuated by what was known as the "Chicago window," a central window with smaller, movable windows on either side. The 1922 Gothic-style **Tribune Tower** across the street from the Wrigley Building at the foot of the Magnificent Mile, (435 N. Michigan Ave.) was built after a well-publicized contest in which the newspaper's owner, the powerful Colonel Robert McCormick, rejected more modern designs. Look for chunks of great buildings through the ages, such as Westminster Abbey, St. Peter's Basilica, and even the Berlin Wall, embedded into the tower's base. Ludwig Mies van der Rohe, who fled Nazi Germany and settled in Chicago, much to the city's great advantage, designed many important buildings—as well as most of the **Illinois Institute of Technology** on the South Side—but none as important, perhaps, as the two glass-and-steel apartment houses at **860–880 North Lake Shore Drive**, which he designed in 1952. Their distinctive box-like profile became the basis for hundreds of other high-rise buildings around the city and the world.

The Wright stuff... Chicago is a Frank Lloyd Wright-o-phile's dream. Wright's uncluttered Prairie School look stood in direct opposition to the ornamentation popular in his day, particularly the Victorian style. He strove for a design that was functional, in harmony with its natural surroundings, and still aesthetically pleasing. Not only did he live and work in suburban Oak Park, which has a superb collection of his homes, but his work survives throughout the city of Chicago as well. He built the **Robie House** (and designed all its interior furnishings), now a National Historic Landmark, in 1909 near the University of Chicago campus. (It now houses the university's admissions office, but it's open for daily tours.) Lined with leaded-glass windows and topped with a low-slung cantilevered roof, the house exemplifies the Prairie Style. Also in **Hyde Park**, other Wright houses include **Blossom House** (4858 S. Kenwood Ave.) and **MacArthur House** (4852 S. Kenwood Ave.), both built in 1892 when Wright was only 25 years old and an employee of Louis Sullivan, and the **Heller House** (5132 S. Woodlawn Ave), which dates to 1897. All are privately owned, but at least you can walk by and gawk. Wright designed more than 30 buildings between 1899 and 1913 in nearby **River Forest** and **Oak Park**, suburbs 10 miles due west of the Loop. **His home and studio** (951 Chicago Ave., Oak Park), where he lived and worked from 1889 to 1911, is open daily for tours. The **Unity Temple** (875 Lake St., Oak Park) was built from 1905 to 1908 and, like many of his buildings scattered throughout the Chicago area, is a National Historic Landmark. Both the **Oak Park Visitors Center** and the **Chicago Architecture Foundation** offer guided tours of Wright's Oak Park work (see "Tour Time," below).

Home sweet historic home... The **Prairie Avenue Historic District** (South Prairie Avenue between 18th and 20th streets) was a once-fashionable neighborhood known as "Millionaire's Row," lined with many fine homes built from the 1870s to the 1890s by the city's wealthiest families, from George Pullman to Marshall Field. Unfortunately, most of them were torn down years ago; the few that remain are being, or have been, restored, along with the street itself, which is cobblestoned and lit by gaslights just as it was in the nineteenth century. There are two star attractions here. **Clarke House** (1800 S. Prairie Ave.), built in 1836, is Chicago's oldest still-standing building. While the wooden structure is original, the location isn't—in fact, it's been moved twice, once after the 1871 fire, which it miraculously survived. Today it's a museum, still boasting some of its original furniture. The only surviving house by the great Boston architect Henry Hobson Richardson—built in 1886 for John J. Glessner, founder of International Harvester—is today known as **Glessner House** (1801 S. Prairie Ave.). With a large interior courtyard, the 35-room house's exterior seems to turn away from the street, punctuated by small windows. On the unbelievably ugly University of Illinois campus, **Hull House** (800 S. Halsted St.) is where Benny Goodman

DIVERSIONS | CHICAGO

learned to play the clarinet. It's even better known as the building where social worker Jane Addams performed her good works. If you find yourself in the Bridgeport neighborhood, drive or walk by the bungalow at **3536 S. Lowe Avenue**, former home of the pasha of Chicago politics, the late Richard J. Daley, who also happens to be the father of the city's current mayor.

Blasts from the past... On the streets nearest the lake on the North Side, once lined with beautiful houses and today mostly with apartment houses and condos, **Hutchinson Street** (4200 north, at the lake) stands out as a real prize. Most of the houses there were designed and built from 1894 to 1913 by architect George W. Maher and reflect the changing tastes of the time. Nearby **Hawthorne Street** (3400 north at the lake) is another mansion-lined street well worth strolling down. Most of the houses were originally built between 1880 and the 1930s. A few blocks away, **Alta Vista Terrace** (3800 north at Grace St.), built between 1900 and 1904, is another one of those streets that look as if it could be "the English Street" at an amusement park. Known as the "Street of 40 Doors," it's lined with 40 tiny but beautiful rowhouses with facades representing various eras—Gothic, Georgian, Palladian—and was designated an Architectural Landmark District in 1972. Each house faces its twin across the street. It's beautiful and sort of weird.

Lincoln Parking... The residential neighborhood of Lincoln Park is named after—you guessed it—Lincoln Park. Half park, more or less, and half neighborhood with stores, restaurants, clubs, and over-the-top gentrified residential areas, it is a virtual yuppeteria of all things good and expensive. The vast park itself remains its heart, with its zoo, conservatory, and loads of sports facilities (see Getting Outside). Just because you've finished hiking the park, though, doesn't mean you've "done" Lincoln Park. Them thar streets are paved with gold, or at least with houses lived in by people who make a lot of it, and almost every one is a delight. There's no dominant architectural style; rowhouses or single-family dwellings, built of brick, clapboard, or stone, they're invariably well-tended, with gardens often in the front and back. Most are old and rehabbed, but the few brand-new houses tend to be showy. Just walk around, point at the ones you like best, and imagine how if you had a million dollars you'd buy this one or that. And then go shopping. There are stores galore along the neighborhood's streets—not just the regulars like **The Gap** and **Banana Republic**, but scores of unique shops as well—such as **2nd Hand Tunes** (2604 N. Clark St.), which sells used albums (yes, vinyl LPs) and CDs; **Raymond Hudd** (2545 N. Clark St.), a ladies' (yes, ladies') hat shop; and **Blake** (2448 N. Lincoln Ave.), a drop-dead chic women's boutique that should probably be on Oak Street. (See Shopping.) When it's time for "coffee and…," try **Starbucks** (Webster and N. Halsted St.) or any of the other latté cafes that have sprung up like so many toadstools around town. For great dogs and fries hit **The Wiener Circle** (2622 N. Clark St.); for something more substantial (and French) put on some decent clothes and eat at **Un Grand Cafe** (2300 N. Lincoln Park West); or, if you feel like blowing your wad, **Ambria** (also at 2300 N. Lincoln Park West)—all three are listed in Dining.

It's a small world… Walk around **Andersonville** and you'll see remnants of what is still thought of as the city's Swedish neighborhood, from the **Swedish-American Museum Center** (tel 312/728–8111, 5211 N. Clark St.) to the sweet-smelling **Swedish Bakery**, the **Svi Restaurant**, **Wikstrom's Gourmet Foods**, and a branch of **Ann Sather** (which serves beautifully thin Swedish pancakes with lingonberries), all of which line the 5200 block of North Clark. But try finding an actual Swede. Today the neighborhood, while housing a Swede or two or three, is home to a mixed ethnic group that includes Vietnamese, Thais, and Arabs, as well as a growing gay population. **Rogers Park**, the old **Jewish neighborhood** around Devon Avenue (6400 north), while maintaining some of its delis, bakeries, and butchers with window signs in Hebrew, has in the past decade been become very international, with immigrants from India, Russia, and elsewhere living in what appears to be relative harmony. Here you'll find some of the city's best Indian restaurants, sari shops (which, mysteriously, often sell small appliances, too), and video stores renting and selling the best and the worst the Indian film industry has to offer. A few Korean restaurants and Russian groceries dot the street as well.

CHICAGO | DIVERSIONS

The **Southwest Side** around **Marquette Park** is home to many Lithuanians. Vietnamese immigrants have settled in what has recently been dubbed **Little Saigon** around Argyle Street and Broadway, which houses restaurants, shops, and the **Vietnam War Museum** (954 W. Carmen St., tel 312/728–6111). Though Poles have spread throughout the city, Polish businesses, restaurants, and nightclubs still line the area around **Milwaukee Avenue** from Division Street to Irving Park Road. Highlights include the **Polish Museum of America** and the **Busy Bee Restaurant** (see Dining), which serves cheap and, well, let's just say hearty Polish "cuisine." **Bridgeport**, known the world over as the home of the powerful Daley family (though the current Mayor Daley moved his family to a fancy townhouse development in the South Loop), centers on Thirty-fifth Street and Halsted; just southwest of there is **Canaryville**, also still largely Irish. Around **Lincoln Square**, near Lawrence and Western avenues, you can still hear German spoken, and you can still buy homemade sausage. There's a bustling but small **Chinatown** on the **South Side**, with Cermak and Wentworth avenues as its focal point, filled with restaurants, retail, and Chinese people. A very little **Little Italy** along Taylor Street (around 1500 west) is still populated by many Italians and home to a slew of restaurants. **Greek Town**, on Halsted between Adams and Monroe streets, has several restaurants but is really an invention of clever marketing, not an authentic neighborhood.

Up-and-comers... **Pilsen** has come full circle, from Bohemia to bohemian. Settled from about 1870 to the early 1950s by immigrant Czechs (the name Pilsen comes from what was once Bohemia's second-largest city), it evolved into a Mexican neighborhood, and its main drag, Eighteenth Street, is still lined with Mexican diners and tacquerias, small, family-owned grocery stores, bakeries, and music shops blaring the latest salsa onto the street. The **Mexican Fine Arts Center Museum** is here, as well as many colorful outdoor murals, and side streets around the intersection of Eighteenth and Halsted streets are lined with generally well-kept narrow row houses and tenements, their stoops serving as places for old people, kids, and families to sit and watch, as well as be a part of, the lively passing parade. In recent years, however, lower-case-b bohemians have returned in the form of local artists who have discovered Pilsen's large loft-like spaces and reasonable rents. Now as you stroll the streets, in addition to salsa wafting through the air and families shopping and kibitzing in Spanish, you'll also see a healthy number of pierced-nosed, goatee-ed people who you can bet aren't rolling tortillas in their spare time. **Wicker Park**, **Bucktown**, and **Ukrainian Village**, all of which are northwest of the Loop, were also originally home to various Eastern European immigrant groups. But, like Pilsen, in the past decade these neighborhoods have been "discovered" by artists and others seeking cheaper rents—which of course attracted real-estate developers who rehabbed apartment after apartment, which jacked up the rents, forcing many of the second wave of settlers to move elsewhere. Still, the neighborhoods have a funky, urbane, feel; while still home to many artists, they're getting yuppier by the day, creating an odd mix of small clubs featuring loud live music, coffee houses sponsoring poetry readings and performance art, art galleries, antique stores, and upscale restaurants attracting BMW-driving suburbanites.

An offbeat place to get your hair cut... Big Hair (tel 312/348–0440, 2012 W. Roscoe St.) is a decidedly strange place with thrift store decor, music, and stylists dedicated to, well, really big hair, all for only $5.

You bowl me over!... Chicago has two of the neatest bowling alleys around. Tiny, four-lane **Southport Lanes** is housed in an old Schlitz tavern and fortunately still looks it. No newfangled things like automatic pin resets here—there are actual and *live* pin-boys to do the job. There are pool tables, too, and an outdoor cafe. For a more *moderne* experience, try the **Diversey River Bowl**, a more traditional-looking alley that's known to insiders as the "rock 'n' bowl"—its sound system blares everything from Motown to Melissa Etheridge, for a real party atmosphere. Completely fun.

School daze... Chicago has many universities within its borders, but three really deserve a visit. The **Illinois Institute of Technology** may not be the city's most prestigious institution of higher learning, but it's definitely its most architecturally significant one—in fact, in 1976 it

CHICAGO | DIVERSIONS

was designated one of the 200 most important works of architecture in the United States by the American Institute of Architecture. Designed from 1942 to 1958 primarily by the great Mies van der Rohe, it is a classic example of a then very un-classic modernist style which has since become classic. **Crown Hall** (3360 S. State St.) and the **Robert F. Carr Memorial St. Savior Chapel** (65 E. 32nd St.) are the most distinguished buildings on the 100-acre campus. It's not particularly pretty—frankly, it's a fairly monotonous collection of boxy low-rise buildings laid out one after another like children's building blocks. Talk about "less is more." Still, there is an undeniable look to the place—clean and spare, and oddly satisfying in its rectilinear-ness. For a different take on campus life, stroll around the urbane 175-acre **University of Chicago**, founded in 1892 by John D. Rockefeller, in Hyde Park. A Gothic-style fantasia, with many buildings adorned with intricate gargoyles, fine-pitched arches, and towers, the campus seeks to copy its British rivals, Oxford and Cambridge. Many of the buildings have lushly planted courtyards, as well, and benches throughout make terrific spots for a lazy day spent reading out-of-doors. There are some big, ugly, modern buildings, too, but they're well integrated into the campus. Don't miss the extraordinarily beautiful **Rockefeller Chapel** (1156 E. 59th St.), which houses the world's second-largest carillon. Both the **Oriental Institute**, with its fine collection of archaeological finds, and the **David and Alfred Smart Museum of Art** are worthwhile stops as well. Hyde Park itself is one of the best-integrated middle-class neighborhoods in any urban area, with some Frank Lloyd Wright masterpieces scattered about, but one word of warning: It borders some very nasty places, so meandering around at night is not a very good idea. You can take the el to **Northwestern University** in Evanston, but if you have a car, use it—the ride north along the lakeshore is beautiful. Founded in 1855, the campus is filled with Gothic buildings and looks just as you imagine a college should look: bucolic, impressive, daunting, solid. Tours are available, whether you're considering sending Junior there or not.

Lake views in Lake View... Just north of Lincoln Park lies Lake View, bordered by the lake, Ashland Avenue, Diversey Parkway, and Irving Park Road, an also-gentrified neighborhood of funky stores, even funkier small theaters, and beautiful tree-lined residential streets. Broadway, Halsted and Clark streets are the area's main north–south drags; Diversey Parkway and Belmont Avenue are the main east–west streets. Each of these is lined with stores and boutiques specializing in everything from condoms to ultra-chic fashions to adorable cafes to high-rent restaurants. And, of course, **Lincoln Park** snakes along Lake View's eastern edge, with the **Waveland Golf Course** (see Getting Outside), tennis courts, baseball diamonds, and other recreational facilities. A lot of people might warn you to stay away from the five square blocks that surround **Wrigley Field** on a game day (that is, when the Cubs are at home, generally losing) unless you're actually attending the game—the traffic is at a standstill, the sidewalks are jammed, there are honky-tonk bands playing on the corners, and souvenir hawkers everywhere. But for the adventurous that's exactly when to go, because it's fun, plain and simple. There's electricity in the air, anticipation of a good time, and hope that maybe the Cubs will pull it off. Your best bet is to go to the game, but even if you're just walking around before heading elsewhere, it's a scene worth being a part of. A bit south of the ballpark lies what is considered **"Boys' Town,"** the city's sort of gay ghetto. On any given night the sidewalks along Halsted Street between Belmont Avenue and Irving Park Road are jammed with gay men in search of everything from a good time at the clubs to a quart of milk at the 24-hour 7–11. So, while there are gay people and gay bars throughout the city (see Nightlife), the epicenter of gay life is here, on Halsted and the side streets that fan off it. Here you'll find restaurants (like **Oo-La-La!**), bars (like the grandpappy of Chicago's gay scene, **Little Jim's**), dance clubs (like **Vortex**, known for featuring the latest disco divas such as RuPaul and Markey Mark), boutiques (like **We Are Everywhere**, which specializes in T-shirts, sweatshirts, cards, mugs, and other paraphernalia), and even a sex club or two (like the **Unicorn** bath house). The streets nearest the lake, though now mostly lined with apartments, used to be lined with beautiful houses; see "Residential streetscapes," above, for descriptions of **Hutchinson Street** (4200 North, at the lake), **Hawthorne Street** (3400 north at the lake), and **Alta Vista Terrace** (3800 north at Grace St.).

Where to dog-watch... You wouldn't expect a city with mile after mile after mile of beaches not to have one devoted exclusively to dogs, would you? **Doggy Beach** is where all the best dogs go—or, at least, where all the best dog-owners go—a fenced-off beach midway between Belmont Avenue and Addison Street, at the lake (obviously). Every summer day literally dozens of dogs from sleek weimaraners to teensy Chihuahuas run wild in the sand and water, much to the delight of passersby, much to the chagrin of the Chihuahuas. It's a terrific sight.

Overhyped experiences... "Taste of Chicago," an annual week-long feast that culminates July Fourth weekend, started out as a way to sample some of the finest food Chicago's restaurants had to offer, but it has evolved over the years into a hyperbolic and not-too-cheap outdoor gorge-fest. Much of the food is fried and fatty and messy, as well as astonishly mundane, considering that some of the city's best restaurants ply their delicacies here—though lately the grocery chain Dominicks was represented, and there was even a Maxwell House coffee booth. The food festival—the world's largest—is not only a pig-out, it becomes a pigsty, as more than four million people jam into Grant Park on Columbus Drive between Jackson and Randolph streets. Both the **Gold Coast Art Fair** and the **Old Town Art Fair** are losers, too, unless you like sentimental color photographs of the city's skyline, pastels of children and dogs, abstract oil paintings that defy description, landscape watercolors, and lots and lots and lots of pottery. Artlovers are better off going to galleries in River North. Both **Planet Hollywood** and the **Hard Rock Cafe** (see Dining for both) have better food than you'd expect, but what, ultimately, is the point? And if anyone tells you to go to the **Biograph Theater** to see anything other than a movie, don't listen. Yes, it's true that gangster supreme John Dillinger was tricked into attending a screening of *Manhattan Melodrama* on July 22, 1934, and instead became the object of his own real-life drama when tricky-fingered government dicks gunned him down in the alley next door. But there aren't any blood stains remaining or a faded chalk outline for you to gawk at—all that remains is...an alley. Unless you want to take a snapshot of the garbage cans from the Mexican restaurant next door, don't bother. There were such high expectations when the Chicago White Sox moved into the new **Comiskey Park** in 1991, it probably would have been impossible for it to live up to them. The park was supposed to be a modern show palace, a place to see baseball with the whole family. Well, yes, it is that, of course, but the whole experience is so false, so phony, and so expensive. You get the feeling that even though baseball is being played, way down yonder (most of the time you're watching the game through your toes), what's really going on is that you're getting your pockets picked. The **Baton Show Lounge**, Chicago's supposedly glitzy, glamour-filled drag show popular with tourists and suburbanites alike, is, if you'll excuse the expression, a real bust. You get shown to your table; you order over-priced, watered-down drinks (you're required to purchase at least two of these); and you think you're settling in for a fabulous Las Vegas-style evening of drag. Instead, you get a bunch of robotic she-males strutting around lip-synching songs you'd rather not even hear at the gym, let alone a nightclub. These men don't merely dress like women, walk and talk like women, and wear slit-to-here gowns that show off a pair of great gams—some of these guys *are* women, having artificially provided themselves with many of the opposite sex's physical attributes. So where's the illusion? Hell, shoot up Sam Donaldson with hormones and silicone, give him a dress, put "Mame" on the record player, and he, too, could work at the Baton.

Tour time... It's not unusual to see red double-decker tour buses moving slow as snails through bumper-to-bumper traffic on Michigan Avenue, as tourists from who-knows-where get told who-knows-what by who-knows-whom. Here are some of the tours that are worth your time: **Art Encounters** (tel 708/328–9222) offers specific programs throughout the year, from tours of the gallery district to visits to artists' and collectors' homes and studios. Well-planned and thought-out art "walks" are generally held 11am to 12:45pm the second Saturday of every month except May, for about $15. Though there are undoubtedly still gangsters in town, the **Untouchable Tour** (tel 312/881–1195) brings Chicago's gangland past alive, concentrating on the hoodlum hangouts of such guys as John Dillinger, Al Capone, "Bugs" Moran, and others, as well as the site of the St. Valentine's Day massacre (which is now in the shadow of a retirement home)

CHICAGO | DIVERSIONS

and the hotel from which Al Capone ruled his evil empire. Richard Crowe, who claims he's the only "full-time professional ghost hunter in the Midwest," runs **Chicago Supernatural Tours** (tel 708/499–0300), which feature legends, lore, and ghost stories of Chicagoland cemeteries, murder sites, gangsters, and haunted pubs, all while cruising the city on a bus or, as he likes to call it, a "luxury highway coach." The five-hour daytime or evening tours cost $28 per person and include a snack stop. In the summer, Crowe offers two-hour supernatural cruises on a boat called the *Mercury Skyline Queen*. The first-rate **Chicago Architecture Foundation** (tel 312/922–3432) organizes regular tours of the Prairie Avenue District, including the Glessner and Clarke houses, as well as river cruises, bus tours, and scores of walking tours of specific buildings, streets, districts, and neighborhoods, from the Loop to Hyde Park to the Gold Coast. The foundation also offers both walking and bus tours of Frank Lloyd Wright's greatest hits, a bike tour of suburban Winnetka, and scores of others, more than 50 tours in all. Tour fees vary from $5 for a walking tour of, say, Alta Vista Terrace, to $17 for river cruises (daily, May–October) to $25 for bus tours covering 30 miles of the Loop, Hyde Park, the Gold Coast, and other historic districts. You may also want to stop by the foundation's shop (224 S. Michigan Ave.), one of the best places to buy souvenirs that actually mean something. The **Oak Park Visitors Center** (tel 708/848–1500) offers daily tours of that suburb's incredible collection of the work of Frank Lloyd Wright, a former resident who designed many homes, as well as his internationally renowned Unity Temple, here.

The Index

Adler Planetarium. Besides the great Sky Show in the domed theater, the Adler offers three floors of interactive exhibits about space exploration, the solar system, and the galaxies. History, too: The newest permanent exhibit, "The Universe in Your Hands," recreates the scientific and social setting of Europe and Asia of the Middle Ages, showing how they used sundials, astrolabes, and other seriously low-tech tools.... *Tel 312/322–0304; Sky Show information, tel 312/332–0300. 1300 S. Lake Shore Dr. Open 9–5, until 9 on Fri. Planetarium is free; admission charged for Sky Show.*

Art Institute of Chicago. Weary feet are the denouement of a day spent here, checking out every picture you ever studied in art history class, including those by Vermeer, Renoir, Cézanne, and Rothko, to name just a few. The 1892 building is a wonder in itself, with a grand staircase up the center giving it that perfect big-city museum touch. There are furniture galleries, modern art galleries, a Children's Museum, gardens, and unique exhibits such as the Rubloff paperweight collection and the miniature Thorne rooms (which are weird but not-to-be-missed). Not to mention the zillion-square-foot gift shop.... *Tel 312/443–3500. Michigan Ave. at Adams St., Adams St. el stop. Open weekdays 10:30–4:30 (Tue until 8), Sat 10–5, Sun noon–5. Admission charged.*

Brookfield Zoo. Spread out over 200 acres, 14 miles due west of the Loop, Brookfield's 2,000 animals (representing 425 species) are housed in naturalistic settings. There's a children's zoo and a tram circling the grounds. Take a Burlington Northern train from Union Station to Hollywood and walk to zoo (follow signs). By car, take I-55, I-290, or I-294 to the Brookfield Zoo exits.... *Tel 708/485–0263. 8400 W. 31st St., Brookfield. Open 10–6. Admission charged.*

CHICAGO | DIVERSIONS

Buckingham Fountain. Donated to the city in 1927 by Kate Sturges Buckingham, this ornate pink marble confection is surrounded by a pool of water inhabited by four bronze sea horses (representing the four states that border Lake Michigan—Illinois, Wisconsin, Michigan, and Indiana). A computer-generated light show plays over the dazzling sprays of water at night.... *Grant Park, at Congress Parkway, Van Buren el stop.*

Chicago Architecture Foundation Shop and Tour Center. This first-rate organization devoted to Chicago's architecture and design operates scores of tours (by bus, boat, bike, or on foot) of specific buildings, streets, districts, and neighborhoods. Superb gift shop, too.... *Tel 312/922–8687 for recorded tour information, 312/922–3432 to talk to a human being. 224 S. Michigan Ave., Jackson el stop.*

Chicago Board of Trade. If Chicago had a Wall Street, this would be it. Not only stocks and bonds but all sorts of tangible commodities like wheat are traded here (it's not for nothing that on the roof there's a sculpture of Ceres, Roman goddess of grain). You can watch the wild behavior of the traders from a gallery.... *Tel 312/435–3590. 141 W. Jackson Blvd., Van Buren el stop. Visitors gallery open weekdays 9–2. Admission free.*

Chicago Board Options Exchange. The country's largest stock option exchange—the goings-on can be viewed from a gallery.... *Tel 312/786–7492. 400 S. LaSalle St., Van Buren el stop. Open weekdays 9–3. Admission free.*

Chicago Historical Society. This Gold Coast museum has neat Civil War and Lincoln artifacts, dioramas of Illinois history, and some lively, imaginative temporary exhibits.... *Tel 312/642–4600. Clark St. at North Ave. Open Mon–Sat 9:30–4:40, Sun noon–5. Admission charged.*

Chicago Mercantile Exchange. Known as "the Merc," this is where futures and options on agricultural commodities (like pork bellies), and financial products (like gold), are traded. The traders put on a great show in what is called the "open outcry" system, in which they shout at each other like animals—literally—to make their trades. Millions, if not billions, of dollars are at stake every minute of the day. Don't miss the show, so to speak, from the visitors gallery.... *Tel 312/930–1000. 10 and 30 S. Wacker Dr., Quincy/Wells el stop. Visitors gallery open weekdays 7:30–3:15. Admission free.*

Clarke House. Chicago's oldest surviving building, dating back to 1836, this Greek Revival house displays period furniture and decorative objects. There's a beautiful heirloom herb and vegetable garden, as well, in spring and summer. Tours start at coach house behind Glessner house (see below).... *Tel 312/922–8687. 1801 S. Prairie Ave. Tours Wed–Sun at noon, 1, and 2. Admission charged.*

David and Alfred Smart Museum of Art. This museum displays the University of Chicago's encyclopedic art collection, which spans from the Renaissance to today—paintings by Degas and Matisse, sculptures by Rodin and Henry Moore, furniture designed by Frank Lloyd Wright, an incredible collection of ancient Greek vases, and thousands of other works.... *Tel 312/702–0200. 5550 S. Greenwood Ave., METRA train to 57th St. and Lake Park Ave. Open Tue–Fri 10–4, weekends noon–6. Admission free.*

Diversey River Bowl. This bowling alley is know as the "rock 'n' bowl" for its lively piped-in music.... *Tel 312/227–5800. 2211 W. Diversey Ave., Diversey el stop.*

DuSable Museum of African American History. In Hyde Park, the DuSable traces the history of the black experience in America through an extensive collection of art, artifacts, and displays honoring Martin Luther King, Jr., Rosa Parks, Sojourner Truth, and others. Fine library and gift shop, too.... *Tel 312/947–0600. 740 E. 56th Pl., METRA train to 57th St. and Lake Park Ave. Open 10–5 (until 6 Thur). Admission charged.*

Field Museum of Natural History. Lions and tigers and bears, dead and stuffed and on display, along with dinosaurs and enormous interactive exhibits devoted to other cultures and environments.... *Tel 312/922–9410. Roosevelt Rd. and Lake Shore Dr. Open 9–5 daily. Closed Christmas, Thanksgiving, New Year's Day. Admission charged.*

Glessner House. Chicago's only surviving house by the great Boston architect Henry Hobson Richardson is beautifully restored. Some rooms, furnished with original period furniture, feature reproduction William Morris wallpaper.... *Tel 312/922–8687. 1801 S. Prairie Ave. Tours start in the coach house, Wed–Sun at 1, 2, and 3pm. Admission charged.*

Harold Washington Library Center. The largest municipal library in the nation, it houses more than two million books, most in open stacks. The 18,000-square-foot children's library is the country's best.... *Tel 312/747–4050. 400 S. State St., Van Buren el stop. Open Mon 9–7, Tue and Thur 11–7, Wed and Fri–Sat 9–5. Admission free.*

Hull House. Home of social worker Jane Addams and her American settlement-house movement, the house today is a fine historical museum, still furnished with some original pieces, maps, and photographs.... *Tel 312/413–5353. 800 S. Halsted St. Open weekdays 10–4, Sun noon–5. Admission free.*

Illinois Institute of Technology. Mies van der Rohe's Chicago masterpiece, this 100-acre campus is a Bauhaus collection unlike any other in the country.... *Tel 312/567–3025. 3300 S. Federal St. Guided tours leave from admissions office (Pearlstein Hall, 10 W. 33rd St.) Mon–Fri at 11am and 1pm.*

International Museum of Surgical Sciences. Housed in a couple of 1917 mansions on Lake Shore Drive, the museum showcases medical devices through the ages, as well as a recreation of a turn-of-the-century drugstore.... *Tel 312/642–6502. 1524 N. Lake Shore Dr. Open Tue–Sat 10–4, Sun 11–5. Admission charged.*

John Hancock Center Observation Deck. Located on the skyscraper's ninety-fourth floor, the Skydeck provides unparalleled views for miles and miles and miles. Prepare for your ears to pop in the express elevator up.... *Tel 312/751–3681. 875 N. Michigan Ave., Michigan Ave. bus. Open 9am–midnight. Admission charged.*

Lincoln Park Zoo. The most visited zoo in the country, located in the middle of Lincoln Park, it has more than 1,700 animals, ranging from elephants to bats, all on a 35-acre site. Highlights include a great 260,000-gallon polar

bear tank and the kid-friendly Farm-in-a-Zoo, which houses horses, cows, sheep, and other farm animals.... *Tel
312/294–4660. 2200 N. Cannon Dr. Open 9–5. Admission free.*

Merchandise Mart. With more than four million square feet of
space, this is one of the world's largest buildings, but it's
mostly off-limits to anyone not "in the trade"—meaning that
unless you're a decorator, designer, or architect, all you can
do is roam its enormous halls and peer into the windows of
the main furniture and fabric showrooms.... *Tel 312/527–
7600. 350 N. Wells St., Merchandise Mart el stop. Tours
weekdays at noon. Admission charged.*

Mexican Fine Arts Center Museum. In Pilsen, this small but
well-respected and popular museum showcases contemporary Mexican and Mexican-American art. Really good gift
shop.... *Tel 312/738–1503. 1852 W. 19th St. Open 10–5;
closed Mon. Admission charged.*

Museum of Contemporary Art. Moving to a new and more
lush building in 1996, this for-too-long-small museum will no
longer have to hide its terrific permanent collection of 4,400
pieces of artwork. Expect the same high-level temporary
exhibits of contemporary masters working in various fields,
from on-the-edge video and computer-related works to pho-
tography to painting.... *Tel 312/280–2660. As of summer
1996: 234 E. Chicago Ave.; until then, 237 E. Ontario St.
Open Tue–Sat 10–5, Sun noon–5. Admission charged.*

Museum of Science and Industry. With its host of high-tech
interactive displays, an actual World War II Nazi U-505 submarine, a coal mine into which you descend 50 feet, a
huge, pulsating heart that you can walk through, and a sim-
ulated space shuttle that you can ride, there shouldn't be a
child who won't love, love, love this museum; adults love it
too. The Henry Crown Space Center houses the domed
futuristic Omnimax Theater. Great gift shop.... *Tel 312/
684–1414 or 800/468–6674. 57th St. and Lake Shore
Dr., METRA train to 57th St. and Lake Park Ave. Open
9:30–4 (until 5:30 weekdays, Memorial Day–Labor Day).
Admission charged.*

Northwestern University. Just what you think a university
should look like, with its idyllic lawns, huge imposing Gothic

buildings, and fresh-faced students walking around with books under their arms. Founded in 1855, the campus spreads out along the lake for an entire mile. Maps of the campus are available at the Tudor Revival mansion at the intersection of Sheridan Road and Clark Street; you can also take a tour designed by the undergraduate admissions office. Stop by the university's fine art museum, the Mary and Leigh Block Gallery, and the outdoor sculpture garden next door, filled with pieces by Henry Moore, Joan Miró, and other big names.... *Tel 708/491–4000. Sheridan Rd. and Clark St., Evanston. Tours run frequently, starting from admissions office.*

Oak Park Visitors Center. Frank Lloyd Wright not only lived in suburban Oak Park, he forever put it on the map by designing many of its finest homes, as well as the Unity Temple. The visitor's center offers daily tours of both his home and studio, as well as the temple, and a walking tour of the exteriors of 13 other privately owned Wright homes. Take the Lake Street/Dan Ryan el to Marion; walk down North Boulevard (it'll be obvious) to Forest Avenue, turn left another block to Lake Street. The center is on the corner.... *Tel 708/848–1500. 158 Forest Ave., Oak Park. Admission free; fee for tours. Call ahead for tour schedule.*

Oriental Institute Museum. Housed in a Gothic building on the University of Chicago campus, the Oriental Institute showcases the art and artifacts of the Near East from about 9000 B.C. to the tenth century A.D. Good souk-cum-gift-shop.... *Tel 312–702–9521. 1155 E. 58th St., METRA train to 57th St. and Lake Park Ave. Open 10–4 (until 8:30 on Wed, opens at noon Sun). Closed Mon. Admission free.*

Polish Museum of America. One of the largest museums in the country devoted to one ethnic group's art and history, the Polish Museum of America highlights both traditional and modern Polish and Polish-American art, including the Stations of the Cross from the first Polish church in America.... *Tel 312/384–3352. 984 N. Milwaukee Ave. Open noon–5. Admission charged.*

Prairie Avenue Historic District. The Prairie Avenue Tour Center is located in the coach house behind Glessner House. You can tour it and Clarke House (see above); each house tour takes an hour.... *Tel 312/922–3432. S. Prairie*

Ave. between 18th and 20th streets. Tours Wed–Sun afternoons. Fee for tours.

Robie House. One of Frank Lloyd Wright's greatest works, the house exemplifies the Prairie Style for which he is famous. Beautiful leaded-glass windows, the low-slung cantilevered roof, the built-in storage, it's all there.... *Tel 312/702–8374. 5755 S. Woodlawn Ave., METRA train to 57th St. and Lake Park Ave. Tours daily at noon. Admission free.*

Sears Tower Skydeck. The observatory deck here is located on the 103rd floor, eleven floors higher than the one at the Hancock Center (see above). More than 100,000 people every day soar to the top in two express elevators. Be prepared to be wowed, and to hear everyone say "Wow!" over and over.... *Tel 312/875–9696. 233 S. Wacker Dr., Quincy/ Wells el stop. Open 9am–10pm Oct–Feb, 9am–11pm Mar–Sept. Admission charged.*

Shedd Aquarium. The world's largest aquarium, it features Beluga and Pacific black whales, sharks, turtles, eels, and sea anemones, and a 60,000-gallon penguin habitat. More than 6,000 live things abide here peacefully under one roof.... *Tel 312/939–2438. 1200 S. Lake Shore Dr. Open 9–6. Admission charged.*

Southport Lanes. Housed in an old Schlitz tavern, this tiny four-lane bowling alley is about as charming as a bowling alley could be. No newfangled things like automatic pin resets here—there are live pin-boys to do the job. There are pool tables, too, and an outdoor cafe.... *Tel 312/472–1601. 3325 N. Southport Ave., Southport el stop.*

Spertus Museum of Judaica. Jewish art and artifacts, from ritual objects to paintings and sculpture, as well as a Holocaust memorial and a children's museum, trace the history of the Jews from ancient times until today.... *Tel 312/922–9012. 618 S. Michigan Ave., Harrison and State el stop. Open Sun–Thur 10–5, until 3 Fri, closed Sat. Admission charged.*

Terra Museum of American Art. One of the few museums in the country devoted to U.S. artists, with pictures by many of the grand poobahs of American art—Homer, Cassatt, Hopper, and Audubon. Gift-shop aficionados will be sorely disappointed at the one here.... *Tel 312/664–3939. 666 N. Michigan Ave., Michigan Ave. bus. Open 10–5, until 8 Tue; closed Mon. Admission charged.*

University of Chicago. 175 acres of gorgeous Gothic buildings (with a few modern ones in between) define one of the country's finest universities. Both art museums—the Oriental Institute and the David and Alfred Smart Museum—are alone worth the trip, but also check out the gargoyles, the courtyards, and the passing parade of brains walking from class to class—the University of Chicago has been associated with more than 60 Nobel Prize winners.... *Tel 312/753–1234. METRA train to 57th St. and Lake Park Ave. Guided tours Mon–Sat at 10am from Ida Noyes Hall, 1212 E. 59th St.*

Hyde Park Diversions

David and Alfred Smart Museum of Art **2**
DuSable Museum of African American History **1**
The Museum of Science and Industry **6**
Oriental Institute **4**
Robie House **5**
University of Chicago **3**

118

Chicago Diversions

Mexican Fine Arts
Center Museum **27**
Museum of
Contemporary Art **8**
Newberry Library **10**
Northwestern
University **1**
Oak Park Visitors
Center **32**
Polish Museum of
America **11**
Prairie Avenue Historic
District **26**
Sears Tower
Skydeck **15**
Shedd Aquarium **23**
Southport Lanes **2**
Spertus Museum of
Judaica **20**
Terra Museum of
American Art **9**

getting

4 outside

Chicago may be a
big city, but it's a
big city on a
lake—on a big
lake—and what
a difference
that makes.

Chicagoans never get blasé about Lake Michigan sparkling on their doorstep. It is literally the city's living room, where people of all different races and classes meet, mingle, play together, listen to music together, eat together. Chicago uses its lake like no other major city in the world, thanks in large part to forward-thinking urban planning of a century ago. Today, particularly in the summer months, the lakefront takes on the feel of one big urban resort, with boating, swimming, biking, beach volleyball, whatever your pleasure. Forget Club Med. Two huge green parks, named Grant and Lincoln, fan off from the lake, and a string of public beaches within city limits invite one and all to enjoy the water. There's no need to drive to the suburbs or faraway rural area in search of a golf course or bike path, either. It's all here.

The Lowdown

Parks... At one time, it was possible to walk in a huge arc through the city without touching pavement, via parks and boulevards. Accordingly, the city's motto is *Urbs in Horto*, which means City in a Garden. Nice sentiment—too bad it's no longer true (slums fill much of the city's borders, not flowerbeds and hedgerows). But Chicago does have incredible parks—in fact, it has more than 6,700 acres of parkland. Take 220-acre **Grant Park**, for instance. Spreading out on landfill between Michigan Avenue and the lake (tel 312/747–2200, East Randolph St. to E. McFetridge Dr., at Lake Michigan) it was designed in the 1920s by Daniel Burnham and supposedly inspired by the gardens at Versailles. With the Loop's skyscrapers looming so near, Versailles may not be your first thought when you see Grant Park; it's more like the Luxembourg Gardens in Paris, a highly civilized green space plunked down right in the middle of a big city. Grant Park offers everything a grand city park should—impressive formal gardens, baseball diamonds, tennis courts, ice skating in winter and rollerskating in summer, the Petrillo Music Shell for free summertime concerts and festivals, and vast areas of grass for lounging and loafing, picnicking, or protesting (remember the 1968 Democratic Convention?). Grant Park's most notable feature is the baroque Buckingham Fountain, as seen in the opening credits of the TV show *Married...With*

Children. It's a well-known make-out spot and setting for many a marriage proposal.

Even bigger than Grant Park is **Lincoln Park**, running right along the lake north of North Avenue. Here, on 1,200 acres of near-perfect parkland, are meadows, sports facilities, extraordinary formal gardens, extraordinary wildflower gardens, beaches, harbors… the list goes on and on. Since the park borders on several thriving residential neighborhoods, it attracts all sorts of people. For a dizzying burst of humidity, walk into the Lincoln Park Conservatory (tel 312/742–7736, 2400 N. Stockton Dr.), three acres of greenhouses erected in 1891, including a palm house, a fern house, a tropical house, and a show house. There's something weirdly Victorian about prowling around here, sniffing out some of the more exotic species in this hothouse. Just outside the conservatory's entrance lies the park's main garden, almost 300,000 dazzling square feet of flowers. By far the biggest attraction in the park is the zoo (see Diversions). Another park well worth visiting is **Jackson Park** (E. 63rd St. and Stoney Island Ave., tel 312/643–6363), built on landfill originally used for the 1893 World's Columbian Exposition. Designed by Frederick Law Olmsted, who also created

---

A few good men in Lincoln Park

In Lincoln Park alone you'll find nine famous people further immortalized in sculpture (some, of course, more famous than others). Politicians proliferate, everyone from president **Ulysses S. Grant** *(near 1900 N. Lake Shore Dr.) and statesman* **Alexander Hamilton** *(near Diversey Pkwy.) to* **John Peter Altgeld**, *a former governor of Illinois, immortalized in bronze near Lake Shore Drive. Then, of course, there's inventor and all-around good American* **Benjamin Franklin** *at LaSalle Street and Stockton Drive. Our favorite German poet and thinker,* **Johann Wolfgang von Goethe**, *has been set down at Diversey Parkway, looking proud and very German—and blindingly bright, after a recent re-gilding. His compatriot, poet and playwright* **Friedrich Schiller**, *sits near Stockton Drive and Webster Street. The Bard himself,* **William Shakespeare**, *poses near Belden Avenue, surrounded by flowers. Kid's fave* **Hans Christian Andersen** *is near Armitage Street, and look for the Italian stallion,* **Giuseppe Garibaldi**, *between Stockton and Lake Shore drives.*

CHICAGO | GETTING OUTSIDE

Central Park in New York City, this bit of greenery is home to one of the city's greatest attractions, the Museum of Science and Industry (see Diversions), which is housed in a stone recreation of the exhibition's Palace of Fine Arts. Jackson Park also features baseball diamonds, basketball courts, two dozen tennis courts, bicycle and bridle paths, and an 18-hole golf course and driving range (see "Par for the course," below). After visiting the museum, stroll down to the tranquil Japanese garden on the park's southern end. It's a great spot for contemplation, with a soothing waterfall, rocks, water lilies, and a teahouse.

Mittless softball... Chicago is the only place where 16-inch softball has elbowed out the 12-inch version. This variant of the old sandlot game uses no mitts, a slow pitch, and, obviously, a larger ball than the 12-inch variety. Lots of beer and jammed fingers are involved, especially if the ball is new, and for some reason, people with massive beer bellies and really tall thin guys are the only ones who can drive the ball deep. On the evolutionary scale of softballs, the 16-incher is a ceolecanth, a vestige from the days of the game's invention as an indoor winter sport. Leagues play in the parks; to watch a game, try Lincoln Park, or Oz Park in the western sector of the Lincoln Park residential neighborhood.

Playing pick-up... Grant Park (tel 312/747–2426) is known for softball and soccer, on weekends in the playing fields south of the Art Institute and the bandshell. There are more than a dozen fields in the Upper and Lower Hutchinson areas, many of which will be taken by organized office teams or leagues. But come looking prepared—in other words leave your glove at home—and you could get lucky. In addition, there is a three-on-three basketball tournament—sponsored by the Bulls in past years—which features local Be-Like-Mikes and takes place every August on a special temporary court near 900 south, on the lake. You can also find a game of pick-up b-ball on virtually any school playground in the city—after school hours and on weekends. Levels of ability vary; if you're, say, a youngish guy who loves to play but can't jump, you might want to try a playground in the tamer Lincoln Park or Lake View neighborhoods. The courts in the park a short walk south of the zoo are another good place to look for a pick-up game. Lincoln

Park (tel 312/742-7726) has great touch football games near Belmont Avenue, usually on Sunday mornings, and organized by league. Two of the latter, Sports Monsters and Command Performance (tel 312/327-1348 and 312/975-6624, respectively) can clue you in on schedules and the chance of getting off the bench. According to legend, luminaries such as former Bears back-up QB Mike Tomczak and assorted college linemen have been known to drop in. Every Sunday afternoon in spring and summer, the gay crowd at Hollywood Beach (5800 north on the lake) has pick-up volleyball games.

Hitting the beaches... One of Chicago's greatest summertime assets is the beaches that almost continually line Lake Michigan. Some are smooth and sandy, others are craggier and not well-kept, so beware. If there's a sign that says "no swimming," heed its advice. Beaches are open Memorial Day through Labor Day, 9am to 9:30pm. Various beaches have distinct sensibilities. **North Avenue Beach**, for instance, attracts volleyball players, young families, and lots and lots of singles. **Oak Street Beach** is one of the most popular, due no doubt to its easy-to-get-to location near the Magnificent Mile and lots of hotels; its crowd seems to have arrived there right off the set of "The Bold and The Beautiful," an alarming number of people with svelte bodies, sleek bathing suits, and slick tans. Farther up in the neighborhoods, **Foster Avenue Beach** (5200 north) attracts families, with convenient parking, a huge grassy area perfect for barbecuing, and a Rollerblading path on the shore just inland from the sandy beach. The most popular gay beach isn't even a beach in the traditional sense—for instance, there is no sand. Located just south of **Belmont Harbor**, though, a large green space has been annexed, more or less, by hordes of gay men (a few lesbians, too, but really, this is a gay male beach) in bathing suits, picnicking, tanning, cruising, and yammering. The last few summers have seen the gay population gradually shift to **Hollywood Beach** (5800 north), where every Sunday there are pick-up volleyball and frisbee, as well as just a lot of sitting around in the sun. To find it, look for the big rainbow flag that's usually flying from one of the volleyball nets.

Ahoy there... It shouldn't come as a surprise that, between the lake and the river, Chicagoans are gaga for boating—

CHICAGO | GETTING OUTSIDE

on sailboats, cigarette speedsters, powerboats, houseboats, rowboats, even kayaks and canoes. At Belmont Harbor, you can take sailing lessons and rent sailboats from the **Chicago Sailing Club** (tel 312/871–7245), which offers a two-week basic course for around $350 or instruction at $40–50 an hour for more experienced sailors; **Sailboats, Inc.** (tel 312/861–1757 or 800/826–7010), which has a wider range of boats to rent, also runs two- or three-day clinics for various levels, which may set you back up to $500. If you have your own boat, the **Belmont Yacht Club** (tel 312/477–7575) is for members only, but members of yacht clubs in another cities can have reciprocal use of the facilities. Though the club doesn't look all that fancy, to belong here you do have to own a boat, and owning a boat at Belmont Harbor isn't cheap, so you should be in pretty well-heeled company. If that's too rich for your blood, boaters can also dock for about $10 a person at **North Pier** (tel 312/527–2002), alongside sightseeing cruise boats.

Can you canoe?... For a truly fresh perspective on Chicago's downtown, how about paddling your way between the skyscrapers that line the Chicago River? **Friends of the Chicago River** (tel 312/939–0490) organizes a wide variety of guided canoe trips—some out in the northern and southern suburbs, but some actually on the downtown stretches of the river. There's a least one trip a week in summer; book a week ahead if possible. All ages and sorts of people sign onto these outings, not just weathered pros. If you're more the seasoned canoer, know that the **Chicagoland Canoe Base** (tel 312/777–1489, 4019 N. Narragansett Ave.) not only sells both antique and new canoes but rents them as well—$30 for one day, $15 for additional days. Don't expect to negotiate whitewater, but about an hour's drive from the city, the lower Fox River or the Kishwaukee River out near Rockford are good canoeing rivers.

Sightseeing afloat... There's no dearth of boat tours on both the lake and the river. The most popular is the 90-minute **Wendella Sightseeing Boats tour** (400 N. Michigan Ave., tel 312/337–1446; $10 adults, $5 kids under 12), which sets off April through October from the Wrigley Building. The route cruises along the Chicago River as it cuts through the Loop, then along the lake from the Adler Planetarium to Oak Street; take it at night for really stunning views. June through September, **Mercury Skyline Cruises** (Wacker Dr. and Michigan Ave., tel 312/332–1353) and **Shoreline Marine** (departing from the Shedd Aquarium, tel 312/222–9328) give Wendella competition. The narration on these boats is pretty much your standard sightseeing spiel, however; for something a bit different, book a seat on one of the weekly sightseeing boat tours run by **Friends of the Chicago River** (tel 312/939–0490), whose focus is, predictably, the ecology of the Chicago River system. The **Chicago Architecture Foundation** (tel 312/922–3432) offers insightful narrated boat trips on the river too, focusing not only on the landmark buildings on its shore but also on the history of the river and the city's relation to it. It's best to buy tickets in advance (TicketMaster tel 312/902–1500), as this tour is gaining in popularity. Tickets are $15 weekdays, $17 weekends.

Pedal pushers... There's no better way to see the city than by biking through it. A blacktop path stretches for about 20 prime lakefront miles, **from 7100 south to 5700 north** taking in spectacular views of the lake, museums, parks, harbors, and the skyline. Considering the views, it's no surprise that the path is often crowded with walkers, Rollerbladers, joggers, parents with baby carriages, dog-walkers, and others. If possible, avoid this route, or at least try to avoid it on Saturdays and Sundays after 8am and weekdays after 3pm. A word of warning: From McCormick Place on north, the path is pretty safe, and riding alone during daylight hours poses no real threat. But much of the path south of McCormick Place runs through areas where few people congregate, and despite city-run bike patrols along the entire length of the path, muggings have been known to happen. One easy way to avoid trouble is the most obvious: Don't ride alone. Another great bike path is the 7-mile **Evanston-Lake Shore trail**, along Sheridan Road in nearby north-suburban Evanston, from about Main Street north to the Evanston-Wilmette border. It's about a half-hour drive from the Loop to the starting point; you can also take the Evanston Express el, or ride your bike up there. The route more or less traces the lakeshore, passing Northwestern University; the northern end of the trail follows on pedestrian sidewalks. For more information on these and other bike trails in the metropolitan area, call the **Chicago**

Bicycle Federation (tel 312/427–3325). For a detailed map of the lakefront path, call the Chicago Park District at 312/747–2200. Public bike rental is available along the lakefront at Oak Street Beach, Lincoln Park Zoo, at Cannon Drive, and at Buckingham Fountain. In addition, several stores rent bicycles by the hour and day, including **Turin Bike Shop** (435 W. Illinois St., tel 312/923–0100) at North Pier, **The Bike Stop** (1034 W. Belmont Ave., tel 312/868–6800) in Lake View, and **Wheels & Things** (5210 S. Harper Ave., tel 312/493–4326) in Hyde Park.

Out on a swim... With the lake at your doorstep, or at least steps away from where you're probably staying, there's no real reason to swim in a pool (unless your hotel has a particularly fine one, such as the beautiful pool at the **Four Seasons** or the **Hotel Inter-Continental**'s 13th-floor Italianate junior Olympic-size pool—see Accommodations). But if you must, the Chicago Park District operates dozens of outdoor neighborhood swimming pools, two dozen indoor pools, and a couple of swimming lagoons. Just beware—kids swim in all of these, and you know what that means. The lagoons are at **Douglas Park** (1401 S. Sacramento Ave., tel 312/521–3244) and **Humbolt Park** (1400 N. Sacramento Ave., tel 312/276–0107), both open June through Labor Day, 9am to 11pm. Wednesday nights at 7pm, the gay swim team known as the Smelts practices (all are welcome) at Gill Park's public pool (tel 312/281–4692 for other times and dates, 825 W. Sheridan Rd.).

Par for the course... City duffers got a gift from the golf god in July 1994, when one of the city's ugliest patches of land—a pocket of dirt and sand between the Chicago River and Grant Park, overlooked by some of the most expensive real estate in the city—was converted into the **Illinois Center Golf Course and Driving Range** (221 N. Columbus Dr., tel 312/616–1234). A *downtown* golf course, no less—perfect for sneaking in a quick nine holes between business meetings. Designed by Perry Dye (son of famous course designer Pete Dye), the nine-hole, par-three course includes hitting stalls, a 65-person driving range, and, of course, locker rooms, a pro shop, and a bar and grill. The center is open year-round (it has heated driving stalls and indoor teaching stalls) and there's even valet parking. A bucket of about 80 balls will run you $9, while green fees are $22 for nine holes. If you're registered at the Swissotel next door, you're guaranteed a tee time (reserve through the concierge). The **Sydney Marovitz Course** (3600 N. Lake Shore Dr.), which many Chicagoans still call Waveland, is a pretty nine-holer right on the lake, which is convenient for visitors; there's also an 18-hole course in **Jackson Park** (63rd and Stoney Island Ave.), as well as a municipal driving range, and a 35-tee range in **Lincoln Park** (Lake Shore Dr. at Diversey Pkwy.). All city-run courses are open mid-April through November, dawn to dusk; for information on green fees, location, and hours, call the **Chicago Park District office** (tel 312/747–2200; automated phone reservation system at 312/245–0909).

The tennis racket... Right in the dreamy shadows of the city's skyline, there are hundreds of courts to choose from, several of them lighted for night play. City courts are open mid-April through November; some charge fees and take reservations—reserve if you can, since facilities tend to get very crowded on weekends and in the after-work hours. Two convenient locations with lighted courts are **Daley Bicentennial Plaza** in Grant Park (tel 312/742–7648, Randolph St. and Lake Shore Dr., $5 an hour, reservations accepted) and **Waveland** (tel 312/742–7674, Addison St. and Lake Shore Dr., $3 per person daily pass guarantees you one hour on courts, on a first-come-first-served basis).

Rollerblade runner... Stores renting in-line skates have sprung up all over the city, especially along the streets within a block or two or three of the lake, where throngs of Rollerbladers cheerfully mow down runners, strollers, bikers, and dogs. The lakeshore path all the way from Shedd Aquarium north to Hollywood beach is fantastic for skating; of course, as always along the lake, the farther north you go the less crowded it will be. Try **Londo Mondo Motionwear** (tel 312/751–2794, 1100 N. Dearborn St.,), **Windward Sports** (tel 312/472–6868, 3317 N. Clark St.), and **City Sweats** (tel 312/348–2489, 2467 N. Clark St.), all of which rent in-line skates by the hour and the day. A skate rental booth sprouts up during the summer at **North Avenue Beach** (North Ave. and Lake Shore Dr.) and **Oak Street Beach** (Oak St. and Lake Shore Dr.). If it rains and you've still got the yen to Rollerblade, head to the **Rainbo Sports Club** (tel 312/ 271–5668, 4836 N. Clark St.), an indoor Rollerblading and rollerskating rink. It offers nightly open skating, with special times set aside for kids, adults over 25, families, and teens. There's even an adult late night skate that goes until 3am, and Monday night is unofficially for gays. Rent roller skates and in-line skates here for use on site only. Call ahead for current schedule and fees.

What's nice on ice... One good thing about the brutal winters here is that you can ice-skate outdoors—the city maintains more than 100 outdoor ice-skating rinks (call the park district at 312/747–2200 for locations). For a totally cool urban experience, head downtown (or up, depending on where you're coming from) for the Loop's **Skate on State** (tel 312/744–3315, State St. between Randolph and Washington streets.). This wintertime outdoor rink is surrounded on three sides by Loop office towers and Marshall Field's grand State Street store on the fourth. It's free, and if you don't own skates, you can rent them there for $2. There's a warming shelter and a food concession, too, and hokey music wafting through the air. If scenic vistas are more to your liking, the 80-by-135-foot rink at the **Daley Bicentennial Plaza** (tel 312/294–4790, Randolph St. at Lake Shore Dr.) has gorgeous views of the lake and beyond. It's open December through March, assuming the weather is cold and blustery enough. There's skate rental and a warming shelter; a small fee is charged. For year-round skating, damn the weather, try the practical indoor rink at the **McFetridge Sports Center** (tel 312/478–0210, 3843 N. California Ave.). Open hours vary depending on the day and season, so call ahead.

Run for your life... In Chicago, figuring out *where* to run is dead easy. Something about the sight of Chicago's lakeshore paths makes even nonrunners yearn to lace up their Nikes and sprint away. The stretch from Oak Street north to Foster is superb, and therefore very crowded on weekends; go early, late, or on weekdays. Most of the path is blacktop, but there's a separate gravel running path for about a mile from Belmont to Irving Park. If you want to run in a group, call the **Chicago Area Runners Association** (tel 312/922–4420). On the north side, the **Lincoln Park Pacers** (tel 312/665–4640) meet in Lincoln Park at Diversey Parkway and Lake Shore Drive every Tuesday at 6:30pm and Saturday at 8am; on the south side, the **Rainbow Road Runners** (tel 312/324–5524) meet Saturday at 7am at 55th Street and the lake. **Front-runners/walkers** (tel 312/409–2790), the gay and lesbian running group, meets every Tuesday at 6:30pm and Saturday at 9am at the totem pole at Addison Street and the Lake Shore Drive. All three organizations, pre-dictably, run along the lake. Where else? For serious run-ners, there's the **Chicago Marathon** every October—call 312/527-1105 for registration and information.

The wind's beneath my wings... Windsurfing on Lake Michigan is cool beyond belief, but also dangerous if you don't know what you're doing. And you probably don't. **Windward Sports** (tel 312/472–6868, 3317 N. Clark St.) offers windsurfing classes from late April through August; meet at the store Saturday at 10am or Sunday at 2pm. A two-day course, complete with certification, costs $125; a one-day class is $65.

You sleigh me!... Romantic, fun, jolly, toasty: these are a few words that could describe the winter sleigh rides offered at **Forest View Farm** (1/2-mile west of Cicero Ave. on 167th St., tel 708/560–0306) in suburban Tinley Park. Park your carcass on the velvet seats under a warm blanket, and let the horses pull you and your love slave in an antique carriage into another world; or pile the whole family in the sleigh and raise a rowdy chorus of "Over the River and Through the Woods." (The sleigh drivers must have heard it a gazillion times.) Rides last about 40 won-derful minutes; reservations (and snow) required.

shop

5

ping

In Chicago, shop-
ping is as much a
pastime as voting
twice, walking
through the giant
heart at the
Museum of

Science and Industry, or sitting in the bleachers at Wrigley Field watching the Cubs lose another game. As the hub of the Midwest, it draws millions of people to its shores, many of whom visit to do nothing but spend, spend, spend. Even jaded jet-setters from L.A., Paris, and Rome will find the experience of shopping in Chicago entirely satisfying. Service here is generally peppy, too. The New York assumption that people like to be abused by snotty saleshelp just doesn't exist in Chicago.

Target Zones

Michigan Avenue, from Oak Street on its northern tip, down to the Chicago River, is hands-down the most important shopping street in the city, justly known as the **Magnificent Mile**. Once a sleepy thoroughfare lined with elegant five-story limestone buildings, it has in the past few decades become a marble canyon of sky-high towers, home to the fanciest of the fancy, such as Chanel and Cartier, as well as embarrassing middlebrow fixtures like Victoria's Secret. It is home, as well, to all the best department stores—Marshall Field's, Lord & Taylor, Neiman Marcus, Saks Fifth Avenue, Bloomingdale's—and almost every well-known chain. In 1995, there was a big brouhaha when a Filene's Basement, known as the mother of all things discounted, opened across from the Water Tower Place shopping mall: Around the corner from Michigan Avenue, however, is **Oak Street**, Chicago's own Madison Avenue, Ginza, and Rodeo Drive all rolled up into one. Only one block long, it houses the most important designer boutiques (usually in beautiful brownstone settings), including Giorgio Armani, Sonia Rykiel, Betsey Johnson, Gianni Versace, Jil Sander, and Hermès, not to mention Barneys New York. You'll find a lot of the funkier boutiques, from vintage to fashion forward, as well as the hippest record stores, in **Lake View** and **Lincoln Park**. The main strolling streets there include Broadway, Clark Street, and Halsted Street. **State Street** in **the Loop** used to be the shopping mecca for Chicagoans, but no longer. Other than the mother store of Marshall Field's—admittedly a big deal—a Crate & Barrel (not as good as Michigan Avenue's), Carson Pirie Scott & Co., and Carl Fischer (the city's best source for sheet music), there's not much there in the way of quality-time shopping, unless you like schlock shops.

Vertical Malls

For better or for worse, Chicago has perfected the urban shopping mall. Michigan Avenue is lined with huge, generally pretentious marble monuments to the almighty dollar, ugly on the outside and, well, pretty ugly on the inside, too. But Chicago's towering malls at least are filled with scores of stores and restaurants that provide for a lot of good shopping—and great people-watching. Built in 1976, **Water Tower Place** (tel 312/440–3165, 835 N. Michigan Ave. at Pearson St.) is the leader of the proverbial pack, with both Marshall Field's and Lord & Taylor weighing it down at its base, and the Ritz-Carlton Hotel (see Accommodations) perched on top. Walk into its impressive marble-walled, marble-floored lobby, go up the escalator past waterfalls and lush foliage to the mezzanine, and just wander. There's more than enough to see and do, whether you're a window-shopping kind of person, an inveterate bargain-hunter (yes, you will find some bargains here), or just a browser. With about 100 stores, the only limit is your budget. If you get bored shopping—is that even a possibility?—there are six shoebox-size movie theaters, too. Across the street, Bloomingdale's anchors the **Atrium** at 900 North Michigan Avenue (tel 312/ 915–3916), a way-upscale mall with Gucci, Christofle, Henri Bendel, Charles

Auction action

*The fun begins when Leslie Hindman steps up to the podium at **Leslie Hindman Auctioneers**. Next to her, an assistant holds up a porcelain lamp. "Do I hear $1,000?" she asks. Dead silence. "Do I hear $900?" Another dead silence. "Oh come on, people. Think retail!" Paddles finally rise and the bidding begins, with Hindman increasing the price until she reaches $1,800. "Sold!" she shouts, banging the gavel. At the Midwest's premier auction house (tel 312/670–0100, 215 W. Ohio St.), savvy shoppers sit on rickety folding chairs, hoping to get for a song that pair of Frank Lloyd Wright leaded-glass windows or a painting that might be a Picasso. Admission's free, and exhibitions are held for three to five days before the actual auction (for dates, call 312/ AUCTION). Don't worry— unless you arrange before-hand, no sneeze or mop of the brow will be misconstrued as a bid. And Hindman takes the fear out of bidding with her wise-cracking Eve Arden-like personality; during Bears games she even announces the scores. But novice buyers should beware: a 15% sur-charge is added to each puchase. Hey, the lady's got to make money somehow.*

CHICAGO | SHOPPING

Jourdan, and about 80 other stores, as well as direct access to the Four Seasons Hotel (see Accommodations). When the mall first opened it took a lot of guff for being too upscale and too controlling. For instance, the way the escalators were positioned forced shoppers to walk for what seemed like miles, passing store after store after store, to catch the next one going down. People balked (and didn't spend money), so eventually the owners of the mall installed more escalators, making it more user-friendly. One warning: if you suffer from vertigo, don't look down from the mall's walkways—it's a treacherous view. There is, however, a particularly good view of Michigan Avenue and beyond from the huge round window on the eastern side. Although eight-story **Chicago Place** (tel 312/642–4811, 700 N. Michigan Ave.) has a few good stores—such as Room and Board for furniture, The Real Nancy Drew for inventive children's clothes, Louis Vuitton, and a Williams-Sonoma—otherwise, the place is sort of a low-energy bore. Even the Saks Fifth Avenue on the ground floor is a snooze.

Another washout is the **Shops at the Mart** at the **Merchandise Mart** (tel 312/527–4141, 450 N. Wells St.), which is crowded with secretaries, furniture- and fabric reps, designers, and office workers during the week (mostly eating lunch in the greasy-smelling food court), but eerily empty on weekends. No wonder, either, since its selection of stores can all be found elsewhere. The Mart itself is a gargantuan and wonderful building, but most of it—in fact, the interesting parts—are off-limits to the hoi polloi unless they have card-carrying interior designers leading the way.

Lots of locals groan when the shopping mall at **North Pier Chicago** (tel 312/836–4300, 435 E. Illinois St.) gets mentioned—it was built expressly for tourists, after all—but don't pay attention to the fulminations of jaded Chicagoans. North Pier's setting along the scenic Ogden Slip alone is worth the trip; the building itself—a rehabbed commercial pier—is a terrific success. It's bright, light-filled, and designed to afford the best views of the outside. Granted, there's the cheesy **Baja Beach Club** dance club (see Nightlife), but there are almost 50 specialty and novelty stores, too, some of which are unique. Just don't expect to find Back-to-School sales, sensible shoes or a Chanel suit.

Farther north, in Lake View, is the neon-frenzied **Century Shopping Center** (tel 312/929–8100, 2828 N. Clark St.), filled with fast-food joints, sunglasses stores, jeans, electronics, lingerie shops, and a health club on the top floor. The mall's advertisements claim it's where "progressive people shop," which says it all.

Money Matters

Chicago's merchants know they don't live by locals alone, so they are generally as accommodating as possible to out-of-towners. All the major department stores will hold merchandise for a reasonable amount of time and will ship your purchases home to you. Writing personal checks is an iffier proposition—and at some stores, especially department stores, it takes forever. But ask, and as long as you've got a drivers license or some other form of photo ID, most stores will accept your check. Haggling over prices in retail stores is pretty much frowned upon—after all, this isn't the Old Country. But, you've got nothing to lose by trying to get a better price at the various secondhand stores around town. Stores are not required to give refunds if you're not satisfied with your purchase—most will, however, though some will offer it only in the form of exchange credit. One of the best things about **Marshall Field's**, Chicago's most famous retail emporium, is that you can return things long after you've bought them (but, please, not long after you've worn them).

Hours of Business

Most stores, from the small boutiques to the large department stores, open around 10am and remain open until at least 5pm. On Thursdays, stores generally stay open until 9pm. Many bookstores stay open much later, some until 11pm. Many of the owners of vintage stores like to sleep in; hence, those stores often don't open until 11am, or even noon in some cases. Virtually all stores are open on Sunday.

Sales Tax

A state and county sales tax of 8.75% is added to every purchase in Chicago, except groceries and prescription drugs. Tax is waived, however, if you have goods shipped out of state, so have your expensive purchases sent home if you want to save a bundle.

The Lowdown

Landmarks... There are a few stores here whose names are instantly linked with Chicago. Of course, the main event is **Marshall Field's** department store—if nothing else here, you should buy a box of the store's famous Frango Mints, a consummately Chicago ritual practiced by natives as well as visitors. One hint, though: stick to the original flavor, no matter how exotic the lemon, raspberry, and others sound. The offerings at **Carson Pirie Scott & Co.** are nothing special, but the department store's flagship building itself is a don't-miss classic Louis Sullivan extravaganza. Make sure you see its main entrance on the northwest corner. A selection of pipes and other smoking accoutrements is brazenly still on sale in the Loop at **Iwan Ries & Co.**, as it has been since 1857—the second-story Pipe Museum is a hoot. The **Chicago Architecture Foundation Shop**, in the Loop, has beautiful posters and photos, books and, yes, even mugs, that will keep the city's skyline and history alive for you even after you've returned home. **Carl Fischer of Chicago**, a huge dusty, musty place in the shadow of the el in the Loop, has one of the best selections of sheet music in the country. There are **Fannie May** candy stores all over town, and each one of them is an old-timey delight. **Crate & Barrel**, another quintessential Chicago success story, is responsible for more interiors than perhaps any other store in the city. Though it may connote middle-brow, mass taste elsewhere, Chicagoans still remember when it was just a funky little store in Old Town. And none can doubt that **Nike Town**, with its carnival atmosphere and huge selection of sporting goods, has in its so-far short existence on Mag Mile become a retail landmark.

For pampered service... Stick to the Mag Mile/Oak Street nexus and you could hit all these shops in one extremely spoiled day. (Don't laugh—it's been done.) Standing in the handsome dressing rooms of **Barneys New York** while a tailor pins your hem and the saleshelp hurl flattering remarks your way can really help the ego, not to mention how the chic clothing (for both sexes) can help your fashion image. On a much smaller scale, **June Blaker** treats her male and female customers with respect by telling them, if necessary, they look lousy in that particular avant-garde Japanese concoction. After all, not everyone can wear Comme des Garçons. The staff at **Henri Bendel** will go out of their way, running back and forth fetching a different size or color, while ladies luxuriate in their lovely changing rooms, just like the women in *The Women*. The chic salespeople at **Hermés** will spend a surprising amount of time doting on you, as well, even demonstrating how to tie one of their horsy-patterned silk scarves in that insouciant way French women seem to have perfected. (Men may have to figure out on their own what to do with the silk ties.) Chicagoans have long loved the attention they get paid at the **Hino & Malee** boutique, where the store's own label of eminently wearable but unique women's clothes are truly inspiring. Spend a few hours poring over the fancy cosmetics and perfumes at **Marilyn Miglin**—while you may not necessarily depart better-looking than when you entered, the staff is so fawning you'll definitely *feel* better. The well-dressed staff at the **Ultimo** boutique, for men's and women's clothes, is more accommodating than its snooty reputation allows. Buy something and you'll be their friend forever.

Accessorize!... Quirky hats, funny slippers that make you look like a genie, sexy dresses and blouses, and unique hand-crafted jewelry are beautifully displayed at **Krivoy** in the Lincoln Park neighborhood. Whether it's a night-time clutch or a major handbag in which you can schlepp everything but the kitchen sink, you're sure to find it at **Bottega Veneta**, the famous Italian leathergoods shop known for its woven butter-soft leather (and high prices). **Glove Me Tender** may be small in square footage, but then gloves and mittens don't take up much room; the store carries thousands of pairs. Adorning your head with a straw bonnet, pillbox hat, or sleek little cloche from **Raymond Hudd** may look like it would cost an arm and a leg, but the ladies' hats in this Lincoln Park boutique are actually quite reasonably priced. Besides, how often do you buy a hat? And when a button pops, please don't buy one of those little plastic things at Walgreen's—instead head to **Tender Buttons**, a teeny-tiny store with an enormous selection of buttons: new ones, old ones, square ones, round ones, wood, Bakelite, brass, mother-of-pearl, you name it.

Shopping scenes... Don't be surprised on a Saturday morning if housewares-and-furniture mecca **Crate & Barrel** is jammed with preppie-looking couples running around wielding clipboard and wedding registry forms. Things can get pretty hairy on Saturday mornings at **Filene's Basement**, too, with bargain-hunters free from the constraints of their weekday lunch hour battling over some of the best clothing bargains in town. Don't expect to find any cheap deals on the toys and stuffed animals at

F.A.O. Schwarz, though there is the constant din of kids and parents duking it out over the latest Power Rangers, Pocahontas paraphernalia, and Barbie couture dresses. It's a far more civilized scene at **Salvage One**, where do-it-yourselfers with "This Old House" complexes trek to shuffle through five vast floors, discussing the relative merits of this vintage toilet versus that one, these mahogany doors versus those doors in oak, etc, etc.

For foot fetishists... Up in Lake View, **Air Wair/Doc Martens Footwear and Clothing** is the place for what many consider the hippest shoes around. Doc Martens are generally clunky, often black, and usually hated by parents when worn by teenagers. In fact, when said parents were teenagers themselves they were probably running around in the comfy but odd looking sandals sold in Lincoln Park at **Hanig's Birkenstock Shop**, those stout-soled Nordic wonders that today come in all the colors of the rainbow. If you're trying to impress, though, head to **Cole-Haan** for beautifully crafted, sensible-yet-expensive leather shoes. There's nothing sensible about the spiky heels, mules, and other shoes sold at **Stephane Kelian**, the biggest name in French footwear. **Lori's Discount Designer Shoes**, in Lincoln Park, peddles a wide, quickly changing array of bargain-priced designer shoes for women (20% to 40% off Kenneth Cole, Calvin, Joan & David, etc.). In-the-know customers arrive early in the day for the best selection.

For men with Cary Grant complexes... Plan your wardrobe for that deb ball at **Buy-A-Tux**, a south-of–the–Loop store where designer formalwear—including Joseph Abboud and Jhane Barnes—is about a third less than you'd pay anywhere else. Then, perhaps, stop into the gracious portal of the **Giorgio Armani** boutique for a formal black overcoat. Or maybe it's a day at Mummy's club you're planning. In that case, try **Sulka**, which sells the kind of clothes investment bankers might wear on their day off. Then add a little James Bondish élan to your look with a gadget from **Hammacher Schlemmer**, which specializes in high-tech, and often wacky, wizardry. No self-respecting Cary Grant wannabe would appear without a pipe from **Iwan Ries & Co.**, a Loop shop with more than 25,000 pipes in stock, from wood to Meerschaum and everything in between.

For men who would rather resemble Lou Reed...
Go to Lake View's **The Alley** and **99th Floor**, or Lincoln
Park's **Urban Outfitters**—they all sell the kind of clothes
that work well on the wild side, whether that means an
all-nighter at the clubs, a gig with an alternative garage
band, or just a few hours lolling around some see-and-be-
seen outdoor cafe, leaning on your Harley.

Shopping bags to show off... The shiny black bags
with white lettering from **Chanel** are a good start, since
black goes with everything. The discreet, earth-toned
bags from the **Giorgio Armani** or **Jil Sander** boutiques
are also good choices, as they imply not only lots of
money, but lots of taste. The brown-and-white-striped
Henri Bendel bag connotes a youthful flair that few can
match. If folks spy you walking down the street swinging
a **Plaza Escada** bag, they may question your taste, but at
least they'll know you've spent a lot of money. Social
snobs may not appreciate the pretentious navy blue bags
with the embossed gold polo player from **Polo Ralph
Lauren**, but the saleshelp at other stores will—after all, if
you're a Ralph Lauren wannabe, maybe you'll also pay big
bucks on the couture at **Gianni Versace**, **Betsey Johnson**,
or other designer boutiques hereabouts.

Fashion forward... Chicago may not be known as the home
of waif-thin models and ascot-wearing designers, but high
fashion is alive and well here. **Blake**, in Lincoln Park, sells
women's clothes by such on-the-edge Belgian designers as
Dries van Noten and Ann Demeulemeester (try saying
that name three times fast), among others. At **June Blaker**,
a store for both men and women, the eponymous personal-
ity-plus proprietor is usually on hand to offer you guidance
through the hottest of the hot. It's a trip to the future for
men and women at **Gianni Versace**, as well, whose designs
tend toward the flamboyant, the metallic, and the hey-
look-at-me mode (or should that be moda?). The city's
only Ermenegildo Zegna boutique is at **Ultimo**, where
several men's and women's designers meet in a multi-level
store. **Jil Sander**, which sells understated women's clothes
that have been called "architectural," was the German
designer's first freestanding store in the United States. If
you're interested in making a splash, but not the same
splash as everyone else, it's not hard to find the unusual and
sometimes one-of-a-kind at **Hino & Malee** or the Gold

CHICAGO | SHOPPING

Coast's **Krivoy**, both of which are filled with their owners' designs for women. The tatami mats, shoji screens, and beautiful display cases at **Toshiro**, in Lake View, are an indication of the ease and simplicity of the clothes within, which generally come from young, hip designers. Boy-toy club kids do their shopping in Lake View at **Hardwear**, where the clothes are designed to show off those pecs, lats, and glutes they've been working lo these many years. It's the only place in town to buy clothes by favorite gay-guy New York designer Raymond Dragon. At **Sugar Magnolia**, which caters to a youngish, hip crowd of women, you won't find weird hard-to-wear designs by Japanese designers or Belgians with hard-to-pronounce names, but sporty stuff by up-and-coming, mostly American designers.

Key notes... There's such an enormous selection of music available at Lincoln Park's **Tower Records** that you'll probably walk in planning to buy one CD and walk out with a dozen. It has particularly strong classical and show-tune departments and a staff that really knows its stuff, though no one is ever around when you need them. Also in Lincoln Park, the **Jazz Record Mart** not only sells CDs, tapes, and regular albums, but also has old, hard-to-find 45s and even 78s. **2nd Hand Tunes**, on the north side, is rife with collectors, from Judy, Barbra, and Bette fanatics to those seeking rare recordings by the not-for-gotten Clash, Adam Ant, Blondie, and, well, you get the picture. No one over 21 has ever heard of any of the artists whose records are sold at **Wax Trax**, also in Lincoln Park.

Kid stuff, part one... There's often a human "toy soldier" standing in front of **F.A.O. Schwarz**, beckoning families into this frenzied toy palace. Lots of movie tie-in products, and a really kitschy Barbie boutique; but the best things here are the great stuffed animals, so cute they'll break your heart. For a calmer time, go up to Lincoln Park to **Saturday's Child**, whose collection of educational, motivational, and creative toys (none of which are movie tie-ins) is culled from about 300 manufacturers around the world. Most boys and girls will go nuts in the **Chicago Cubs Sports Shop**, though parents might be put off by the high prices.

Kid stuff, part two... If you're looking for clothes that dress up your kids without making them look like baby

Evangelistas, head to **All Our Children**, which sells a sophisticated yet charming collection in sizes infant through 7. **Oilily** carries its own line of bright, adorable kids clothes designed and made in Italy, with a hefty tariff to match. You have to wade through a lot of junk to get to the cute stuff at **Just Kids**, way out on West Belmont, but persevere and you might find great discounted clothes from Baby Gap, Oneita's Soupçon, and other fine name brands.

Book nooks... **People Like Us,** up in Lake View, is the city's only bookstore devoted to gay and lesbian fiction, nonfiction, and periodicals. On Printer's Row in the South Loop, the **Prairie Avenue Bookshop** specializes in books on architecture, design, and engineering, while the **Ginkgo Tree Book Shop** in suburban Oak Park sells books about that town's most famous past resident (not counting Ernest Hemingway), Frank Lloyd Wright. Like the name says, the **Abraham Lincoln Bookstore**, in River North, is devoted to books about Honest Abe, his life and times. At Andersonville's **Women and Children First** you'll find books on women's issues, as well as a good selection of children's books.

Used but not abused books... The Lincoln Park neighborhood is a target zone for secondhand book stores: You'll find thousands of high-quality used hardcover and paperback books at **Bookseller's Row**, **Powell's**, and **Aspidistra Bookshop** (which could use a good dusting). Even better, don't miss the wide selection of contemporary first editions sold at each.

Everything you always wanted to know about sex... Come to the **Pleasure Chest** in Lake View when your needs include sex toys, soft-core porn, skimpy maid's uniforms, and spiked leather dog collars. Decidedly straight, however. **Male Hide**, in Lincoln Park, is for gay guys and lesbians into leather, with all sorts of paraphernalia including vests, chaps, harnesses, along with chains and other items that can turn any evening into a painfully good time. Yee-hah!

For aspiring Martha Stewarts... Given its important role in both the history of design and furniture manufacturing, Chicago is a good place to shop for furniture even if you're just visiting. The light-filled third and fourth floors of the Michigan Avenue **Crate & Barrel** are filled with four-poster beds, big squishy floral-print sofas, club chairs, and all sorts of traditional furniture that, judging from the hordes roaming through the store, seems to appeal to everyone on earth and not just Chicagoans. The sprawling **Room & Board** nearby has similarly appealing furniture, most of it with a more contemporary feel. There are no mass-produced dining room tables, chairs, or sleigh beds at River North's **Sawbridge Studios**, where everything is hand-crafted by individual artisans across the country. Prices rise considerably when you start shopping at **Manifesto**, the city's prime source for architecturally inspired furniture. At **Mario Villa** the furniture design (all created by the store's New Orleans-based namesake) is less architectural than artful, while the overstuffed sofas and chairs at **Shabby Chic** are so plush it's like sitting in a big bowl of pudding. But by far the most fantastical furnishings are sold in River West at **Kleiner Design**, where the sophisticated furniture all looks as if it was designed specifically for a ritzy penthouse high above the city. And in the old Saks Fifth Avenue building on Michigan Avenue, the **Sony Gallery** purveys all things electronic and high-tech. Though it looks off-putting, you really can try out everything—play to your heart's content with all that stereo and TV gadgetry.

Furnishing touches... Antique country pie safes, distressed cupboards, and even vintage umbrellas are available on the third floor of Lake View's **Toshiro** (the first two floors sell lovely women's clothes). If you're trying to re-create a home à la 16th arrondissement, or perhaps in the style of a sun-worn home in Provence, you might want to fill up on the charming French imported dishes, linen, stemware, etc. sold at **La Maison de Nicole**. Don't miss the Limoge. At **Elements** you'll find very expensive cutting-edge designs, including artist-made lamps, picture frames, and some of the most creatively mixed-and-matched tableware in the city. Both the Michigan Avenue **Crate & Barrel** and the **Crate & Barrel Outlet Store** up in Lincoln Park are filled with streamlined, contemporary-styled housewares, including dishes, glasses, bowls, picture frames, pots 'n' pans, and very handsome versions of such practical objects as salad spinners and apple corers. Also in Lincoln Park, **Lill Street Studios** offers one-of-a-kind hand-thrown ceramics—you can actually meet with the individual artists and help design your own tableware. Unspeakably beautiful stationery and paper, much of it imported or made by hand, is available at the **Paper Source**, where you'll no doubt spend more than you intended.

The sporting life... Hollywood might have movie stars and New York has fashion designers, but Chicago has sports gods, and everything and anything to do with them is available at the **Chicago Cubs Sports Shop**. It might look like a shrine to Michael Jordan, Scottie Pippin, and all the rest of the Bulls, but **Nike Town** is a real store selling almost everything the company sells—a cornucopia of footwear and sports clothing. Only tourists actually buy here—the prices tend to be as high as Jordan's jump shot (Nike gear is expensive, but hey, you can buy it for less almost anywhere else). There will be some things you can't get at Nike Town, but don't despair. There's always **Windward Sports**, in Lake View, which specializes in whatever you may need to cut quickly through the elements (i.e., skis, windsurfers, surfboards, snowboards, Rollerblades...).

The vintage vantage point... As you'd expect, funky Lake View is the neighborhood for equally funky vintage clothing stores. A new addition to the used clothing scene, **Disgraceland** has a definite 1960s bent, selling kitschy vintage bellbottoms, chiffon beaded numbers, sandals, and lots of other stuff. It's all very Jackie O. The 1960s are also alive just up the street at **Strange Cargo**, the place to come for vintage clothes à la Brady Bunch, and campy lunch boxes from the Sixties and Seventies (Starsky and Hutch! Bobby Sherman! the Partridge family!). **Flashy Trash** is a bright shop that doesn't sell "used" clothing as much as truly vintage clothes and accessories, with a great selection of winter overcoats, shoes, and party dresses. Drag queens shop here.

Labels for less... The mundane atmosphere at **Buy-A-Tux**, south of the Loop, may not resemble the formal settings where these designer black-tie duds are eventually worn, but the prices are so good you'll be able to afford at least one more charity ball with the savings. You could shop at full-price retail establishments like Barneys New York and Henri Bendel, but if you search hard enough you'll find much of their private-label goods, as well as clothes by designers from Calvin Klein to Anne Klein, steeply discounted at **Filene's Basement**. Those same designers, as well as many others, are also represented at **Lori's Discount Designer Shoes**, a self-serve shoe store in Lincoln Park. For a preppie at-the-shore look for people whose budgets only allow for summer shares, the **Land's End** outlet on the north side is a good place to start. There's a certain timeless solidity in the casual clothes sold at the north side's **The Gap Factory Outlet**, where the discounts can be substantial. Though they claim that much of what's available here is seconds, the flaws are almost impossible to spot. And no outfit would be complete without a great pair of trendy shades from Ray Ban, Vuarnet, or other brand names, which can be found at a discount at **Sun King**.

When you need a sugar fix... Why waste your time or calories on fancy chocolates from Godiva when all over town there are **Fannie May** outlets selling indescribably good chocolate-covered peanuts, creams in all shades of the pastel rainbow, and turtles to die for? Skip the fudge, though, and instead head for the **Fudge Pot**, in Old Town, where the yummiest fudge around comes in many flavors. And don't forget those Frango Mints at **Marshall Field's**!

The Index

Abraham Lincoln Bookstore. Books and paraphernalia relating to the sixteenth president are displayed here as beautifully as they'd be at any museum. Literature about the Civil War is well represented, too.... *Tel 312/944–3085. 357 W. Chicago Ave.*

Air Wair/Doc Martens Footwear and Clothing. Like the name says, the place for combat boots and other thick-soled hip shoes.... *Tel 312/244–0099. 3240 N. Clark St.*

All Our Children. Where the fashion-forward baby gets garbed.... *Tel 312/327–1868. 2217 N. Halsted St.*

The Alley. Motorcycle jackets and all the accoutrements you could ever desire, plus lots of Dead Head paraphernalia, are sold here by salespeople with pierced body parts.... *Tel 312/883–1800. 858 W. Belmont Ave.*

Aspidistra Bookshop. An almost stereotypical-looking dusty old used-book store with an anything-but-stereotypical stock. Disorganized by topic.... *Tel 312/549–3129. 2630 N. Clark St.*

Barbara's Bookstore. A deep stock of recent fiction and non-fiction backlists makes this bright and airy Old Town store a great place to search for that book—you know, the one you've been meaning to get to since you read its review in *Granta*.... *Tel 312/642–5044. 1350 N. Wells St.*

Barnes & Noble. You can browse for hours among the racks of this megastore, which sells almost everything at a 10 percent to 30 percent discount; when fatigue sets in, grab a seat and have a cappuccino in the café.... *Tel 312/971–9004. 659 W. Diversey Pkwy.*

Barneys New York. Make sure you've got a lot of money to blow before you enter these portals, since everything in this fashionable men's and women's clothing store is over-the-top expensive. But if you're into Donna, Calvin, Giorgio, and all the rest, this is the place for you. Friendlier staff than you'd expect, too.... *Tel 312/587–1700. 25 E. Oak St.*

Betsey Johnson. All the best from the new wave designer's funky collection, including cute dresses in the wild patterns she's known for, in fabrics that would make an environmentalist cringe. Gee, that rubber must be sweaty to wear on a hot summer day, but heck, it's *fashion*.... *Tel 312/665–4010. 3341 N. Clark St.*

Blake. A store that's not scared of taking chances, this small discriminating women's boutique sells choice selections of white-hot trendy clothing from designers such as Katherine Hammett and Dolce and Gabenna.... *Tel 312/477–3364. 2448 N. Lincoln Ave.*

Bloomingdale's. Big 'n' glittery, this six-story version of the famed Manhattan emporium sells trendy clothes, great housewares, and gallons of cosmetics. Good luck finding a salesperson to help you, though.... *Tel 312/440–4460. 900 N. Michigan Ave.*

Bookseller's Row. This unusually well-organized (and clean) used-book store sells an impressive, high-end collection. Particularly strong in fiction and history.... *Tel 312/348–1170. 2445 N. Lincoln Ave.*

Borders Books. Another three-story mega-bookstore, this one has a great location going for it—across the street from the Water Tower Place shopping mall.... *Tel 312/573–0564. 830 N. Michigan Ave.*

Bottega Veneta. Purses, briefcases, shoes, and other pricey Italian woven leather goods dyed an array of unusual colors, as well as natural, are the main course here.... *Tel 312/664–3220. 107 E. Oak St.*

Buy-A-Tux. A dreadful name for a formalwear shop selling designer tuxes and black-tie gear for about a third less than the department stores.... *Tel 312/243–5465. 615 W. Roosevelt Rd.*

Carl Fischer of Chicago. There's hardly a song, aria, etude, sonata, show tune, or any other type of sheet music that's not available at this grim-looking but deservedly famous store.... *Tel 312/427–6652. 312 S. Wabash Ave.*

Carson Pirie Scott & Co. How the mighty have fallen! Once one of Chicago's—nay, the Midwest's—great department stores is today just another dreary place that sells pretty much the same conventional clothes and accessories as are available all over. The building, however, is still outstanding.... *Tel 312/641–7000. 1 S. State St.*

Chanel. Coco would be proud of this glamorous two-story boutique where ladies who plan charity events can find suitable suits, little black dresses, hats, shoes, chunky costume jewelry, and, of course, Chanel No. 5.... *Tel 312/787–5500. 940 N. Michigan Ave.*

The Chicago Architecture Foundation Shop. Skip all the tacky souvenir shops around town and head here, where you'll find a great selection of books, small architectural doo-dads, and, if you really must have mugs and T-shirts, ones that'll be worth showing off to your friends back home.... *Tel 312/922–8687. 224 S. Michigan Ave.*

Chicago Cubs Sports Shop. Stuck in a corner of the Tribune Tower (the company owns both the paper and the team), this is the place downtown to get all the Cubs (and other sports team) memorabilia you can carry. Day-of-game and future game tickets on sale, too.... *Tel 312/321–9421. 445 N. Michigan Ave.*

Cole-Haan. Expensive and stylishly conservative men's and women's shoes are sold in an unusually exquisite store.... *Tel 312/642–8995. 645 N. Michigan Ave.*

Crate & Barrel. A home-grown Chicago institution, this store not only sells clean-lined, stylish furniture and kitchenware, but the ultra-contemporary store building is one of the best-looking new structures erected in years on Michigan Avenue. The salespeople here are incredibly nice and helpful, even by Chicago standards. During Christmas shopping season there are actually lines to get in.... *Tel 312/787–5900. 850 N. Michigan Ave.*

Crate & Barrel Outlet Store. With savings anywhere from 20 percent to 70 percent off the prices at the regular store (see above), it's worth braving what is hands-down the worst parking lot in Chicago.... *Tel 312/787–4775. 800 W. North Ave.*

Disgraceland. Secondhand clothes with a decided 1960s bent.... *Tel 312/281–5875. 3330a N. Clark St.*

Elements. Unfairly known as a place with grimacing salespeople, this is truly one of the city's most cosmopolitan tchotchke shops, filled with beautifully displayed and often unique housewares, leather goods, bed linens, bags, and ties.... *Tel 312/642–6574. 102 E. Oak St.*

Fannie May. Old ladies all dolled up in what look like nurse uniforms hand-pack the best chocolates in town at this old-fashioned hometown institution. One hundred types of chocolate candy, with names like pixies, Colonials, and turtles.... *Tel 312/664–0420. Water Tower Place, 835 N. Michigan Ave. (and many other locations).*

CHICAGO | SHOPPING

F.A.O. Schwarz. Over-the-top toy store with about as much warmth as an igloo in Nome, this extravagant and expensive emporium specializes in making kids want everything and parents generally buying it for them just to shut them up.... *Tel 312/587–5000. 840 N. Michigan Ave.*

57th Street Books. Catering to students and professors at the nearby University of Chicago, this great bookstore has an eclectic selection and knowledgable staff.... *Tel 312/684–1300. 1301 E. 57th St.*

Filene's Basement. There are two outlets of this famous bargain-clothing-hunter's delight, though the Michigan Avenue one is, despite the name, on the second and third floors.... *Tel 312/553–1055. 1 N. State St.; and tel 312/482–8918, 830 N. Michigan Ave.*

Flashy Trash. High-end vintage clothing store where the staff will tell you that you look ridiculous if, in fact, you do. Definitely the place to go for party clothes.... *Tel 312/ 327–6900. 3524 N. Halsted St.*

Fudge Pot. Like the name says, this extraordinary-smelling shop sells the most luscious handmade fudge in ten flavors. Hand-dipped caramel apples and candy are knockouts, too.... *Tel 312/943–1777. 1532 N. Wells St.*

Gap Factory Outlet. If you think The Gap is reasonably priced, wait till you see the bargains on high-quality seconds available here, as well as on clothes from Banana Republic, which shares the same parent company.... *Tel 312/252–0594. 2778 N. Milwaukee Ave.*

Gianni Versace. Few people can get away with wearing this designer's often clingy but always flamboyant creations, but if you can, go for it here. They sell it all.... *Tel 312/ 337–1111. 101 E. Oak St.*

Ginkgo Tree Book Shop. It shouldn't surprise anyone that this suburb, which has more examples of Frank Lloyd Wright homes than anywhere else, should also be home to a bookstore specializing in books about the master himself.... *Tel 708/848–1606. 951 Chicago Ave., Oak Park.*

Giorgio Armani. A friendly staff and an incredibly sophisticated, well-chosen selection of the Italian designer's collections make this boutique an elegant shopping experience.... *Tel 312/427–6264. 113 E. Oak St.*

Glove Me Tender. Almost 100 lines of gloves for men, women, and children are sold at this cute little boutique.... *Tel 312/664–4022. 900 N. Michigan Ave.*

Hammacher Schlemmer. When the need arises for self-massagers, high-tech popcorn poppers, watches that do everything from tell the time to remind you of your next appointment, or any other gadget imaginable, this is the place to come. Very James Bond.... *Tel 312/527–9100. 445 N. Michigan Ave.*

Hanig's Birkenstock Shop. What goes around comes around—the mellowest shoes this side of the melée during the 1968 Democratic convention held in Grant Park are baaaack.... *Tel 312/929–5568. 847 W. Armitage St.*

Hardware. Men: If you haven't been to the gym on a regular basis five times a week for the last decade, don't even think of buying these revealing club clothes.... *Tel 312/296–0801. 3243 N. Broadway.*

Henri Bendel. This extravagant four-story store sells women's clothes and accessories to the very rich, the very thin, and the very fashion-forward. Lots of big-name designer clothes, too, as well as the store's private label.... *Tel 312/642–0140. 900 N. Michigan Ave.*

Hermés. Selling everything from its signature silk scarves and men's ties to custom-order saddles that run in the thousands of dollars, this chic little boutique has a helpful staff.... *Tel 312/7887–8175. 110 E. Oak St.*

Hino & Malee. A local treasure, this is the country's only boutique that sells the designing couple's entire collection of avant-garde, Japanese-inspired women's clothes.... *Tel 312/664–7475. 50 E. Oak St.*

Iwan Ries & Co. Decidedly un-p.c., this Chicago institution specializes in tobacco and pipes. It even has a walk-in thermador full of cigars.... *Tel 312/372–1306. 19 S. Wabash Ave.*

CHICAGO | SHOPPING

Jazz Record Mart. Featuring the world's largest selection of jazz recordings, this busting-at-its-seams store is a local fave—and hangout. In addition to American music, there's a terrific selection of salsa and Latin jazz as well. The staff really knows its stuff.... *Tel 312/222–1467. 444 N. Wabash Ave.*

Jil Sander. Devoted to the austere but wearable women's clothes of this German designer. Don't let the severe aesthetic of the shop's design scare you away.... *Tel 312/335–0006. 48 E. Oak St.*

June Blaker. Known as an outpost of the avant-garde, this chic corner boutique sells European and Japanese designer clothes to many of the gallery owners and artists, male and female, who live and work in the neighborhood.... *Tel 312/751–9220. 200 W. Superior St.*

Just Kids. It's a schlepp to get here, but you'll be rewarded with a decent selection of discounted children's clothes.... *Tel 312/202–0203. 4202 W. Belmont Ave.*

Kleiner Design. One of the most creative outlets for furniture in the city, most of which is designed by hip artists chosen by the store's namesake, a local impresario and restaurateur.... *Tel 312/831–0400. 560 W. Fulton St.*

Krivoy. Most everything sold in this highly personal, quirky shop—from the blouses to the shoes to the whimsical hats and bedroom slippers—is designed by the owner.... *Tel 312/248–1466. 1145 W. Webster St.*

Land's End. Overstocks from this well-known clothing catalogue are available at a 20 percent to 40 percent discount.... *Tel 312/281–0900. 2121 N. Clybourn Ave.*

Lill Street Studios. A combination artists' commune, ceramics school, and pottery salesroom, this is the place for one-of-a-kind objects.... *Tel 312/477–6185. 1021 W. Lill St.*

Lori's Discount Designer Shoes. The name pretty much says it all, though it might be worth adding that socks, hosiery, and handbags are available, too.... *Tel 312/281–5655. 808 W. Armitage.*

La Maison de Nicole. Graceful yet usable dishes, stemware, and table linen imported from France are sold in this charming little boutique. They speak French here.... *Tel 312/943–3988. 66 E. Walton St.*

Male Hide. Everything for the man or woman into leather and chains. Great selection of harnesses, for those inclined to like harnesses.... *Tel 312/929–0069. 2816 N. Lincoln Ave.*

Manifesto. This clever two-story furniture store sells original designs evocative of the great masters, like Saarinen, Mies, and Frank Lloyd Wright, in addition to exacting reproductions of designs by the same guys. Contemporary Italian accessories are available, as well.... *Tel 312/664–0733. 200 W. Superior St.*

Marilyn Miglin. Selling the expensive cosmetics and fragrances of the city's own Estée Lauder, this shop is all sugar and spice and everything nice. They specialize in redesigning your make-up routine.... *Tel 312/943–1120. 112 E. Oak St. Closed Sun.*

Mario Villa. Few furniture shops can compete with the exquisite wrought-metal beds, lamps, tables, and chairs sold at this corner boutique specializing in the work of New Orleans-based designer Mario Villa.... *Tel 312/923–0993. 500 N. Wells St.*

Marshall Field's. The legendary Chicago department store selling everything from clothing to housewares to furniture to antique cufflinks, this State Street beauty still can hold its own against upstarts like Neiman Marcus and Nordstrom, though finding someone to help you in any of the more than 140 departments can be difficult.... *Tel 312/781–1000. 111 N. State St.*

Neiman Marcus. A marble-clad tribute to all that's expensive and trendy. But if you're looking for a one-stop couture-a-go-go, this is the place. The gourmet shop is heaven.... *Tel 312/642–5900. 737 N. Michigan Ave.*

Nike Town. This has to be the world's most extravagant sporting goods store, with life-size sculptures of professional athletes dangling from the three-story ceiling, a mini-basketball court in which to test shoes, and shoes and work-out gear displayed as if they were museum exhibitions. The staff is outgoing but not always too helpful.... *Tel 312/642–9525. 669 N. Michigan Ave.*

99th Floor. For club kids and those who haven't realized heavy metal is passé, this store sells leather and vinyl clothing, almost all of which is jet black, and what can only be called alternative-style shoes and boots.... *Tel 312/348–7781. 3406 N. Halsted St.*

Oilily. Shop at this children's clothing store when the sameness of Baby and Kids Gap begins to wear you down. Intensely colorful and creatively designed Italian clothes for junior go for high prices, though.... *Tel 312/642–1166. 900 N. Michigan Ave.*

Paper Source. Handmade and machine-made paper, envelopes, and stationery, as well as a very large selection of rubber stamps, are available at this fascinating corner shop. Very knowledgeable and friendly staff are happy to answer all of your questions.... *Tel 312/337–0798. 232 W. Chicago Ave.*

People Like Us. This is the only bookstore in town devoted exclusively to gay and lesbian literature, nonfiction, and periodicals. Very Oscar Wilde.... *Tel 312/248–6363. 1115 W. Belmont Ave.*

Plaza Escada. Bright, white-marbled, multi-level German-owned boutique plying clothes and accessories for trophy wives.... *Tel 312/915–0500. 840 N. Michigan Ave.*

Pleasure Chest. There's usually a mannequin in some sort of sexy get-up—from nurse's uniform to French maid to a guy in tighty-whities—in the window of this sex-toy palace.... *Tel 312/525–7151. 3143 N. Broadway.*

Polo Ralph Lauren. Everything you'd want from the pasha of prep, including men's and women's clothes.... *Tel 312/280–1655. 960 N. Michigan Ave.*

Powell's. One of the largest used bookstores in town, this is a well-organized and well-lit place, though the staff could try to smile once in a while.... *Tel 312/248–1444. 2850 N. Lincoln Ave.*

Prairie Avenue Bookshop. They say they have the country's largest selection of books and periodicals about art, architecture, design, and engineering, and who are we to doubt them?.... *Tel 312/922–8311. 711 S. Dearborn St.*

Raymond Hudd. This millinery sells handmade and unique ladies hats that remind one of a gentler time.... *Tel 312/477–1159. 2545 N. Clark St.*

Room & Board. One of the only interesting stores in Michigan Avenue's Chicago Place shopping mall, this sprawling two-level place sells contemporary furniture and accessories. Particularly interesting kids' stuff.... *Tel 312/266–0656. 700 N. Michigan Ave.*

Saks Fifth Ave. A far cry from the glamour and chic of its Fifth Avenue namesake, this contemporary, rather grim department store carries much of the same basic designer wear sold all over town.... *Tel 312/944–6500. 700 N. Michigan Ave.*

Salvage One. This gargantuan 100,000-square-foot warehouse has on display literally hundreds of thousands of used bathrooms fixtures, fireplace mantels, doors, wrought-iron fencing, garden accoutrements, and light fixtures salvaged from old buildings and houses.... *Tel 312/733–0098. 1524 S. Sangamon St.*

Saturday's Child. Don't come here looking for the latest Little Mermaid doll. Instead, a delightful collection of toys with which your kids can actually use their imaginations.... *Tel 312/525–8697. 2146 N. Halsted St.*

Sawbridge Studios. The owners here specialize in the unique handcrafted wood furniture designs of individual artisans from around the country.... *Tel 312/828–0055. 406 N. Clark St.*

2nd Hand Tunes. Selling a panoply of used records, CDs, and tapes, this campy little store is overflowing. Don't miss the store windows, which display some of the most hilarious record jackets ever.... *Tel 312/929–6325. 2604 N. Clark St.*

Shabby Chic. Shop here for overstuffed, slip-covered furniture that's so comfortable it redefines the word. But boy, is it expensive.... *Tel 312/649–0080. 54 E. Walton St.*

Sony Gallery. More a museum than a retail outlet—though it is that, too—this severe-looking store displays high-tech Sony products, such as stereos, TVs, personal stereos, etc. The staff knows a lot, so get your questions answered here, but buy somewhere else. It'll be cheaper.... *Tel 312/943–3334. 663 N. Michigan Ave.*

Stephane Kelian. Très bon. This relatively new addition to the city's fanciest shopping street sells women's shoes from one of the most prestigious French names in the business.... *Tel 312/951–2868. 121 E. Oak St.*

Strange Cargo. In addition to used clothing, there's a wide selection of funky furniture and housewares for sale here that looks as if it came directly out of someone's rec room, circa 1963.... *Tel 312/327–8090. 3448 N. Clark St.*

Sugar Magnolia. A women's clothing store that sells clothes that can only be defined as "cute." Much of it is from young, up-and-coming designers, some of it is handmade.... *Tel 312/944–0885. 34 E. Oak St.*

Sulka. For elegantly tailored clothes, formalwear, leisure clothes, and even silk pajamas for men who can afford the best. The staff is very helpful and doesn't seem to mind browsers.... *Tel 312/951–9500. 55 E. Oak St.*

Sun King. Cool shades from Ray Ban, Vuarnet, and others, all sold at a discount. Staff is fairly low in the sycophancy department.... *Tel 312/649–9110. 44 E. Chicago Ave.*

Tender Buttons. As the name implies, this teensy shop sells scads of new and antique buttons.... *Tel 312/337–7033. 946 N. Rush St.*

Toshiro. This dreamy three-story boutique selling simple women's clothes and farm-style antiques and housewares is a local favorite.... *Tel 312/248–1487. 3309 N. Clark St.*

Tower Records/Tower Books. A vast tasteland where records of every conceivable musical type are for sale, neatly divided by style in soundproof areas, so individual managers can play their favorites, all at once.... *Tel 312/477–5994. 2301 N. Clark St.*

Ultimo. The ultimate in designer boutiques, this handsome multilevel men's and women's clothing shop gets everything first. Try to get invited to one of the store's well-known trunk shows, especially designer Issac Mizrahi's annual February visit. It's a hoot, and so is he.... *Tel 312/787–0906. 114 E. Oak St.*

Unabridged Bookstore. One of the few neighborhood book-shops that hasn't been gobbled up by the megastores, this well-stocked store has a fine selection of contemporary fic-tion, cookbooks, and books for a gay and lesbian audience, not to mention a staff that actually knows what they're talk-ing about.... *Tel 312/883–9119. 3251 N. Broadway.*

Urban Outfitters. Ersatz funkdom plying all the clothes, house-wares, and shoes you need to be a hipster once again.... *Tel 312/549–1711. 2352 N. Clark St.*

Wax Trax. The place to buy alternative music, from Nirvana to the sounds normally only heard at the deepest, coolest after-hours clubs.... *Tel 312/862–2121. 1653 N. Damen Ave.*

Windward Sports. Surfboards, snowboards, Tevas, Roller-blades, sunglasses, bathing suits, and all other sleek modes of sports equipment and accessories can be found at this fun store.... *Tel 312/472–6868. 3317 N. Clark St.*

Women and Children First. The only store in town specializing in books and periodicals geared towards women and the issues that concern them, from feminist politics to child-birth. Lots of p.c. children's books, as well. Very Susan Faludi.... *Tel 312/769–9299. 5233 N. Clark St.*

6

tlife

Chicago's bar
scene is organized
a lot like Disney-
land: You don't
really need to
have a specific
destination in

mind, just a theme, a mood, a lifestyle. Then hit the strip that suits those parameters. Conventioneers, suburbanites, and ill-informed visitors patronize the nearly indistinguishable pick-up bars radiating from State and Division streets, the traditional hub of the **Rush Street** area, which has been evolving into a restaurant and retail area in recent years. A few blocks of **Lincoln Avenue**, from Armitage to Fullerton, has sprouted bars and live-music clubs pandering to clean-cut postcollegiate types. The crowd is basically the same farther north along **Clark Street** in Wrigleyville—a few reggae clubs and slacker-ish contingents mix things up a bit, but the sports bar rules here. Just a few blocks away, a passing parade of gays streams up and down **Halsted Street**. African-Americans congregate at a number of well-heeled nightclubs along **Michigan** and **Wabash avenues** in the South Loop. The spit-polished BMWs and motorcycles parked outside a couple of bars on **Damen Avenue** north of North Avenue are a sign of things to come: Lincoln Parkers have found a beachhead in the slacker paradise of Wicker Park, though they leave the neighborhood's rough-hewn artist types undisturbed at their respective dives. All this fragmentation doesn't mean clubbers don't cross a few boundaries: Choose carefully and you'll find a few places where there's plurality on the dance floor.

Sources

Head for Section 3 of the popular free weekly, *Reader*. Live music is listed according to genre, and there are plenty of ads to browse through in search of nightlife options. Less overwhelming, but also less complete, are listings in another alterna-rag, *New City*. In its "Friday" entertainment tabloid, the *Chicago Tribune* publishes an "After hours" column profiling offbeat evening haunts, as well as news of upcoming concerts. The *Sun-Times* provides hints about nocturnal goings-on in its "Friday Weekend Plus" pullout. *¡Exito!* keeps tabs on live music and happenings in the Latino community; *N'Digo*, a free black bimonthly newspaper, covers hot spots patronized by African-American clubgoers. The irreverent gay freebie *Babble*, available at many bars and stores in Lake View, chronicles the gay and lesbian party circuit. Get hip to the underground party scene by studying the flyers and note cards dropped off at **Tower Records** (2301 N. Clark St.) or **Untitled** (2657 N. Clark St.), a hip-hop and rave clothing store in Lincoln Park, or any trendy shop in Lake View or Wicker Park.

Liquor Laws and Drinking Hours

The city liquor-license commissioner has been stingy about awarding new liquor licenses, putting the brakes on a few nightlife districts that turn into veritable street carnivals on weekends. The bar universe is divided into two constellations: those bars with 2am licenses, which allow the taps to flow until 3am on Saturday, and those late-night destinations with 4am licenses, which stay open until 5am Sunday morning and are welcome refuges after the others have closed. In the listings below, we note any place with a 4am license. And remember, Chicago may be home of the blues, but this ain't New Orleans, where revelers tote their beverages in the streets. Drink up before you continue your pub crawl.

The Lowdown

Dressing up... Even if you're not a grown-up, it's fun to dress up like one every once in a while. **Coq d'Or** in the old-money Drake Hotel offers a casual, clubby atmosphere with a crowd of out-of-towners and after-hours business people—for years Buddy Charles has charmed them here on the piano. It's the living room of your dreams at **Seasons Lounge** in the posh Four Seasons Hotel, with well-upholstered furnishings and an outstanding view of North Michigan Avenue from the seventh floor. The **Signature Lounge**, on the ninety-fifth floor of the Hancock Center, has an even better view of the city. You won't even notice the sky-high drink prices. If you're already in the neighborhood to ascend the Sears Tower, make it an evening by stopping next door at **Yvette Wintergarden**, a plush lower-level jazz room.

Calling all slackers... Artists, wannabe rock gods, and pierced-and-tattooed copy-shop employees have created their own exile community in the 'hoods of Wicker Park and Bucktown. At the epicenter is **Rainbo Club**, an unassuming former Polish social club with alternative cachet and a reputation as a hangout for touring rockers. If you can't be bothered with the chain-smoking crowd blocking the door, head over to **The Empty Bottle**, the reigning Ukrainian Village outpost of cool, where you'll find legions of purposefully disheveled twentysomething regulars roosting among the second-hand couches and bar stools.

CHICAGO | NIGHTLIFE

You've got a lot of seating options at **Danny's Tavern**, a warren of rooms in an old Victorian house. Try the faux-fur–covered stools by the bar, or settle into a couch in one of the black-lit rooms in the back. The loafing vibe has been imported to Lake View at **Delilah's**, a dark, somewhat sinister bar where the bartender spins country classics on Wednesdays, and Urge Overkill's drummer Blackie O takes the helm on Sunday nights. A kinder, gentler breed packs the roomy beer garden with its outdoor pool table at **Sheffield's** in Lake View (now if they'd only replenish the critters in the megasize ant farm inside).

Dance fever... Flashy nightclubs open here every few years in spooky warehouses on the edge of downtown, and, yes, it is fun the first few months. The rest of the story is predictable: Carloads of suburbanites join the fun. Scenesters grow bored and flee. Fun is over. One of the first warehouse dance palaces put through the paces was **Shelter**, a labyrinth of theatrically designed rooms illuminated by candles and lava lamps. Desperate gimmicks like outdoor above-ground swimming pools have been added, trying to stir up some excitement again. A line of anxious trendsters snakes down the street on weekends in front of **Crobar**, but the cavernous club's dark Gotham City decor and sprawling dance floor—one of the biggest around—makes the wait worth it. You'll feel like you've stumbled into somebody's loft party at **Red Dog**, a Wicker Park dance club where a diverse aggregation of youngsters grooves to house and hip-hop music on the long, narrow dance floor. Sophisticated African-American patrons discoing at **The Clique** take the downtown club's upscale dress code to heart—if they don't, the tuxedoed bouncers will let them know. It's mesmerizing to watch well-heeled couples at **Club Inta's**, an upscale River North club, dance seemingly choreographed moves to infectious Latin rhythms performed live by a full band on Saturdays. At **Whiskey River**, it takes an equal measure of two-stepping skill to promenade around the dance floor. Don't be put off by **Neo**'s long alley entrance—you'll be surrounded by scrub-faced young professionals out for a nostalgic dose of early eighties tunes at this compact Lincoln Park dance den. Happily, the gay disco **Berlin** has managed to retain its free-wheeling spirit after more than a decade in business, luring nongays and suburbanites on the weekends to a hospitable dance floor inexplicably able to absorb ever more spinning and twirling.

Places to hear live rock... Local acts like Smashing Pumpkins, Liz Phair, and Veruca Salt, before they got too big for their britches, all played the stage at **Metro** (see Entertainment) in Wrigleyville, the city's preeminent rock venue. Owner Joe Shanahan has expanded his franchise into music-laden Wicker Park at **Double Door**, a former biker bar turned rock club with high pressed-tin ceilings and a beautiful long bar. The other major rock outlet in the area is **The Empty Bottle**, an artily decorated club (the light fixtures are made of old paint cans) that usually books bands with impeccable indie credentials. **Lounge Ax** (see Entertainment) in the DePaul neighborhood still sells out for big-name alternative rock performers.

Places to hear live blues... Chicago's famous for smoky blues joints where legendary musicians jam seven nights a week, practically until dawn. At **Kingston Mines**, a fixture for three decades in Lincoln Park, two stages keep the music going without interruption. Female vocalists like Gloria Hardiman and Big Time Sarah are the specialty of **Blue Chicago**, a handsome forties-style room in River North

Where not to hear the blues

For starters, the famed *Rush Street* nightlife zone really isn't Rush Street at all, but *Division Street* between Rush and Dearborn. Rush Street itself used to be home to a slew of great cabarets, bars, clubs, and restaurants—the center of Chicago's nightlife scene—which then spread to Division Street. Eventually the places on Rush closed as the street gentrified. The area is still referred to as Rush Street, but unless your idea of a good time is a keg party, there's no real rush to be found. Division is lined with the most hokey bars—crowded, loud, and obnoxious, with beefy bouncers manning most of the doorways. Wet T-shirt contests, hot legs contests, dollar nights, you name it, it's all depressingly here. But maybe Division Street is going the way of Rush Street—in the last few years a Starbucks coffee shop has opened, as has a huge Gap (the hundred millionth one in Chicago), and other stores that hopefully will squish out the bars. There are better bars to be found, believe me.

CHICAGO | NIGHTLIFE

with a die-hard crowd. Chicago's Queen of the Blues has lent her name to **Koko Taylor's Chicago Blues** on Division Street, which only sees her belting onstage about twice a year. On the southern edge of downtown, **Buddy Guy's Legends** welcomes both local talents and established stars (Dr. John, Junior Wells, and Buddy Guy himself) to its spartan blues room. White college students and black locals share the ramshackle digs of the legendary **Checkerboard Lounge**, where pros like Magic Slim and the Teardrops take the stage seven nights a week.

Places to hear live jazz... The Green Mill, a deco-ish Uptown club once owned by one of Al Capone's henchmen, has made a name for itself as one of the liveliest jazz venues in town. Downtown in the Blackstone Hotel's faded ballroom, **Joe Segal's Jazz Showcase** presents the city's most ambitious lineup of both national and local musicians. A little farther south is **The Cotton Club**, a classy jazz room that has boosted the careers of a number of talents (including saxophonist Art Porter and R&B superstar R. Kelly). The white-walled room decorated with huge photos of jazz legends draws a predominantly black clientele. The **Bop Shop** brings jazz to a younger audience, with an enterprising lineup in an off-the-beaten-path location in Wicker Park. The most intimate jazz room in town, the **Underground Wonder Bar**, draws musicians looking for a pick-up gig on their way home for the night.

Sports and suds... For starters, take your pick of most any place along North Clark Street near Wrigley Field, most notably **Cubby Bear**, which fills up with fans before and after Cubs games, or slick, pennant-festooned **Hi-Tops Cafe**, which overflows onto the sidewalk during Saturday afternoon gridiron games. The prototypical sports scene is **Gamekeepers**, a wood-paneled Lincoln Park bar with every game going on its multitudinous screens. For a more downtown crowd, try **The Hunt Club**, an upscale Rush Street saloon with wide-screen TVs and a large open bar in its airy main room.

Lesbian chic... Chicago's contributions to lesbian chic show their painted lips at the disco **Paris Dance**, a former bait shop, elevated by a softly lit interior decorated with Tamara de Lempicka–inspired murals of fantastically shaped glam gals. No attitude or outfit is necessary to mix with the locals at **The Closet**, your standard-issue neighborhood dive with window-side stools and the famously bleached coif of the bartender.

Where the boys are... An evening stroll down a ten-block strip of North Halsted Street—the Main Street of the lakeside gay enclave known as Boys' Town—will keep any curious club crawler occupied late into the night. Excursions often start from **Roscoe's Tavern and Cafe**, an inviting saloon populated by clean-cut guys in pressed button-down shirts, then continue on to **Sidetrack**, a sleek video bar where the patrons ogle each other as much as the ubiquitous TV monitors. **Gentry**, located in a handsome Gold Coast townhouse, is a popular happy-hour destination with an older, suit-and-tie crowd. Despite its name, **Big Chicks** has been overrun by a rabidly faithful clientele of gay men, drawn to the sparkling two-room Uptown bar by 50-cent midnight shots, a high camp jukebox, and an appreciative staff. Way downtown from the gay ghetto, **The Generator** in **River West** lures a crowd to its sprawling wooden dance floor, packed with African-American men and a handful of women. On the Halsted Strip, **Vortex** draws a youngish, panracial mix of men and women to its maze of bars and dance floors and occasionally brings in national touring disco divas. Located below the Belmont el station, **Berlin** hasn't shown any signs of tiring as one of the city's reigning danceterias.

Neighborhood spots downtown and near North Side... If you're staying in the Loop, you'll have to venture a little farther afield if you don't want to spend the evening in a soulless hotel lobby bar. One downtown exception is **Kitty O'Shea's** at the Chicago Hilton and Towers, a bar that manifests its Irish theme with actual Irish bartenders and traditional Irish music. An authentic spot that has weathered the onslaught of tourists pretty well is **Billy Goat Tavern**, a legendary Chicago dive tucked away on lower North Michigan Avenue (immortalized as the "cheezeburger, cheezeburger" joint on "Saturday Night Live"; see Dining). Another little gem, though not quite as rough, is **The Gold Star Sardine Bar**, a closet-size cabaret hidden in the marbelized lobby of a vintage Streeterville high-rise. In the Rush Street area, young professionals flock to **The Hunt Club**, a ritzy Gold Coast sports bar that adds to the summer street life with its outdoor cafe and rooftop terrace.

Neighborhood spots in Lincoln Park/Old Town... Just as its name suggests, **John Barleycorn Memorial Pub** is a generously proportioned English-style pub that exudes historic charm. The century-old building has functioned as a bar for much of its life, from twenties speakeasy to favored watering hole of John Dillinger. Pleasant, yet considerably less authentic, is the retro Southern roadhouse **Stanley's Kitchen & Tap**, where there are as many fraternity and sorority types underfoot as cracked peanut shells littering the floor. The same well-behaved future leaders of America seem to come unhinged when they step into **The Big Nasty**, a teeming den of hooligans toting around 22-ounce beers.

Neighborhood spots in Lake View/Wrigleyville... If you want to duck the army of dudes donning turned-back baseball caps on North Clark Street, the **Ginger Man Tavern** provides a sanctuary behind its big picture windows. A hipper, more laid-back clientele than you'll find in the rest of the neighborhood clusters around tightly packed tables and chairs up front or shoots pool in the larger back room. TVs are tuned to *Melrose Place* on Mondays at **Hi-Tops Cafe**, where devotees of the Fox soap congregate. The airy front bar at **Schubas Tavern** gets deafeningly loud on weekends when concertgoers attending shows in the back room converge with neighborhood regulars. An extensive beer list and an array of rooms to settle into with friends make **Sheffield's Wine and Beer Garden** a dependable gathering place. An important anchor on the gay scene is **Roscoe's Tavern and Cafe**, a neighborhood haunt often disparaged by snobs who'll still buy a drink and survey the scene to see who's hanging out.

Neighborhood spots on the South Side... Travelers arriving at Midway Airport might consider stopping by **Baby Doll Polka Club**, where local polkaholics have been gathering for forty years. A Hyde Park institution, **Jimmy's Woodlawn Tap**, is a grungy grad student bar that hosts occasional improv performances and prose readings. Operated by the same family for generations, **Schaller's Pump** is the quintessential Bridgeport bar, where locals gather for dinner on vinyl red-checked table-cloths and sit around watching the Sox or the ten o'clock news. One of the last vestiges of a vibrant South Side blues scene is the **Checkerboard Lounge**, where regulars sit in the ramshackle chairs alongside college students.

For people who wouldn't be caught dead drinking a Bud... The chalkboard menu at **Sheffield's Wine and Beer Garden** boasts 60-plus offerings, most of them regional microbrews. This Lake View tavern guides your choice with one recommended and one "bad" beer of the month and a free glossary of beer terms (from aftertaste to wheat beer). Take a peek at the brewing equipment on your way into **Goose Island Brewery**, the city's original microbrewery, which features a fermented repertoire of forty rotating microbrews. They're always ready for a special occasion at **Pops for Champagne**: The elegant Lincoln Park music room stocks more than 125 kinds of sparkling wines. You can buy vino by the glass, or you can train your palate by sampling flights of Merlot, Chardonnay, and Pinot Noir at **Webster's Wine Bar** in Lincoln Park, which provides place mats labeled with the names of each of the four or five samples.

CHICAGO | NIGHTLIFE

The Index

Adagio. Japanese spareness is the aesthetic inspiration for this upscale bar and restaurant popular with the Lincoln Park jet set. Live jazz or lite rock nightly. In summer, the leafy garden patio is a pleasure.... *Tel 312/787–0400. 923 W. Weed St., North and Clybourn el stop. $5 cover for live music Thur–Sun.*

Baby Doll Polka Club. Polka thrives in this chaletlike club where middle-aged men spin their big-haired gals around the small dance floor. It's across the road from Midway Airport—you can listen to "Roll Out the Barrel" while planes roll down the runway. The house band, the Merry Makers, plays on weekends.... *Tel 312/582–9706. 6102 S. Central Ave. Midway el stop, transfer to #63 W bus.*

Berlin. A small room, really, but this gay disco maximizes its real estate with wall-to-wall stimuli: a mix of music from New Wave to techno, nonstop videos, mirrors to see how the light is flattering you, go-go boys atop platforms, and a colorful pansexual crowd.... *Tel 312/348–4975. 954 W. Belmont Ave., Belmont el stop. Until 4am. $3 cover weekends.*

Big Chicks. An out-of-the-way alternative to the Halsted Street party parade, this popular two-room Uptown bar feels like a crowded kitchen at a lively house party on weekends. The owner's idiosyncratic art collection alone makes it worth a visit. Free Sunday afternoon buffets and a DJ spinning dance tunes in the cabaret room on weekends.... *Tel 312/728–5511. 5024 N. Sheridan Rd., Argyle el stop.*

The Big Nasty. A spartan playroom, built for abuse, where drunken post-college types get unapologetically messy. Upstairs there's a sports bar and dance floor; bands play on weekends.... *Tel 312/404–1535. 2242 N. Lincoln Ave., Fullerton el stop. Open Wed–Sun, $2 cover Fri Sat.*

Blue Chicago. This fine blues club recently relocated from a spare room in the Rush Street vicinity to this spiffy joint near the tourist-entertainment bazaar on Ontario Street. Paying cover here admits you to its sister club, Blue Chicago on Clark (536 N. Clark St., closed Mon), two blocks south.... *Tel 312/642–6261. 736 N. Clark St., Chicago and State el stop. Closed Sun. $5–7 cover.*

Bop Shop. An eclectic booking policy gives a boost to emerging local talent at this boho jazz club. Always something brewing, including poetry and occasional theater.... *Tel 312/235–3232. 1807 W. Division St., Division el stop. $3–15 cover.*

Buddy Guy's Legends. The Grammy-winning Chicago guitarist owns this simple, acoustically superb blues hall that also serves up Louisiana-style soul food.... *Tel 312/427–0333. 754 S. Wabash Ave., Jackson and State el stop. $5–16 cover.*

Checkerboard Lounge. Once the heart of a vibrant South Side blues scene, the comfortably decrepit 25-year-old room is a mecca for locals, tourists, and rock stars alike. Music begins nightly at 9:30pm. A secure parking lot is available across the street for minimal or no charge.... *Tel 312/624–3240. 423 E. 43rd St. $3–5 cover.*

The Clique. Something for everyone at this African-American entertainment complex: a relaxed jazz lounge and comedy club downstairs, or jammed discotheque upstairs.... *Tel 312/326–0274. 2347 S. Michigan Ave., Cermak el stop. Until midnight weeknights, 4am weekends with $10 cover.*

The Closet. Lesbians in the neighborhood call this unpretentious video bar home, but gay men and straights mix here too. The jukebox and darts provide a few distractions, but the best seats in this basic black box are the bar stools facing Broadway.... *Tel 312/477–8533. 3325 N. Broadway, Belmont el stop. Until 4am.*

Club Inta's. Elegance translates into sensuality at this stylish nightclub, from the sweet eucalyptus scent in the air to the leggy women in tiny black dresses and men in handsome silk shirts and trousers. The halogen-lit room draws a heavily Latino and African American clientele to its jazz, mambo, and salsa nights; free after-work buffets and dance lessons for the salsa-impaired.... *Tel 312/664–6880. 308 W. Erie St., Chicago el stop. $5–10 cover; min. age 23, some nights 25.*

Coq d'Or. Late nights, customers settle into the wood-paneled bar's red Naughahyde banquettes or crowd around the small piano.... *Tel 312/787–2200. 140 E. Walton St. (Drake Hotel), Chicago and State el stop.*

The Cotton Club. Named for the renowned Harlem club, this downtown jazz spot has an upscale African-American following. The Monday open mike draws big crowds for what are usually some impressive vocalists. Or escape to the dance club in back.... *Tel 312/341–9787. 1710 S. Michigan Ave., Roosevelt Rdo. el stop. Until 4am. $7–10 cover weekends.*

Crobar. This multilevel dance factory presents an array of perches for spying on the roiling sea of bodies on the dance floor—adventure-seeking yuppies and suburbanites disguised in their best alternative rags. A second-story bar pro-

CHICAGO | NIGHTLIFE

vides relief from the ear-splitting tunes. Poorly placed restrooms near the entrance force you to push against a stream of fresh arrivals.... *Tel 312/413–7000. 1543 N. Kingsbury St., North and Clybourn el stop. Until 4am. Open Wed–Sun. $3–10 cover.*

Cubby Bear. One of Wrigleyville's bigger clubs, this playpen absorbs multitudes who come to carouse after games and on weekends. The spacious, multifloor-space keeps them busy with pool, darts, and rock bands.... *Tel 312/327–1662. 1059 W. Addison St., Addison el stop. $5–10 cover.*

Danny's Tavern. A laid-back Bucktown bar in a two-story house. Good beer selection.... *Tel 312/489–6457. 1951 W. Dickens St., Damen el stop.*

Delilah's. Dark and alternative. Find your way to the bar and you'll be greeted with a choice of fifty beers and even more whiskey; follow the exposed electrical wiring upstairs for pinball and pool. On Sundays the Psychotronic Film Society screens locally produced indie films.... *Tel 312/472–2771. 2771 N. Lincoln Ave., Diversey el stop.*

Double Door. A new player on the Wicker Park rock scene, the dark, velvet-draped club has plenty of room for standing near the stage and balcony in the back for early arrivals. Pool tables downstairs.... *Tel 312/489–3160. 1572 N. Milwaukee Ave., Damen el stop. $5–10 cover.*

Drink. Four large rooms for dancing, sitting in swings, and standing around looking at your cohorts: a young, hip crowd looking for big fun on the town. Flavored vodkas and beverages served in buckets and Mason jars make the club's name operative. Live world-beat music once a week.... *Tel 312/441–0818. 541 W. Fulton St., Clinton and Lake el stop. Until 4am. Closed Sun–Mon. $3 cover after 9pm Thur–Sat.*

The Empty Bottle. A grunge clubhouse for twentysomethings in Ukrainian Village. Bands take the stage later in the week, but you can still converse comfortably over the noise with your buddies at the front of the bar or in the pool room. Even better, try the pasta at the attached late-night diner, Bite.... *Tel 312/276–3600. 1035 N. Western Ave.; Western el stop, transfer to #49 Western bus. $5–7 cover.*

Gamekeepers. Television monitors never leave your field of vision at this Lincoln Park sports bar. Kitchen snacks until midnight.... *Tel 312/549–0400. 345 W. Armitage Ave., Armitage el stop. Until 4am. $3 cover for occasional bands.*

The Generator. Nonstop infusions of house music keep the big dance floor at this black gay disco busy. The unadorned warehouse features a long bar and several pool tables.... *Tel 312/243–8889. 306 N. Halsted St. Clinton el stop. Until 4am. Open Wed–Sun. $2–5 cover.*

Gentry. The original location on Rush Street is a cruisy piano bar with a front room dominated by a huge chandelier and a basement video bar that draws younger patrons. Regulars flock to the cabaret room, where music starts at 5pm. The newer Halsted Street outlet is smaller and less formal.... *Tel 312/664 1033. 712 N. Rush St., Chicago and State el stop. Tel 312/348–1053. 3320 N. Halsted St., Belmont el stop.*

Ginger Man Tavern. This unpretentious Wrigleyville bar offers a nice alternative to the frenzied sports bar area. Amenities include a huge selection of mircobrews on tap, a blues/country/rock jukebox, and plenty of elbow room for shooting pool in the back room.... *Tel 312/549–2050. 3740 N. Clark St., Addison el stop.*

The Gold Star Sardine Bar. They certainly got the name right: This Streeterville jazz cabaret will make you feel like a sardine. But the intimate setting gets you up close to the performers.... *Tel 312/664–4215. 680 N. Lake Shore Dr., Chicago and State el stop. Closed Sun. 2-drink min. $5–7 cover, Thur–Sat.*

Goose Island Brewery. Vintage advertising signage provides the visual backdrop for this brew-pub restaurant with a handsome rectangular front bar. Choose from eight beers brewed on the premises.... *Tel 312/915–0071. 1800 N. Clybourn Ave., North and Clybourn el stop.*

The Green Mill Cocktail Lounge. This movie-set–perfect Uptown jazz club draws an eclectic crowd (all ages, classes, and races) to this gritty neighborhood to nestle into cozy velvet booths and perch along the wonderful deco bar to listen to swing, big band, and torch singers. Sundays feature the

the long-running Poetry Slam.... *Tel 312/878–5552. 4802 N. Broadway, Lawrence el stop. Until 4am. $3– 7 cover.*

Hi-Tops Cafe. A nicely renovated former warehouse, this popular Wrigleyville saloon has a large bar up front, leading to an airy raftered room dominated by a big-screen TV. Upstairs there's a slightly more subdued lounge.... *Tel 312/348–0009. 3551 N. Sheffield Ave., Addison el stop. $3–5 cover for bands on weekends.*

The Hunt Club. A hot spot in its early eighties heyday, this upscale nightclub has a new Gold Coast location. Mingle in the main bar or sneak away to the cigar lounge upstairs or the sunken pool room.... *Tel 312/988–7887. 1100 N. State St., Chicago and State el. Until 4am.*

Iggy's. Painted in deep, dark colors, this swank late-night eatery and bar attracts a painfully hip crowd from the surrounding warehouse neighborhood and beyond. Art films are screened on the back patio in the summer.... *Tel 312/829–4449. 700 N. Milwaukee Ave., Chicago el stop. Until 4am.*

Jimmy's Woodlawn Tap. A gritty University of Chicago hangout for smoking, drinking, and intellectualizing.... *Tel 312/643–5516. 1172 E. 55th St.*

Joe Segal's Jazz Showcase. A tuxedoed staff attends to you at one of the city's leading jazz clubs.... *Tel 312/427 4846. 636 S. Michigan Ave. (Blackstone Hotel), Harrison el stop. $10–20 cover.*

John Barleycorn Memorial Pub. The two rooms of this stately Lincoln Park bar are decorated with antique sailing vessels and nautical-themed artwork. Spacious outdoor patio in the summer.... *Tel 312/348–8899. 658 W. Belden St., Fullerton el stop.*

Kingston Mines. With two large rooms, this Chicago institution on the blues scene heats up with capacity crowds.... *Tel 312/477–4646. 2548 N. Halsted St., Fullerton el stop. Until 4am. $8–10 cover.*

Kitty O'Shea's. Traditional Irish duos and trios perform every night at this hotel bar.... *Tel 312/922–4400, ext 4454. 720 S. Michigan Ave. (Chicago Hilton), Harrison and State el stop.*

Koko Taylor's Chicago Blues. A welcome change of pace along Division Street, this newcomer jams all night with local and out-of-town talent. Local musicians are invited to perform with the house band on Sundays.... *Tel 312/337–2583. 7 W. Division St., Clark and Division el stop. Until 4am. $3–10.*

Neo. An ancient club with 16 years under its belt, this dependable dance lair attracts college kids and clean-cut locals. Remember your black eyeliner for the weekly goth night.... *Tel 312/528 2622. 2350 N. Clark St., Fullerton el stop. Until 4am. $2–5 cover.*

Paris Dance. From the prominent sign to the parking lot out front, there's nothing discreet about this elegant lesbian disco. The modest dance floor is ringed by a bar and a small cafe serving sandwiches and desserts. A dressed-up crowd pours in on Saturdays.... *Tel 312/769–0602. 1122 W. Montrose Ave., Montrose el stop. $5 cover Sat.*

Pops for Champagne. This sophisticated Lake View nightclub features pages and pages of champagnes, as well as an array of wines and spirits. Next door the owner has opened Star Bar, going for a younger, more casual crowd.... *Tel 312/472–1000. 2934 N. Sheffield Ave., Fullerton el stop. Most nights $5–9 cover.*

Rainbo Club. The art students clear out on Fridays to make way for slumming yuppies checking out the Wicker Park scene. There's even a photo booth in back to accommodate tourists. Cluster around the bar or sink into one of the clubby round booths. A live music space is slated to open in 1996.... *Tel 312/489–5999. 1150 N. Damen Ave., Damen el stop.*

Red Dog. This sweat-inducing dance pad surveys the burgeoning nightlife scene at North, Milwaukee, and Damen through large second-story windows. A bordello-red loft space above the dance floor offers space to hang out while rehydrating from a dance-floor outing. Thanks for the complimentary pitchers of ice water on the bar.... *Tel 312/278–1009. 1958 W. North Ave. (entrance in alley), Damen el stop. Until 4am. Closed Sun and Tue. $3–5 cover.*

Roscoe's Tavern and Cafe. There's something for everyone at this gay bar: antique-filled front room with a large flowing bar; billiard area; a dark dance floor in back. Things we could

CHICAGO | NIGHTLIFE

do without: gong-show karaoke and communal Star Trek viewing.... *Tel 312/281–3355. 3356 N. Halsted St., Belmont el stop. $2 cover Sat.*

Schaller's Pump. Check out the peephole on a side door for signs of this century-old bar's Prohibition past. Sox fans show up during baseball season to pick from a menu of burgers and steaks (and a corned beef and cabbage special on Thursdays).... *Tel 312/847–9378. 3714 S. Halsted St., 35th St. el stop.*

Schubas Tavern. Live music is the focus of this old Schlitz saloon, but the main bar is a gregarious gathering spot for young people in the neighborhood. Food til 10pm.... *Tel 312/525–2508. 3159 N. Southport Ave., Belmont el stop. $4–15 for live music.*

Seasons Lounge. The large bar area at the Four Seasons Hotel is a restful oasis with a huge fireplace and comfy furnishings. A pianist supplies soft background music during the week, a jazz trio entertains on weekends. There's also a paneled English study for cigar chomping.... *Tel 312/280–8800. 120 Delaware Place, Chicago and State el stop.*

Sheffield's Wine and Beer Garden. It doesn't look like much from the street, but the corner bar accommodates a post-college crowd in a series of spaces given over to pool, occasional theater and live music, and the popular beer garden.... *Tel 312/281–4989. 3258 N. Sheffield Ave., Belmont el stop. $1 cover weekends for beer garden.*

Shelter. The vintage neon hotel sign above the main bar at this River West nightclub appropriately admits "Tourists Welcome." A fresh-faced, multiracial crowd with large contingents from the hinterlands comes to dance, dressed in urban chic. House music propels the dance floor. Clamber your way into the velvet-dripping VIP Paramount Room to plop down on upholstered loveseats beneath five humongous chandeliers.... *Tel 312/648–5500. 564 W. Fulton St., Clinton el stop. Open Thur–Sat until 4am. $10 cover.*

Sidetrack. A place to go when you're alone (or don't want to talk to the people you're with), this high-tech gay bar babysits some of the city's best-looking men with endless video clips of Broadway musicals, Madonna tunes, and "Rose-anne" episodes. Sleek, stainless-steel bathrooms; rooftop deck open in warmer months.... *Tel 312/477–9189. 3349 N. Halsted St., Belmont el stop.*

Stanley's Kitchen & Tap. This lively neighborhood hot spot for Lincoln Park youngsters boasts a strong selection of bourbons.... *Tel 312/642–0007. 1970 N. Lincoln Ave., Sedgwick el stop.*

Underground Wonder Bar. It's clear that everybody really loves music in this funky little jazz club. Three performances a night by an eclectic roster of local musicians and vocalists, including owner Lonie Walker and her Janis Joplin imitation.... *Tel 312/266–7761. 10 E. Walton St., Chicago and State el stop. Until 4am. $2–6 cover.*

Vortex. The biggest dance floor on Halsted Street is a popular late-night destination for a conglomeration of young multicultural partyers. A two-level labyrinth of rooms offers karaoke, videos, and catwalk views of the teeming masses below. Check out the club's ever-changing window displays.... *Tel 312/975–6622. 3631 N. Halsted St., Addison el stop. Until 4am. $5–7 cover.*

Webster's Wine Bar. There's an odd assortment of chairs and tables in this Lincoln Park bar, which caters to both the wine connoisseur and neophyte. The back library, stocked with old books and encyclopedias, is given over to cigar smoking.... *Tel 312/868–0608. 1480 W. Webster Ave., Fullerton el stop. Closed Mon.*

Whiskey River. Enthusiastic Reba and Clint wannabes duded up in hats and boots put on a spirited floor show to a DJ's mix of C&W music at this high-concept club. Big-name acts hit the stage a few times each month. Free dance lessons nightly.... *Tel 312/528–3400. 1997 N. Clybourn Ave., North and Clybourn el stop. Open Tue–Sat. $2–5 cover.*

Yvette Wintergarden. An older, well-dressed crowd shows up at this French restaurant to see local jazz trios and occasional special guests.... *Tel 312/408–1242. 311 S. Wacker Dr., Quincy el stop. Until midnight. Closed Sun.*

CHICAGO | NIGHTLIFE

enterta

7

nment

Forget any
notions you may
have about the
Midwest as hope-
lessly square—
there are plenty of
boundary-pushing

artists in Chicago. The stock of creative folk is constantly renewed by students coming out of the universities and emigrants from all over the Midwest, and not everybody who makes it big here immediately jets off to the coasts—a lot of actors, musicians, and dancers, like regular non-artistic newcomers, find it such a *manageable* place to live that they end up staying. Though big Broadway imports quickly sell out and often run for months, Chicagoans don't hold their breath for out of towners to grace their stages: the city hosts enough home-grown shows to keep more than 100 theater companies busy. In some ways, theaters have replaced bars as a late-night alternative: many of the more offbeat, off-Loop shows don't start until 10:30pm (or later), and some even allow alcoholic beverages, if they don't happen to sell it themselves. Five professional sports teams also confer a certain kind of prestige on the city, while highbrow, world-class institutions like the Lyric Opera and the Chicago Symphony have given Chicago the serious outside validation it craves as the perennial second (now third) city.

Sources

The city's main alternative paper, the *Reader*, gets much of its heft from voluminous reviews, listings, and advertisements for concerts and performing arts. Published on Thursdays, the tabloid prides itself on providing the most complete theater coverage in the city, reviewing even the most obscure productions. More extensive profiles and analyses are carried in the *Chicago Tribune's* daily arts section and its "Friday" entertainment pullout. The competing *Sun-Times* isn't mandatory reading, but worth a look in its Friday "Weekend Plus" and Sunday "Showcase" sections. Look to the entertainment pullout section in *N'Digo*, a free bimonthly tabloid, for an African American perspective; *¡Exito!* is a Spanish-language free weekly that offers a weekly calendar of events of Latino-related events; and the city's predominant lesbian and gay newspaper, *Windy City Times*, offers its own spin on both gay and non-gay events. Tune into **WBEZ** (91.5 FM), the local National Public Radio affiliate, for erudite discussions of the latest happenings, during arts programs aired Friday and Saturday afternoons.

Getting Tickets

We're not sure what bothers us more about **Ticketmaster**: the teeth-gnashing service charges or the way the telephone ticket reps repeat the logistics of your event ad nauseum. But if you're looking for tickets to concerts, Broadway imports, or sporting events, the monolithic ticket agent is still the only game in town. You can charge tickets on a credit card by calling 312/559–1212, or pay with cash only at one of their outlets at **Carson Pirie Scott & Co.** (1 S. State St.), **Tower Records** (2301 N. Clark St.), or the three **Hot Tix** locations (see below). If you're willing to pay even bigger bucks, you can get tickets to just about any event by thumbing through the Yellow Pages for one of more than forty **ticket brokers** (all must be licensed by the state). Two reputable ones are **Tower Ticket Service** (tel 312/454–1300) and **Gold Coast Tickets** (tel 312/644–6446). They take credit card orders by phone and deliver overnight or the same day (of course, adding various commissions based on availability, demand, etc.). Less legitimate, and a misdemeanor in Illinois, is selling scalped tickets. But take a walk around Wrigley Field or the United Center on a game day and you'll see that the law hasn't exactly driven the illegal ticket trade underground. Be wary of what you buy on the street: you don't want to find that you've bought a ticket to last week's game. You don't always have to resort to such desperate measures, especially if a theater outing is on your agenda. Besides full price Ticketmaster events, **Hot Tix** (tel 312/977–1755), run by the nonprofit **League of Chicago Theatres**, also sells half-price, day-of-show tickets to many theatrical productions, concerts, and dance performances in the city and suburbs. Available by credit card, check, or cash, tickets can be purchased in person at one of three locations:

Chicago in the movies, part 3—The Suburbs

Director/writer/producer John Hughes was responsible for a raft of movies that immortalized the lakeshore Chicago suburbs: Sixteen Candles *(1984),* The Breakfast Club *(1985),* Home Alone *(1990); in* Ferris Bueller's Day Off *(1986), an impish Matthew Broderick borrowed his pal's dad's Porsche for a joy ride into the city. The great* Ordinary People *(1980), directed by Robert Redford and starring Mary Tyler Moore, Judd Hirsch, and Timothy Hutton, was filmed mostly in affluent Lake Forest. Then, of course, there's* Risky Business *(1983), in which Tom Cruise popularized parading around in your underwear (gay bars in Chicago now have underwear parties where everyone wears nothing but their skivvies). Mike Meyers and Dana Carvey played pubescent public-access heroes in* Wayne's World *(1992), but to Chicagoans the real star was former Blackhawks hockey star Stan Mikita, who made a cameo appearance as the owner of a donut shop.*

CHICAGO | ENTERTAINMENT

the sixth level of the **Chicago Place** mall (700 N. Michigan Ave.), across from Marshall Field's in the **Loop** (108 N. State St.), and at the **City Parking Garage** in **Evanston** (1616 Sherman Ave.). Getting there early always helps ensure that you get to choose from the widest selection of shows; ticket availability varies from day to day, but most don't sell out until later in the day. The outlets are open daily, and tickets to many Sunday performances are sold on Saturday. For members, **Hot Tix by Mail** offers 40–50% discounts by mail, for up to 30 different shows every eight weeks. For a $10 annual membership, subscribers can order tickets to selected shows in advance through a bimonthly newsletter. In general, it's pretty easy to see smaller off-Loop shows simply by leaving your name on the theater's answering machine; your place usually will be guaranteed if you show up at least 15 minutes before showtime, and someone will return your call if they're already sold out. Larger theaters guarantee seats by using plastic over the phone, though you might want to save on the minimal service charge by stopping by the box office. A few theaters, including the biggest ones in town, offer discount or half-price tickets at the box office the night of the performance. Many others regularly reduce the price of admission for students and seniors.

The Lowdown

The theater establishment... Every year, scads of theater grads dream of following the trajectory of the highly regarded **Steppenwolf Theatre Company**, which was born out of a North Shore church basement in the Seventies and has settled down into its own $8 million theater complex in Lincoln Park. Many of the founding members (Gary Sinise, John Malkovitch, and "Roseanne" star Laurie Metcalf, among them) have been preoccupied with projects in New York and Hollywood, and in recent years the company has had a few local bombs and mixed results from its forays onto Broadway, after its *The Grapes of Wrath* took home two Tonys. But these perpetrators of the "in your face" Chicago acting school are still one of the most dynamic companies anywhere. The other biggie in town is the **Goodman Theatre**, the city's oldest and largest resident theater, which offers a season of crowd-pleasing plays and musicals; often premieres by the likes of David Mamet, director Frank Galati, and Edward Albee—with edgier works in its smaller studio theater. Lavish Broadway musicals trucking into town put up their tents at the **Auditorium Theatre**, a Louis Sullivan-designed architectural gem with wonderful acoustics; a 1906 vaudeville house, the **Shubert Theatre**; and a refurbished 1921 movie palace, the **Chicago Theatre**, which recently weathered a seven-month siege by Donny Osmond in Andrew Lloyd Webber's *Joseph and the Amazing Technicolor Dreamcoat*. For the works of an Englishman with more impeccable theater credentials, check out **Shakespeare Repertory**, which mounts three solid productions a year, including a freebie at the end of the summer in Grant Park.

On the fringes... The Chicago theater scene really came alive during the Eighties—you can hardly walk a block on the North Side without stumbling across a storefront theater. On any given night, a small production is guaranteed an audience of, say, eight people: actors' moms, actors' friends who are also actors, and perhaps even a few non-acting innocent bystanders. Though some of the stuff can be raw or amateurish, a few of the more original, exciting shows in town toil for months in modest, out-of-the-way theaters until a word-of-mouth buzz attracts the notice of the downtown critics and vaults the show onto a higher-profile stage. Spawning ground for Dennis Franz and Joe Mantegna, Lake View's **Organic Theater Company** has been an important player in the Chicago theater over two decades, producing original works and literary adaptations, including some offbeat sci-fi and horror-based shows. Among the next generation, **Lookingglass Theatre Company**, an ensemble of twentysomething Northwestern theater grads, has earned its media-darling status with highly physical, lyrically staged productions of literary works, as well as original works rooted in company members' personal obsessions. They even have a certified star in their founding ranks: sensitive guy David Schwimmer of NBC's sitcom "Friends." Tired of Hollywood's pillaging of old TV shows? Blame the scandalous improvisers at **Annoyance Theatre**, who still haven't lived up to (or lived down) the runaway success of their *The Real Live Brady Bunch* a few years back. One of our favorite things about this Wrigleyville theater is its goofy

CHICAGO | ENTERTAINMENT

show names (*Shake, Shake, Shake, Shake, Shake, Shake, Shake Your Ass, Brainwarp, the Baby Eater*). They claim the city's longest-running musical, *Coed Prison Sluts*, a sophomoric parody of jailhouse films—introduced as being "just like *Annie*, except she's in prison and she's a whore"—that's chockful of anal-sex jokes and other naughty pranks guaranteed to get the frat boys in the audience laughing. Much easier on delicate ears is the late-night hit *Too Much Light Makes the Baby Go Blind*, performed by the **Neo-Futurists**. They promise "30 plays in 60 minutes," an entertaining evening (Friday or Saturday at 11:30pm) with much left to chance: audience members pay $3 plus the roll of a six-sided die (therefore, $4–$9) and determine the random order of short skits by shouting out their assigned numbers to performers. The group has written more than 2,000 plays, so no evening is ever the same. It's a mixed bag at nearby **Cafe Voltaire**, a vegetarian eatery in Lake View that draws amateur playwrights and performers out of the woodwork to try out their stuff in a subterranean theater furnished with thrift store couches. Also in the neighborhood is **Bailiwick Repertory**, a busy theater space that gives young companies a chance to develop their craft. Next door is the **Theatre Building**, another rental complex that nurtured Bailiwick before it moved into its own the-ater. Wicker Park has a number of small spaces, among them the converted firehouse where **Latino Chicago Theater Company** plays to artsy theater folk rather than the local Latino community, with a repertoire emphasiz-ing Nuyorican playwrights. They toss a few Spanish phrasings into the English texts of plays by Latin writers, along with making some overtures to magical realism. It's a hike down to 75th Street for the city's most prominent African-American theater, **ETA Creative Arts**, well-respected for its topnotch staging of serious dramas by black playwrights.

Classical sounds... It's easy to slip into hyperbole when referring to the **Chicago Symphony Orchestra**, but we'll do it anyway: The 110-member body, now under the baton of musical director Daniel Barenboim, is one of the country's top orchestras, in large measure because of a peerless brass section chaired by one of the world's finest trumpeters, Adolph Herseth, and its principal horn player, Dale Clevenger. A traditionally strong wind section also makes the CSO popular among fans of Strauss, Mahler, and late Beethoven. Their home base, **Orchestra Hall**, is undergoing a major renovation that should finesse the acoustics. (People like to say that CSO founder Theodore Thomas died a few weeks after Daniel Burnham's concert hall debuted in 1905, so horrified was he by the acoustics, but don't believe them—the sound has always been just fine.) Along with the CSO, Orchestra Hall hosts a series of jazz, classical, and chamber music concerts, piano recitals, and the occasional pop singer. Also playing at Orchestra Hall, the **Chicago Civic Orchestra**, the CSO's "farm team" of students and semiprofessional musicians, has a similar repertoire, but experiments more with new works by young composers—it's easier for them to do that, since their tickets are free. The CSO shares its summer home, the pastoral North Shore music venue **Ravinia**, with visiting orchestras, chamber music ensembles, and soloists. Though the music ostensibly draws people to this idyllic, tree-covered park, there's also the competition to out-Martha-Stewart everyone else with your outdoor concert accoutrements: to bring the china or not to bring the china? The **Grant Park Music Festival**, the last free classical concert series in the country, offers afternoon concerts at the **Petrillo Music Shell** in downtown Grant Park a couple of days a week, and special evening performances by the **Grant Park Symphony Orchestra** and the **Grant Park Symphony Chorus**, composed of members of the **Lyric Opera** and other vacationing musicians. Skip the grass and move up front to avoid the amplified version of events on stage. Here's a tip: Empty seats in the season ticket-holders' section are released 15 minutes before each performance.

What's opera, doc?... You gotta love a woman who has the chutzpah to fire Luciano Pavarotti. A legend-in-the-making herself, **Lyric Opera of Chicago** boss Ardis Krainik gave the heave-ho to the superstar tenor in the late Eighties after he had cancelled one too many performances. She's done just fine without him, putting together a string of financially successful and artistically ambitious seasons from works that range from sturdy museum pieces to 20th-century operas, as well as a few experi-

CHICAGO | ENTERTAINMENT

mental pieces, just to keep audiences on their toes. They've vaulted the company into the ranks of the opera world's heavy hitters. There are no supertitles at productions of the **Chicago Opera Theater**—all its operas (mostly American works, as opposed to the Lyrics's more traditional repertory) are sung in English. Instead, they spend their bucks on professional singer-actors and fanciful costumes and sets. In its new downtown space, more comfortable seating is provided; tickets are cheaper, and easier to get, than Lyric tickets.

Men in tights... Using a variety of venues around town for its shows and festivals, Chicago dance (which usually flowers in the springtime) often gets lost in the shuffle among other performing arts. That should change in 1997 with the completion of a new mid-size $28 million **Chicago Music and Dance Theatre** downtown. Classical ballet, which has long struggled to find a foothold in Chicago, now has two companiexs: the nationally lauded **Joffrey Ballet**, which fled New York for Chicago in 1995; and **Ballet Chicago**, a blip on the cultural radar with no permanent corps of dancers and only one scheduled production in 1996. Aggressive marketing, featuring stylish Victor Skrebneski photos, has lifted the profile of globe-trotting **Hubbard Street Dance Chicago**. Guided by Broadway veteran Lou Conte, the 19-member ensemble's technical mastery has earned it star status, though its blend of jazz, ballet, and modern dance is crowd-pleasingly safe. Hubbard Street dancers often make the leap from the **River North Dance Company**, a younger, hipper troupe strong on jazz, that performs commercial, though highly skilled, MTV-inspired choreography. Vibrant tribal costumes, energetic drumming, and traditional dance stress the African and African-American experience in performances by the widely touring **Muntu Dance Theater of Chicago**. The center for modern dance in the city, the **Dance Center of Columbia College**, provides a venue for a lot of hometown performers as well as touring guest artists from around the world. If you enjoy getting close enough to feel dancers sweat, tiny **Links Hall Studio** presents sometimes great, sometimes not-so-great performances by young dancers and choreographers, as well as returning veterans.

In concert... **New World Music Theatre** is your basic theater-under-the-stars—it's fine when you feel like driving a million miles out to the suburbs and indulging in a rock concert spectacle with thousand of others. More rarefied is **Ravinia Park**, summer home of the Chicago Symphony and an eclectic menu of dance, opera, jazz, and entertainers from Mel Torme to Mary Chapin Carpenter. A mix of music, dance, and theater moves front and center at the **Skyline Stage**, a 1,500-seat open-air theater under a pristine white canopy on Navy Pier. The **Chicago International Film Festival** also screens second-run films here. Unfortunately, commotion from the nearby entertainment center can intrude at times. Before they hit stadiums (or perhaps on the long slide down), a lot of testosterone-infused rock acts come through **The Vic**, a Lake View theater dating to the teens that doubles as a second-run movie house. Another mid-size venue, **Park West**, is a more upscale nightclub that brings in an assortment of alternative rock, reggae, and jazz acts; there's not a bad seat in the house. Right up the street from Wrigley Field, **Metro** is the granddaddy of rock clubs, a former theater that's a good place to see many touring acts before they're booked into bigger venues. Get there early to claim a seat in the balcony, unless you want to join the mosh pit at center stage. The creative booking of **Lounge Ax**'s Sue Miller has made this DePaul rock club a place to check out upcoming acts, both local bands and touring artists, though popular shows pack the narrow rock room so tight that it's tough to see much of anything if you're not ensconced up front. A challenger for the same type of acts is **The Empty Bottle**, which is also home to periodic queer punk shows organized by Homocore Chicago. Tip: The best seat in the house is a raggedy couch stowed on top of a pool table. Country acts saunter through **Whiskey River Saloon**, a dancehall with a devoted clientele. You can practically make eye contact with singer-songwriters from the Austin-Nashville axis that appear on stage at **Schubas Tavern**, a former Schlitz beerhall (see Nightlife). You'll find a mix of folk, country, bluegrass, and other traditional forms at concerts sponsored by the **Old Town School of Folk Music**, the oldest training ground for folk music in the country. It is making plans to expand to larger quarters from its 300-seat house, since lately it's had to schedule larger events at other venues

CHICAGO | ENTERTAINMENT

around town. An eclectic newcomer, the **Lunar Cabaret and Full Moon Cafe**, was established by a collective of bohemian actors and performers with a dual mission: Tired of working as waitstaff at other people's restaurants, and needing a place to perform, they set up their own cabaret space for a refreshing, adventurous mix of avant-garde theater and music.

Comedy tonight... Improvisational comedy has spawned a bit of a cottage industry in Chicago. Of course, tourist magnet **Second City** looms large over the burgeoning scene, with its comedy revues skewering local politics and pop culture, capped each night by improvised sketches. The show's format—sketch, blackout, sketch—had gone stale in recent years, until the company shook things up by hiring away some of the city's best improvisers and borrowing a few tricks from other improv groups. But you'll often find more experimental stuff from a number of quick-witted newcomers. **ImprovOlympic** has energized the improv scene with long-form productions—wholesome, clean-cut twentysomethings taking improv workshops invent full-length plays from single audience suggestions. Enterprising graduates of the group often turn up with their own spin-off projects at **Cafe Voltaire**'s basement space, **Annoyance Theatre**, and the two studio spaces at the **Organic Theater Company's Greenhouse**. Another group taking up the long form is **The Free Associates**, an ensemble that hilariously sends up anything from Tennessee Williams plays *(Cast on a Hot Tin Roof)* and Brontë novels *(Blithering Heights)* to detective mysteries and TV hospital melodramas. While the standup comedy rage has (blessedly) ebbed, Raymond Lambert figured there was still something missing from the scene: he opened **All Jokes Aside** to showcase some very funny African-American and Latino comics who weren't getting gigs at other clubs in town. **Zanies** reigns as the big professional comedy club in town by hosting marquee-name comedians from TV.

The spoken word... The thriving performance and poetry scene here is noted for the number of women doing monologues. Since the demise of a legendary club called Lower Links a few years ago, performers have scattered across a number of theater spaces and clubs. They've been welcomed by The **Lunar Cabaret and Full Moon Cafe**, a homey Lake View restaurant and performance space that counts local songstress and performance artist Jenny Magnus among its owners. If you have a pen, a crisp cocktail napkin, and an urge to share your pain, that's all you need to participate in the long-running Sunday-night "Poetry Slam" at **The Green Mill** (see Nightlife), a vintage jazz club. The raucous evening features an open mike, followed by a competition pitting street poets against each other. Former champs have gone on to performance careers, but many in this democratic show go back to their drinks after the judges are through with them. **Guild Complex** sponsors a weekly poetry performance every Wednesday in Wicker Park, as well as a wide range of readings and workshops. Performance artists do off-the-wall work at **Randolph Street Gallery**, a cutting-edge art gallery that often sandwiches intimate artist-led workshops between two back-to-back weekends of performances.

Da sports... "Saturday Night Live" has made sure that Chicago will forever be linked in popular imagination with rib-eating, beer-slurping, linguistically challenged sports fans. Of course, come to think of it, in a lot of cases SNL wasn't too far off the mark. Just try making your way through one of the brats and Old Style tailgate parties in Soldier Field's parking lot before a **Bears** game. Chicago fans can be codependent in many ways—how else to explain the way Michael Jordan's 1995 return to the **Chicago Bulls** gave renewed meaning to the lives of so many citizens? Bulls fans are a fair-weather lot; they lost interest when Jordan retired in 1993, but now that he's playing again, you're lucky if you can get a seat inside the spanking-new **United Center**, the successor to the famously ear-splitting Chicago Stadium, which now rests in stadium heaven along with the old Comiskey Park, former home of the **Chicago White Sox** baseball team. Now in a new mall-like stadium, also called **Comiskey Park** ("Sox Park" to locals), the Sox traditionally attract blue-collar, South Side, and south-suburban fans. The Sox made it to the American League championship a few years ago, but the team has a fickle following. Sox fans tend to be hardcore baseball lovers, who often deride the North

Side's **Chicago Cubs** as a yuppie team. But the Cubs and **Wrigley Field**, one of baseball's oldest parks, occupy a special place in people's hearts, not only in Chicago but all over the country (thanks to cable transmitted WGN-TV). The lovable losers haven't made it to the World Series since before the second World War (even then they lost the Series), but ducking work to sit in the bleachers for an afternoon game is a summer ritual. While baseball divides the city, football brings it together: the **Chicago Bears** still enjoy the goodwill brought by NFL founder and former owner George Halas Sr.; his son, coach George "Papa Bear" Halas Jr.; and a tradition of big-name players from Dick Butkus to William "Refrigerator" Perry. It's been a few years since he led the team, but Mike Ditka, the prototype for the SNL gag, still retains the moniker "Da Coach." And then there is the cult of **Chicago Blackhawks** hockey fans—hard-working people from factory workers to CEOs—who with their impassioned vocalizing made the old Chicago Stadium a death-defyingly loud place for visiting teams. The larger United Center has diluted things a bit, but you should still observe three rules at a Blackhawks game: 1) Hate the long-time owners, the Wirtz family, and never, *never* forgive them for trading away Bobby Hull more than two decades ago; 2) When the players set up for a power play, shout "SHOOT! SHOOT!" at the top of your lungs; and 3) No matter how much the team sucks, stick by the hard-working players, knowing that you love hockey and no one else in town really cares.

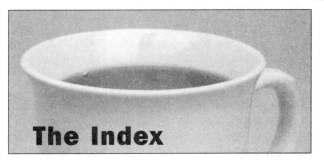

The Index

All Jokes Aside. This comedy club on the Near South Side features a predominantly African-American roster of local acts and occasional out-of-town celebs five nights a week (including three shows on Saturdays). Phone reservations are accepted, or buy tickets in person through the box office after 6pm; jeans and gym shoes are frowned upon.... *Tel 312/922–0577. 1000 S. Wabash St., Roosevelt el stop. $10—16 and two-drink minimum. Wed–Sun.*

Annoyance Theatre. Going to a performance in this troupe's wide-open warehouse theater is akin to sitting in the bleachers at Wrigley Field down the street: You can drink beer (it's BYOB), smoke, and otherwise misbehave without disturbing the gross-out antics onstage.... *Tel 312/929–6200. 3747 N. Clark St., Addison el stop. Tickets $5–10 (no reservations).*

Auditorium Theatre. The original home of the symphony and the opera, Adler and Sullivan's 4,000-seat masterpiece offers the finest acoustics in the city. These days it often hosts touring Broadway blockbusters.... *Tel 312/559–2900 (Ticketmaster Arts Line). 50 E. Congress Pkwy., Jackson and State el stop.*

Bailiwick Repertory. The stage lights rarely go dark in the complex's three theater spaces, with a constant stream of adventurous plays opening here.... *Tel 312/883–1090. 1229 W. Belmont Ave., Belmont el stop. $15–20.*

Ballet Chicago. This small classical ballet company's precarious situation is even shakier now that the Joffrey Ballet (see below) has come to town.... *Tel 312/251–8838. Offices at 185 N. Wabash Ave., suite 2300. Tickets $10–40.*

Cafe Voltaire. It's a crapshoot quality-wise for the independently produced shows fermenting in the basement of this veggie

CHICAGO | ENTERTAINMENT

restaurant. But there's plenty to choose from: Shows are scheduled seven nights a week, with two to three different shows back-to-back on weekends.... *Tel 312/528–3136. 3231 N. Clark St., Belmont el stop. Tickets $3–10 (first-come, first-seated).*

Chicago Bears. Season tickets passed down through the generations have contributed to years of sold-out games at Soldier Field. If you miss the early summer offering of single tickets, your best bets are going through a ticket broker, showing up at the game hoping to find a few (scalped) extras, or packing a parka for a frigid late-season game when saner fans stay home by the TV.... *Tel 708/615–2327. Soldier Field, Lake Shore Dr. and 16th St., Roosevelt el stop. $30–50. Aug–Dec.*

Chicago Blackhawks. The defense-oriented Blackhawks have made the playoffs several times in recent years, but a poor draft over the last decade has kept the team in the NHL's second tier. Still, don't think of showing up to root for the other team. Just don't.... *Tel 312/559–1212 (Ticketmaster). United Center, 1901 W. Madison St. $15–75. Sept–Apr.*

Chicago Bulls. Just another NBA team with a forward named Mike and a bunch of other guys who've won the championship two or three times. Tickets are nearly impossible to get, even in the team's roomy new digs.... *Tel 312/455–4000. United Center, 1901 W. Madison St. $15–65. Oct–June.*

Chicago Civic Orchestra. This training body of the Chicago Symphony Orchestra, and a stepping-stone to other major professional orchestras, performs with many of the same conductors in frequent sold-out concerts at Orchestra Hall. Tickets are free, but must be reserved in advance.... *Tel 312/435–6666. 220 W. Michigan Ave., Jackson el stop. Sept–June.*

Chicago Cubs. They've pretty much been in a slump for the last half-century, but no matter—the bleachers are filled every game, day or night, with fans drawn by Wrigley Field's ivy-covered outfield, manually operated scoreboard, and the legendary announcer Harry Caray.... *Tel 312/404–*

2827. *Wrigley Field, 1060 W. Addison St., Addison el stop. $6–15. Apr–Oct.*

Chicago Opera Theater. Opera for the rest of us. The company emphasizes American performers and composers and uses a mid-size theater with the goal of making the genre inviting to the non-black-tie crowd.... *Tel 312/292–7578. 60 E. Balbo Ave. Tickets $17–55. June–July.*

Chicago Symphony Orchestra. This top-ranked orchestra has a devoted audience that follows them from their downtown home at Orchestra Hall to their summer residence at north-suburban Ravinia. Even when concerts are sold out, turned-back tickets from subscribers are often available the night of the performance. Students and seniors get a discount as well.... *Tel 312/435–6666. 220 W. Michigan Ave., Jackson el stop. $6.50–75. Sept–June (Orchestra Hall); June–Sept (Ravinia).*

Chicago Theatre. Shamefully, Chicago has bulldozed most of its once-grand movie palaces, but it managed to restore this 4,000-seat house at the head of State Street as a performing arts center used for visiting musicals and occasional concerts.... *Tel 312/902–1500 (Ticketmaster). 175 N. State St., Washington el stop.*

Chicago White Sox. The city's South Side team has played consistently better than the Cubs over the years, but even Saturday night fireworks can't compete with the devotion Chicagoans hold for the crosstown ball club. That said, Sox fans show up to watch *the game*, so it's beside the point that they've been saddled with a soulless ballpark.... *Tel 312/924–1000 or 312/831–1769 (Ticketmaster). Comiskey Park, 333 W. 35th St., Sox/35th el stop. $8–18. Apr–Oct.*

Dance Center of Columbia College. This hub for modern dance in the city keeps a busy year-round schedule of 50-plus performances by both resident companies and guest artists and choreographers. Though the center occasionally utilizes other venues around town, the college's 250-seat Uptown theater offers a serviceable yet intimate setting.... *Tel 312/271–7928. 4730 N. Sheridan Rd., Lawrence el stop. $14–16. Sept–May.*

The Empty Bottle. This hipster club keeps the indie flame burning bright with a mix of touring and local bands. Cheap admission at the door, sometimes in advance for bigger events.... *Tel 312/276–3600. 1035 N. Western Ave.; Western el stop, transfer to #49 Western bus. $5–7.*

ETA Creative Arts Foundation. This highly regarded African-American company stages serious drama in its 200-seat theater, including a variety of productions geared toward families and children.... *Tel 312/752–3955. 7558 S. Chicago Ave. $15.*

The Free Associates. Practitioners of long-form improvisational comedy, the troupe uses audience input to concoct one-act plays based on a good ear for literary genres.... *Tel 312/975-7171. Ivanhoe Theater, 750 W. Wellington St., Belmont el stop. $8–10.*

Goodman Theatre. You'd expect an institutional theater to worry about pleasing subscribers, but Goodman doesn't seem afraid to take a few risks even on its mainstage, a comfy 700-seat theater with pleasing sightlines and a proscenium-arch stage. A well-kept secret is the theater's "Tix by Six" offering of half-price, day-of-performance tickets. The theater begins selling extra tickets (often excellent turned-back subscription passes) at 1pm for matinees and 6pm for evening shows. Rarely is anyone turned away.... *Tel 312/443–3800. 200 S. Columbus Dr. (eastern side of the Art Institute), Monroe el stop. Tickets $25–38 mainstage, $19–25 studio.*

Grant Park Music Festival. The Chicago Park District's summer concert festival features frequent free performances by the Grant Park Symphony Orchestra and soloists such as illustrious Van Cliburn.... *Tel 312/819–0614. Petrillo Music Shell, Grant Park, Columbus and Jackson drives, Jackson el stop. June–Aug.*

Guild Complex. A spin-off of a now-defunct DePaul area independent bookstore, this literary organization hosts poetry readings, open-mike nights, and workshops.... *Tel 312/ 278–2210. Chopin Theater, 1543 W. Division St., Division el stop. $4–10.*

Hubbard Street Dance Chicago. One of the only companies in the country to perform Twyla Tharp's pieces, the city's premiere dance troupe, founded in 1978, will be based at the Chicago Music and Dance Theatre when it opens in 1997; until then it performs at various sites around town.... *Tel 312/663–0853. $12–38. Apr–May.*

ImprovOlympic. Co-owned by a former Second City director, this theater hosts Chicago's top improvisers together on Monday nights, as well as more structured shows staged upstairs in a 100-seat space. In the cabaret theater, workshop students give some entertaining unscripted performances a few times a week.... *Tel 312/880–0199. 3541 N. Clark St., Addison el stop. $7–9.*

Joffrey Ballet of Chicago. Led by co-founder and artistic director Gerald Arpino, this 30-dancer classical ballet troupe incorporates members of the former New York company and a few dancers stolen from Ballet Chicago (see above).... *Tel 312/739–0120. Offices at 70 E. Lake St., suite 1300.*

Latino Chicago Theater Company. Presenting original productions by Latino writers, the theater is located in the gentrifying Wicker Park/West Town area.... *Tel 312/486–5120. The Firehouse, 1625 N. Damen Ave., Damen el stop. $12–15.*

Links Hall Studio. Local choreographer Bob Eisen is a fixture in this 50-seat room, which is also a popular performance space for other established modern dancers and emerging choreographers.... *Tel 312/281–0824. 3435 N. Sheffield Ave., Addison el stop.*

Lookingglass Theatre Company. The group takes its name from one of its early productions, an adaptation of Lewis Carroll's *Through the Looking Glass*, which followed an earlier adaptation of *Alice's Adventures in Wonderland*, first staged when the performers were undergraduate theater majors. The young company presents at a variety of venues and offers a limited number of $10 tickets before performances.... *Tel 312/477–9257. $10–16.*

Lounge Ax. A dependable neighborhood club that's the place to hear bands only you and your coolest friends have heard of. Tickets are occasionally sold in advance.... *Tel 312/525–6620. 2438 N. Lincoln Ave., Fullerton el stop. $3–10.*

Lunar Cabaret and Full Moon Cafe. If you feel like you've stumbled into someone's home, you're right: Most of the artist owners/members of the offbeat musical and performance group **Maestro Subgum and the Whole** live upstairs. The restaurant's menu is mostly veggie, while the theater, performance, and music (jazz, folk, klezmer) presented in a cabaret setting is gathered from the fringes.... *Tel 312/327–6666. 2827 N. Lincoln Ave., Diversey el stop. Closed Mon.*

Lyric Opera of Chicago. A-list singers, spectacular sets, and the regal Civic Opera House make the Lyric one of the toughest-to-find tickets in town. The season regularly sells out long in advance, but check with the box office for turned-back tickets in advance or the day of a performance.... *Tel 312/332–2244. 20 N. Wacker Dr., Randolph and Wells el stop. $21–107. Sept–Feb.*

Metro. A Chicago institution, this sturdy old theater can be crowded, sweaty, and smoky when you pack throngs of alterative-rock fans into the small space. But any discomfort is mitigated by the way the crowd feeds off a band's onstage energy. Save on Ticketmaster fees by buying advance tickets at the club's box office. Shows sell out quickly.... *Tel 312/549–0203. 3730 N. Clark St., Addison el stop. $6–20.*

Muntu Dance Theatre of Chicago. The popular ethnic dance company communicates the culture of the African and African-American experience, drawing upon tradtional and contemporary dance styles.... *Tel 312/602–1135. Offices at 6800 S. Wentworth Ave. $7–15.*

Neo-Futurists. Located above the Nelson Funeral Home, this theater group offers one-acts and other experimental stuff. They don't take reservations, so show up early for their long-runnung hit, *Too Much Light Makes the Baby Go Blind*.... *Tel 312/275–5255. 5153 N. Ashland Ave., Montrose el stop, walk to #9 Ashland bus. $4–9. Fri–Sun.*

New World Music Theatre. Well, at least you're outside. The view from the pavilion seats isn't all that bad, while the cheaper grass plots in back offer close-ups of teenagers making out while big-name rockers take the stage.... *Tel 312/559–1212 (Ticketmaster). 19100 S. Ridgeland Ave., Tinley Park.*

Old Town School of Folk Music. This long-established school has welcomed all the major players, from Peter Seeger to Alison Krauss, to its 300-seat concert hall and other venues in the city. The offerings now also embrace jazz, world music, Native American, Celtic, Latin, and Cajun. A Sunday showcase series introduces emerging artists.... *Tel 312/525–7793. 909 W. Armitage Ave., Armitage el stop. $8–18.*

Orchestra Hall. This sublime 1905 hall designed by Daniel Burnham is home to the Chicago Symphony Orchestra, the Chicago Civic Orchestra, and visiting jazz, classical, and chamber artists.... *Tel 312/435–6666. 220 W. Michigan Ave., Jackson el stop.*

Organic Theater Company. The Lake View acting company has a rich history, but the original plays, improv shows, and performance pieces programmed into the two Greenhouse spaces upstairs at times supersede its own productions. The company stages the latter in a pleasant 350-seat room with good seats for everybody.... *Tel 312/327–5588. 3319 N. Clark St., Belmont el stop. $12–15 company, $5–15 Greenhouse.*

Park West. This intimate, cabaret-style club has a way of focusing attention on the stage, and offers a nice balcony perch from which to take in the show.... *Tel 312/929–5959. 322 W. Armitage Ave., #151 bus from Michigan Ave. or State St.*

Randolph Street Gallery. Heavy on conceptual art, this River West gallery is also a performance art mainstay for locals and name artists coming through town. Shows often sell out in the narrow black-box theater.... *Tel 312/666–7737. 756 N. Milwaukee Ave., Chicago el stop.*

Ravinia. This tree-covered music idyll is a romantic spot to relax on the lawn with a spread of wine and cheese on a summer evening. If you're not equipped for some moonlight picnicking, you can also rent chairs ($3.50 each) and pick up a boxed meal at the well-stocked concession area. During the rest of the year, recitals featuring musicians under age 30 are held in the park's **Bennett Hall** ($15).... *Tel 312/ RAVINIA (728–4642). Lake-Cook and Green Bay roads, Highland Park; Metra train to Ravinia Park stop. $7 for lawn seats, $15–40 for covered pavilion seats. June–Sept.*

River North Dance Company. Performing at various venues, this 12-member jazz-oriented company gives a lot of local artists a shot at choreographing.... *Tel 312/944–2888. $15–25. Oct–May.*

Second City. Who hasn't come through Second City? The Old Town institution has been a launching pad for comedic careers from Ed Asner to Gilda Radner to the voice of Homer Simpson (Dan Castellaneta). There's no drink minimum, so all ages are welcome in the company's two theaters.... *Tel 312/337–3992, 642–8189. 1616 W. Wells St., Sedgwick el stop. $5–15.*

Shakespeare Repertory. The Bard is all the ten-year-old company does and they do him well. The audience surrounds the stage on three sides of the 333-seat theater.... *Tel 312/642–2273. Ruth Page Theater, 1016 N. Dearborn Pkwy. Tickets $17–31. Oct–May.*

Shubert Theatre. Beware the second balcony and a few obstructed seats in this otherwise magnificent 2,000-seat theater.... *Tel 312/902–1500. 22 W. Monroe St., Monroe el stop.*

Skyline Stage at Navy Pier. Part of the reinvigorated Navy Pier entertainment complex, this open-air theater cuts a profile on the cityscape that's compared (a bit generously) to the Sydney Opera House.... *Tel 312/595–7437. Grand Ave. at Lake Michigan, Grand el stop, transfer to #65 Grand or #29 State buses. $15–30 tickets for concerts, $6 for films.*

Steppenwolf Theatre Company. After moving from a series of transient spaces over much of its life, this widely admired, risk-taking company still hasn't adjusted to its grown-up building containing a 500-seat mainstage and upstairs studio space. You can snap up half-price tickets to shows by calling or stopping by the box office after 5pm the night of a performance.... *Tel 335–1650. 1650 N. Halsted St., North and Clybourn el stop. $22.50–35 mainstage; $10–20 studio.*

Theatre Building. Shows sometimes gravitate to this beehive of play-making after finding audiences in smaller houses around town. More than a dozen theater companies, including some promising young upstarts, use the three spaces.... *Tel 312/327–5252. 1225 W. Belmont Ave., Belmont el stop. $5–20.*

The Vic. Kids stand outside for hours waiting to get the best seats for the occasional general-admission show. You'll practically have to shoehorn yourself into the tight cabaret seating.... *Tel 312/472–0366. 3145 N. Sheffield Ave., Belmont el stop. $12–20.*

Whiskey River Saloon. This cavernous club remains dedicated to bringing in national country and country-folk hybrid acts a few times a month.... *Tel 312/528–3400. 1997 N. Clybourn Ave., North and Clybourn el stop. $5–20.*

Zanies. Big name talent and suburbanites' birthday parties fill the room at this Old Town club, which hits you with a standard two-drink minimum.... *Tel 312/337–4027. 1548 N. Wells St., Sedgwick el stop. Closed Mon.*

hotlines &
other basics

Airports... O'Hare Airport, as everybody knows, is the
world's busiest airport. And though technically located in
the city of Chicago, it's actually 17 miles northwest of the
Loop, tethered to the city by a narrow corridor of land.
Much of the airport has been refurbished since it was originally built, or totally built new in recent years—there's
even a Starbucks out there now. The international terminal
is a high-tech addition; the United terminal, designed by
Helmut Jahn, has a great light show and an eerie sound system that makes you feel like you're on your way to Pluto,
even if you're just heading to Dayton. The city's other airport is the small **Midway Airport**, 10 miles southwest of
the Loop, off the Stephenson Expressway on South Cicero
Avenue. In some ways it's more convenient to deal with
than O'Hare, serviced by a lot of smaller airlines such as
KIWI and MarkAir.

Airport transport to downtown... While both airports
are jammed with cabs vying for your business, Chicago is
blessed with a subway system that allows travelers to get to
and from both O'Hare and Midway for only $1.50 (a cab
from O'Hare to downtown will run about $35, including a
$1 surcharge, while from downtown to Midway it can cost

up to $20). From O'Hare, the O'Hare/Congress/Douglas line runs 24 hours a day and transports you directly to the North Side and into the Loop. (If you're heading to Lincoln Park, Lake View, or another neighborhood, you can get off at any point along the way and take a bus or cab either east toward the lake or west away from it; just make sure you get a transfer for an extra 30¢ when you pay your fare at O'Hare.) The trip can take about a half hour but it's still faster than any other mode of transport. At O'Hare, follow the signs that look like the front of a subway car to get to the station. The line that runs to Midway is less convenient because once you get to the airport the walk to the terminal is a long one and there are no moving sidewalks as there are at O'Hare. The Midway line only runs until 11pm. Other modes of transportation include **Continental Airport Express** *(tel 312/454–7799)*, which offers door-to-door bus service from either airport to most downtown hotels. From O'Hare it costs $14.75, or $25 round trip; from Midway it's $10.75, $19 round trip. In addition, all the major car rental agencies are available at both airports, with courtesy buses running between the terminals and lots.

American Express... Travel service offices are located at 34 N. Clark *(tel 312/263–6617)*, 122 S. Michigan *(tel 312/435–2595)*, 230 S. Clark *(tel 312/629–0685)*, and 625 N. Michigan *(tel 312/435–2570)*. All are open Mon–Fri 9–5.

Baby-sitters... In the mood to dump the kids and trip the night fantastic? **The American Registry for Nurses & Sitters** *(tel 312/248–8100)*, a state-licensed service that's been around since 1950, may be able to help. All sitters have passed background checks, must have at least three references, and must be certified in child and infant CPR. You're responsible for the sitter's transportation home if it's after 10pm. Cost varies.

Buses... The **Chicago Transit Authority** operates more than 100 bus routes in the city, though riding them can be somewhat more complicated than the el. The fare structure certainly is more complex: during both the morning and evening rush hours a ride costs $1.50, paid with either a token or exact change (Chicago buses are equipped to accept dollar bills, bless 'em). At other times, the fare is $1.25. Transfers cost 30¢ extra and must be used within two hours of purchase; they must be purchased *as you board the bus*—the drivers are sticklers about this and no amount of whining will get them to back down. There's generally a bus stop every other block along each individual route, marked by a blue-and-white sign illustrating the route itself. If it says there's "night owl service," that route runs 24 hours. Many don't, though, so always check (and frankly, for safety's sake, you probably shouldn't ride the buses late at night anyhow).

Car rental... All major car rental agencies are represented in Chicago, with outlets throughout the city and at both airports. Prices vary widely, so ask in advance. And take note, the city of Chicago levies an 18% tax on car rentals. Call for locations; here are the phone numbers: **Alamo** *(tel 800/327–9633)*; **Avis** *(tel 800/331–1212)*; **Budget** *(tel 800/527–0700)*; **Dollar** *(tel 312/686–2030)*; **Hertz** *(tel 800/654–3131)*; **National** *(tel 800/227–7368)*; **Rent-a-Wreck** (tel 800/535–1391*)*; **Thrifty** *(tel 800/367–2277)*.

Chicago Office of Tourism... Tel 312/744–2400, 800/ITS–CHGO. The office staffs a visitor information desk at the Water Tower Pumping Station, 163 E. Pearson Street (at North Michigan Ave.), open Mon–Fri 9:30–6, Sat 10–6, and Sun 11–5.

Chicago Park District... Tel 312/747–2200.

Chicago Transit Authority (CTA)... Call the **CTA** *(tel 312/836–7000)* for information on how to take the subway from where you are to where you want to go.

Children's Emergency Services... Internationally recognized as one of the finest—if not *the* finest—children's hospital in the country, **Children's Memorial Hospital** *(tel 312/880–4000, Fullerton and Lincoln Aves.)* operates the city's only emergency room geared toward children.

Convention centers... McCormick Place *(tel 312/791–7000, 2300 S. Lake Shore Dr.)* is one of the biggest and most important convention complexes in the country; when the expansion of its South Building is completed in early 1997, it will have 63 meeting rooms and over 2.2 million square feet of exhibition space.

Dentists... The **Chicago Dental Society** *(tel 312/476–4321)* makes free referrals 24 hours a day.

Doctors... The **Chicago Medical Society** *(tel 312/670–2550)* makes free referrals weekdays, 8:30am to 4:30pm.

El... see Subways, below.

Emergencies... Most Chicago hospitals have 24-hour emergency rooms. Call **911** for ambulance, paramedics, and police, or to report a fire or an animal bite. **Northwestern Memorial Hospital** *(tel 312/908–2000, 233 E.*

Superior St.), generally considered the best emergency room in the city, is near many Magnificent Mile hotels. Other vital numbers: **Children's Memorial Hospital Emergency Room** *(tel 312/880–4000)*; **Coast Guard Search and Rescue** *(tel 312/768–4093)*; **Poison Control** *(tel 312/942–5969)*.

Events hotlines... Desperate for something to do? Call the **City of Chicago Events Hotline** *(tel 312/744–3370)*; **Jazz Hotline** *(tel 312/427–3300)*; **Dance Hotline** *(tel 312/419–8383)*; **JAM Concert Line** *(tel 312/666–6667)* for pop, country, and rock music information; **Classical Music Alliance** *(tel 312/987–9296)* for classical music and opera information; **Hot Tix Hotline** *(tel 312/977–1755)* for a recorded message listing all shows for which tickets are available on that day (calls on Friday also receive weekend information).

Festivals and special events...

January: **Chicago Boat, Sports, and RV Show** *(tel 312/567–8500, McCormick Place)*; **Sports, Fishing, and Outdoor Show** *(O'Hare Expo Center, tel 312/692–2220)*.

February: **Chicago Cubs Fans Convention** *(tel 312/951–CUBS)*; **Azalea Flower Show** *(tel 312/742–7736, Lincoln Park Conservatory)*; **Camellia Flower Show** *(tel 312/746–5100, Garfield Park Conservatory)*; **Chinese New Year Parade** *(tel 312/326–5329, Wentworth and Cermak Aves.)*; **Chicago International Auto Show** *(tel 312/692–2220, McCormick Place)*.

March: **St. Patrick's Day Parade**, March 17 *(Dearborn St. at Wacker Dr.)*.

April: **Cubs Opening Day**, Wrigley Field *(tel 312/404–CUBS, see Entertainment)*; **White Sox Opening Day** *(tel 312/924–1000, Comiskey Park, see Entertainment)*; **Spring and Easter Flower Show** *(tel 312/742–7736, Lincoln Park Conservatory)*; **International Kennel Dog Show** *(tel 312/237–5100, McCormick Place)*.

May: **Buckingham Fountain Color Light Show**, runs through September *(Grant Park at Congress St. and Lake Shore Dr.)*; **Polish Day Parade** *(tel 312/744–3315, Clark St. at Wacker Dr.)*; **Greek-American Parade** *(tel 312/744–3315, Michigan Ave. at Wacker Dr.)*; **International Theater Festival** *(tel 312/527–4832)*, held in even-numbered years at various theaters throughout the city; **International Mr. Leather Contest** *(tel 312/878–6360)*, at several concurrent venues.

June: **Gay and Lesbian Pride Week Parade** *(tel 312/348–8243, Halsted St. at Belmont St.)*; **Chicago Blues Festival** *(tel 312/744–3315, Petrillo Music Shell, Grant Park)*; **57th Street Art Fair** *(tel 312/684–8383, Hyde Park)*; **Old Town Art Fair** *(tel 312/337–1938 or 312/744–3315, Lincoln Park W at Orleans St.)*; **Puerto Rican Day Parade** *(tel 312/744–3315, Clark St. at Wacker Dr.)*; **Andersonville Midsummerfest** *(tel 312/728–2995, Clark St., between Foster and Catalpa Aves.)*; **Printer's Row Book Fair** *(tel 312/987–1980, Dearborn St. at Harrison St.)*.

July: **Chicago Country Music Festival** *(tel 312/744–3370, Petrillo Music Shell, Grant Park)*; **Chinatown Summer Fair** *(tel 312/225–6198, Wentworth Ave. at 22nd St.)*; **Sheffield Garden Walk and Festival** *(tel 312/929–9255, Webster and Sheffield Aves.)*; **Halsted Street Market Days** *(tel 312/868–3010, Halsted St. at Belmont Ave.)*; **Taste of Chicago** *(tel 312/744–3315, Grant Park)*; **Fourth of July Celebration**, July 3 *(Grant Park)*; **Chicago-Mackinac Island Boat Race** *(tel 312/861–7777, starts at Monroe Harbor)*.

August: **Medieval Fair** *(tel 312/880–5200, Oz Park, at Webster, Larrabee, and Lincoln Aves.)*; **Sandcastle Competition** *(tel 312/670–7770, North Ave. Beach)*; **Gold Coast Art Fair** *(tel 312/787–2677, River North)*; **Festa Italiana** *(tel 312/829–8888, North Pier)*; **Venetian Night** *(tel 312/744–3315, Monroe Harbor)*; **Bud Billiken Parade**, the largest African-American parade in the country, celebrating the beginning of the school year *(tel 312/225–2400, 39th St. and King Dr.)*; **Air and Water Show** *(tel 312/744–3315, North Ave. Beach)*.

September: **Chicago Jazz Festival** *(tel 312/744–3315, Petrillo Music Shell, Grant Park)*; **"Viva! Chicago" Latin Music Festival** *(tel 312/744–3340, Petrillo Music Shell, Grant Park)*; **Octoberfest** *(tel 312/427–3170, Adams St. between Dearborn and State Sts.)*; **Mexican Independence Day Parade** *(tel 312/744–3315, Michigan Ave. at Wacker Dr.)*.

October: **Chicago Marathon** *(tel 312/951–0660 or 312/527–2300)*, which starts in Grant Park and runs throughout the city; **Columbus Day Parade** *(tel 312/828–0010, Dearborn St. at Wacker Dr.)*; **Chicago International Film Festival** *(tel 312/644–3400)*; **Chicago International Antique Show** *(tel 312/787–6858, Navy Pier)*.

November: **Chrysanthemum Show** *(tel 312/746–5100, Garfield Park Conservatory, and tel 312/742–7736, Lincoln Park Conservatory)*; **Veterans' Day Parade** *(tel 312/744–3315, the Loop)*; **Christmas Tree Lighting** *(tel 312/744–3315, Daley Plaza, the Loop)*.

December: **Christmas Flower Show** *(tel 312/746–5100, Garfield Park Conservatory, and tel 312/742–7736, Lincoln Park Conservatory)*.

Gay guys and lesbians... **Anti-Violence Project** *(tel 312/871–2273)*; **Horizons Community Services** *(tel 312/472–6469)*; **Horizons Helpline** (offers gay youth services, *tel 312/929–HELP)*; **Rodde Center** (gay and lesbian community center, *tel 312/271–4155)*; **ACT UP/Chicago** *(tel 312/509–6802)*; **Queer Nation** *(tel 708/581–3200)*; **Chicago Professional Networking Association** *(tel 312/296–2762)*; **Cook County AIDS Hotline** *(tel 708/445–AIDS)*; **NAMES Project/Chicago** *(tel 312/472–4460)*; **Test Positive Aware Network** *(tel 312/404–8726)*; **Chicago Gay Men's Chorus** *(tel 312/275–7294)*; **Windy City Gay Chorus** *(tel 312/404–9242)*; **Lesbian Book Discussion Group** *(tel 312/327–7431)*; **Chi-Town Squares** (square-dancing, *tel 312/357–3100)*; **Congregation Or Chadesh** *(tel 312/248–9456)*; **Dignity Chicago** *(tel 312/296–0780)*; **Unity Church of Chicago** *(tel 312/973–0007)*; **Metropolitan Sports Association** *(tel 312/665–8008)*; **Windy City Athletic Association** *(tel 312/509–2977)*; **Front Runners/Front Walkers** *(tel 312/409–2790)*; **Women's Sports Association** *(tel 312/975–6101)*; **Northwestern University Bisexual, Gay, and Lesbian Alliance** *(tel 708/491–2375)*; **Chicago Area Republican Gay Organization** *(tel 312/943–4731)*.

Hearing-impaired services... **Chicago area interpreter referral** *(voice, tel 708/797–0002)*. **City of Chicago Events Hotline** TDD number for the hearing impaired *(tel 312/744–8599)*.

Newspapers and magazines... The big kahuna is the *Chicago Tribune*, for which uber-Chicagoan Mike Royko writes. The daily paper costs 50¢; the Sunday edition is $1.50. The "Friday" section is good for nightlife and entertainment listings. The *Chicago Sun-Times* has equally good Friday listings and, since it's a tabloid, is easier to read on the el. It's cheaper than the *Trib*, too, at 35¢ for the daily and $1.25 on Sunday. Both have a fairly conservative political slant. If you still can't decide on which paper to read, remember Gene Siskel writes for the *Trib*, while his full-figured counterpart Roger Ebert flips his thumb at the *Sun-Times*. The ***Chicago Reader,*** which comes out on Thursdays, has the city's most comprehensive nightlife listings; it's available, free, at bookstores and other stores throughout the North Side. Another freebie, upstart ***New City,*** is a terrific blend of service information, listings, reviews, and in-your-face journalism. ***Chicago*** magazine ($2.50) carries 120 or so restaurant reviews every month; though its reviewers don't dish the restaurants as much as merely list the dishes, they still hold a lot of sway among the foodie cognoscenti. The magazine's also a good resource for dozens of theater reviews, gallery listings, and special events.

Parking... If you're willing to pay for it, there is parking galore in Chicago. Municipal lots, where the rates are comparatively low ($5 for each 24-hour period, believe it or not), are generally located downtown; privately owned lots are sprinkled throughout the city. Municipal lots include: **East Monroe Underground** *(tel 312/294–4740, 350 E. Monroe St.)*; **Grant Park Underground North** *(tel 312/294–2437, N. Michigan Ave. at Monroe St.)*; **Grant Park Underground South** *(tel 312/294–4593, S. Michigan Ave. at Congress)*; **McCormick Place Underground** *(tel 312/294–4600, 23rd St. and S. Lake Shore Dr.)*; **Midcontinental Parking Garage** *(tel 312/986–6821, 55 E. Monroe St.)*; **Navy Pier Parking** *(tel 312/791–7437, 600 E. Grand Ave.)*; **Soldier Field** *(tel 312/294–2437, 14th St. and Lake Shore Dr.)*.

Pharmacies... **Walgreens** has more than 100 branches throughout the city, with 17 of them open 24 hours a day. The 24–hour branch *(tel 312/664–8686, 757 N. Michigan Ave.)* holds claim to being one of the world's busiest pharmacies, for whatever that's worth. Another big chain, **Osco** *(tel 312/477–3333)*, has a number of 24-hour branches, too.

Pro sports... The **Chicago Bears** NFL football team *(tel 708/615–2327)*; the **Chicago Blackhawks** hockey team *(tel 312/455–7000)*; the **Chicago Bulls** NBA basketball team *(tel 312/455–4000)*; and the **Chicago Cubs** *(tel 312/404–2827)* and the **Chicago White Sox** *(tel 312/924–1000)* for baseball. For more details on these teams, see Entertainment.

Radio stations... WBEZ (91.5 FM), local National Public Radio; WFMT (98.7 FM), classical music; WLUP (97.9 FM and 1000 AM), rock; WXRT (93 FM), traditional and alternative rock.

Restrooms... Like any huge urban sprawl, Chicago rarely supplies a bathroom when and where you want one. Still, plenty of clean bathrooms exist if you know where to look. Try department stores, from **Marshall Field's** to **Neiman Marcus**, even **Crate & Barrel** on Michigan Avenue, or scout out the bathrooms off the lobbies of any of the downtown hotels. The **Starbucks** coffee bar on Rush Street is another handy pit-stop spot. You can generally disregard signs in restaurant and bar windows that say "restrooms for patrons only." There are public restrooms at the **Water Tower Pumping Station**, at the corner of Michigan Avenue and Pearson Street.

Subways... Four subway lines are operated by the **Chicago Transit Authority (CTA)**, though the entire system, whether below-ground or above, is generally referred to as the "el." Most trains run 24 hours a day, though some stations are closed at night and some routes run limited hours on Sundays (it's always wise to check first). Stations generally alternate "A" and "B," with the major stations being both; still, it's a good idea to check your map when making plans. There's nothing worse than being on a train that only makes "A" stops when you want to get off at a "B." The city claims the trains run every 5 to 15 minutes, and that's probably true during the morning and evening rush hours, but at other times the wait can be a drag. Fortunately, many of the outdoor el platforms have heat lamps that actually work, a real lifesaver in winter. You must use tokens to ride the system—buy them at any station. Some stations are unmanned, especially at night, in which case you're supposed to pay the conductor on the train after boarding. As in any big city, there's the constant threat of raising the fare, but tokens are currently $1.50, with a 30¢ transfer available if you want to switch to any bus route (the transfer must be used within two hours). Ten-packs of tokens can be purchased for $12.50 at many token booths, currency exchanges, and at two grocery chains, Jewel and Dominick's. There are reduced fares for children under 11 and seniors over 65. Always check maps to make sure you can find transfer points between lines;

most el stations have maps posted, and you can get your own individual map from almost any token booth. Call the surprisingly useful **CTA hotline** *(tel 312/836–7000)* for information on how to get from where you are to where you want to go.

Taxes... Chicago sales tax is 8.75% on everything but groceries and prescription drugs, for which there is, thankfully, no tax at all.

Taxis... A necessary evil, Chicago taxis are often dirty, unpleasantly aromatic, and driven by men and women who neither know the city well nor care to learn. It's not unheard-of to get in a cab, give your destination, and have the driver ask *you* for directions. Supposedly, a light on the top of a cab indicates that the cab is available, but lit cabs zoom by with riders all the time, while dark ones roam the streets with no fares. You might as well hail any cab you see coming—the worst that can happen is that it passes you by. The farther you go away from the Loop and the Michigan Avenue area, the more difficult it becomes to get a cab; in many neighborhoods you simply have to phone ahead *(tel 312/TAXICAB)*. As with the public transportation system, cab fees are in constant flux. Currently they're fixed at $1.20 as the meter starts, $1.50 for each additional mile. There's a surcharge (or rip-off, depending on your attitude) of 50¢ for each additional person in the cab.

Ticketmaster... Tel 312/559–1212 for tickets to theater, music, and sports events. *773 831·CUBS*

Time... Tel 312/976–1616.

Trains... Train service to Chicago's suburbs is fast and relatively convenient. **METRA** *(tel 312/836–7000)* operates commuter lines to almost all of them, departing from various stations in the city, including the Northwestern Station *(Madison St. and Canal St.)*, Union Station *(Adams St. and Canal St.)*, LaSalle Street Station *(LaSalle St. and Van Buren St.)*, and the Randolph Street Station *(Randolph St. and Michigan Ave.)*. **The Illinois Central-Gulf Railroad**, or IC *(tel 312/755–7500)*, commutes to Hyde Park. **Amtrak** *(tel 800/872–8245)* trains use grand old Union Station, which just happens to have a nifty children's playroom to help make long waits a little more bearable for train-traveling families.

Travelers with disabilities... For information, (tel 312/744–4016).

TV stations... The networks: CBS is channel 2, NBC is channel 5, and ABC is channel 7. Local stations: Chicagoland Television (local 24-hour news) is on channel 10, Fox-WFLD is on channel 32, WGN is on channel 9. The PBS affiliate, WTTW, is channel 13. For channel-surfers, the Chicago area is wired with the usual host of cable-TV options.

Visitor information... **Chicago Convention and Tourism Bureau**, tel 312/567–8500; **Chicago Office of Tourism**, tel 312/744–2400; **Illinois Bureau of Tourism**, tel 800/223–0121.

Weather... Tel 312/976–1212.

Western Union... Tel 800/325–6000.

FROMMER'S COMPLETE TRAVEL GUIDES

(Comprehensive guides to sightseeing, dining and accommodations,
with selections in all price ranges—from deluxe to budget)

FROMMER'S $-A-DAY GUIDES

(Dream Vacations at Down-to-Earth Prices)

FROMMER'S COMPLETE CITY GUIDES

(Comprehensive guides to sightseeing, dining, and accommodations in all price ranges)

Amsterdam, 8th Ed.	S176	Miami '95-'96	S149
Athens, 10th Ed.	S174	Minneapolis/St. Paul, 4th Ed.	S159
Atlanta & the Summer Olympic		Montréal/Québec City '95	S166
Games '96 (avail. 11/95)	S181	Nashville/Memphis, 1st Ed.	S141
Atlantic City/Cape May,		New Orleans '96 (avail. 10/95)	S182
5th Ed.	S130	New York City '96 (avail. 11/95)	S183
Bangkok, 2nd Ed.	S147	Paris '96 (avail. 9/95)	S180
Barcelona '93-'94	S115	Philadelphia, 8th Ed.	S167
Berlin, 3rd Ed.	S162	Prague, 1st Ed.	S143
Boston '95	S160	Rome, 10th Ed.	S168
Budapest, 1st Ed.	S139	St. Louis/Kansas City, 2nd Ed.	S127
Chicago '95	S169	San Antonio/Austin, 1st Ed.	S177
Denver/Boulder/		San Diego '95	S158
Colorado Springs, 3rd Ed.	S154	San Francisco '96 (avail. 10/95)	S184
Disney World/Orlando '96		Santa Fe/Taos/	
(avail. 9/95)	S178	Albuquerque '95	S172
Dublin, 2nd Ed.	S157	Seattle/Portland '94-'95	S137
Hong Kong '94-'95	S140	Sydney, 4th Ed.	S171
Las Vegas '95	S163	Tampa/St. Petersburg, 3rd Ed.	S146
London '96 (avail. 9/95)	S179	Tokyo '94-'95	S144
Los Angeles '95	S164	Toronto, 3rd Ed.	S173
Madrid/Costa del Sol, 2nd Ed.	S165	Vancouver/Victoria '94-'95	S142
Mexico City, 1st Ed.	S175	Washington, D.C. '95	S153

FROMMER'S FAMILY GUIDES

(Guides to family-friendly hotels, restaurants, activities, and attractions)

California with Kids	F105	San Francisco with Kids	F104
Los Angeles with Kids	F103	Washington, D.C. with Kids	F102
New York City with Kids	F101		

FROMMER'S WALKING TOURS

(Memorable strolls through colorful and historic neighborhoods, accompanied by detailed directions and maps)

Berlin	W100	San Francisco, 2nd Ed.	W115
Chicago	W107	Spain's Favorite Cities	
England's Favorite Cities	W108	(avail. 9/95)	W116
London, 2nd Ed.	W111	Tokyo	W109
Montréal/Québec City	W106	Venice	W110
New York, 2nd Ed.	W113	Washington, D.C., 2nd Ed.	W114
Paris, 2nd Ed.	W112		

FROMMER'S AMERICA ON WHEELS

(Guides for travelers who are exploring the U.S.A. by car, featuring a brand-new rating system for accommodations and full-color road maps)

Arizona/New Mexico	A100	Florida	A102
California/Nevada	A101	Mid-Atlantic	A103

FROMMER'S SPECIAL-INTEREST TITLES

Arthur Frommer's Branson!	P107	Frommer's Where to	
Arthur Frommer's New World		Stay U.S.A., 11th Ed.	P102
of Travel (avail. 11/95)	P112	National Park Guide, 29th Ed.	P106
Frommer's Caribbean		USA Today Golf	
Hideaways (avail. 9/95)	P110	Tournament Guide	P113
Frommer's America's 100		USA Today Minor League	
Best-Loved State Parks	P109	Baseball Book	P111

FROMMER'S BEST BEACH VACATIONS

*(The top places to sun, stroll, shop, stay, play, party, and swim—with each
beach rated for beauty, swimming, sand, and amenities)*

California (avail. 10/95)	G100	Hawaii (avail. 10/95)	G102
Florida (avail. 10/95)	G101		

FROMMER'S BED & BREAKFAST GUIDES

*(Selective guides with four-color photos and full descriptions of
the best inns in each region)*

California	B100	Hawaii	B105
Caribbean	B101	Pacific Northwest	B106
East Coast	B102	Rockies	B107
Eastern United States	B103	Southwest	B108
Great American Cities	B104		

FROMMER'S IRREVERENT GUIDES

*(Wickedly honest guides for sophisticated travelers and
those who want to be)*

Chicago (avail. 11/95)	I100	New Orleans (avail. 11/95)	I103
London (avail. 11/95)	I101	San Francisco (avail. 11/95)	I104
Manhattan (avail. 11/95)	I102	Virgin Islands (avail. 11/95)	I105

FROMMER'S DRIVING TOURS

*(Four-color photos and detailed maps outlining
spectacular scenic driving routes)*

Australia	Y100	Italy	Y108
Austria	Y101	Mexico	Y109
Britain	Y102	Scandinavia	Y110
Canada	Y103	Scotland	Y111
Florida	Y104	Spain	Y112
France	Y105	Switzerland	Y113
Germany	Y106	U.S.A.	Y114
Ireland	Y107		

FROMMER'S BORN TO SHOP

*(The ultimate travel guides for discriminating
shoppers—from cut-rate to couture)*

Hong Kong (avail. 11/95)	Z100	London (avail. 11/95)	Z101

irreverent notes

irreverent notes

irrevent notes

irreverent notes

irrevrent notes